WHITE WEEKENDS

BANTAM PRESS

LONDON · TORONTO · SYDNEY · AUCKLAND · JOHANNESBURG

For Jill and Pelly

TRANSWORLD PUBLISHERS
61–63 Uxbridge Road, London W5 5SA
A Random House Group Company
www.rbooks.co.uk

First published in Great Britain
in 2008 by Bantam Press
an imprint of Transworld Publishers

This book is a work of non-fiction based on the experiences and recollections of the author. The author has stated to the publishers that, except in such minor respects not affecting the substantial accuracy of the work, the contents of this book are true.

A CIP catalogue record for this book
is available from the British Library.

ISBN 9780593060155

Addresses for Random House Group Ltd companies outside the UK can be found at: www.randomhouse.co.uk
The Random House Group Ltd Reg. No. 954009

The Random House Group Limited supports The Forest Stewardship Council (FSC), the leading international forest-certification organization. All our titles that are printed on Greenpeace-approved FSC-certified paper carry the FSC logo. Our paper procurement policy can be found at www.rbooks.co.uk/environment

Typeset in Myriad Pro and Bell Gothic
Designed by Bobby Birchall, Bobby&Co, London
Printed and bound in Germany

2 4 6 8 10 9 7 5 3 1

OFF-PISTE SKIING Many chapters in this book describe skiing off piste, and in some cases mention particular routes. Skiing off piste is an inherently dangerous activity and it goes without saying that it must only be done by those in a group with the correct equipment – shovels, probes and transceivers – and with adequate training and experience, or a fully qualified guide. This book is not intended as a route guide.

PRICES The price of flights, hotel rooms and just about everything else associated with ski trips can vary wildly according to time of year. Prices given in *White Weekends* are for 'standard season', which in practice usually means January. During 2008, turmoil in European exchange rates and the price of oil has led to holiday prices fluctuating more than usual, so while prices in this book were correct at time of writing, clearly they may have altered by the time you travel.

THANKS TO Sarah Emsley, my editor at Transworld, who was kind enough – even after a long afternoon on the terrace of the Mooserwirt – to listen to a swaying man in salopettes with a large stein of beer and an idea for a ski book. Also to Bobby Birchall, our designer; Rebecca Jones, Sarah Day, Tom Poland and Sam Jones at Transworld; Joanne O'Connor, travel editor of the *Observer*; Philippa Sutton at Visit Sweden; Amanda Monroe at Rail Europe; Richard Rigby and Susie Westwood at BGB; Deborah Zani at Südtirol Marketing; Heidi Reisz at Switzerland Tourism; Betony Garner at the Ski Club of Great Britain; Richard Seymour at Salomon; Claire Bernard at Mango PR; Rowen Gower at Born PR; Moira Clarke at Esprit Ski; Lisa Holm at the Austrian National Tourist Office; Eva McBride and Claire Ashman at Get Involved; Claire Burnet in Chamonix; Wilma Himmelfreundpointner and Anna Stefanitsch in St Anton; Mountain Jo, Kev and Andy, also in St Anton; Keith Garvey in La Grave; George Reid in Aviemore; Charlotte Wilmots at lastminute.com; Alison Reeson at HSL; Rob and Sue Freeman; Silvia de Leon Torres at Turespaña; Jenny Glumoff at Visit Scotland; Samantha Day at Easyjet; Sam Lawson at LDR; Jemma Hewlett; Lorna Farren of Ryanair; Philip Addicott at 3x1; Iain Wilson at First ScotRail. But most of all to David and Rae Robbins for taking me skiing and giving me a life-long love of the mountains.

SKIS AND CLOTHING were kindly provided by Salomon (www.salomonsports.com). Thanks also to Gore-tex (www.gore-tex.co.uk) for providing additional clothing.

ALL PICTURES are © Robin Gautier, except for that on page 88, which was provided by Skierslodge, and those in chapter 14: pages 212, 215, 216 and 217 were kindly supplied by Nissan (www.nissansportsadventure.com), and pages 210 and 220 were kindly provided by Yak & Yeti heliskiing (+33 (0)4 50 53 53 67; www.yak-yeti.com); all others in the chapter are by Tom Robbins.

WHITE WEEKENDS

TOM ROBBINS

PHOTOGRAPHS BY ROBIN GAUTIER

UNDERGROUND
BANK STATION

Introduction

SO WHAT DID YOU DO AT THE WEEKEND?

Go to Ikea? Mow the lawn? Iron all your shirts with nice sharp creases ready for the week ahead? Maybe you can't quite remember.

Or did you spend it floating through deep powder, kicking up a plume of snow that sparkled in the alpine sunlight leaving wisps of white smoke spinning and playing on the hillside long after you'd disappeared from view? Perhaps there were long lunches in cosy mountain huts, raucous moments of shared bonhomie in après-ski bars and nights spent watching a billion stars above the silhouetted mountains in the cold, clear sky.

Pipe up with all that at the water-cooler on Monday morning and your colleagues will probably think you've gone mad, but then there is something thrillingly unreal about going skiing for the weekend. You step outside your workaday existence for a fleeting glimpse of a totally different world, one of fresh air, stunning scenery and exhilarating exercise. It's almost like being teleported – suddenly, there is soft snow underfoot instead of tarmac and paving stone. The air carries the smell of pine forests and woodsmoke, not the whiff of traffic. It's all quite deliciously disorientating.

Yet pulling off this alchemy – turning a humble weekend into a memory to savour long after – is actually surprisingly straightforward. A decade ago almost everyone who went skiing did so for full weeks, travelling on Saturday charter flights and booking through package-tour companies, but the boom in budget airlines has changed all that. Suddenly, you can choose exactly where you want to fly to and when you want to go. Without paying an arm and a leg, you can tailor-make your ski holidays to fit around your work, and that means you can supplement the traditional annual week in the snow with two or three weekends. Leave work a little early on a Thursday night and come back on Sunday night and you can have three full days on the piste for the price of just one day off work.

You don't have to live next door to Heathrow either. Intense competition between the airlines has prompted a rush into regional airports – you can now fly direct to Geneva from at least twenty British departure points. At the other end, too, the airlines are using an ever-growing range of airports, bringing the whole sweep of the Alps within reach of weekenders for the first time.

Booking the flight is the easy bit – but which resort are you going to head to? What's the best way of getting there from the airport, and where will you stay when you get there? Finding the answers can be tricky, and many people in the travel industry are more than happy to keep it that way. Their traditional business models work far better if everyone pipes down and sticks to fixed, week-long breaks so the hotels, restaurants and ski schools are always full. Try asking some tourist boards or hoteliers about weekends and you can be made to feel like a naughty child. That's where this book comes in – to give the ideas and information to inspire your snowy weekend jaunts for years to come.

Of course, a weekend is always going to be something of a compromise. The travel costs are the same as for a week, the hotels will probably charge a premium for short-breakers, and the downside of maximizing your time on the slopes is that you tend to find yourself in airport luggage halls at ungodly hours of the day or night. But here's the secret – get it right and you come back from your quick fix feeling like you've been away for a week. You'll have crammed so much in that you won't have had a chance to think about work. Plus, there's no time for the Wednesday wobbles of the full-week holiday when you wake up with legs like jelly and the prospect of heading up a freezing-cold mountain seems distinctly unappealing.

Best of all, because you're not committing to sacrificing one of your precious weeks of annual leave, going for a weekend allows you to try something different – ski touring in Scotland perhaps, or a combination of city- and ski-break. Then there's the early pre-Christmas warm-up that makes sure you get the most of your full-week trip later on, the quick blast with a big group of mates, and the late-season jaunt, squeezed in because you can't bear to wait until next winter to make a few more turns.

As I write this on a Sunday afternoon in May, London is sweaty and humid and the sun is beating through the windows. My mind is wandering, north to Riksgränsen in Sweden, up to the heights of Austria's Stubai glacier and the Grande Motte in France, where, even now, some lucky people are skiing. I wish I was with them. Then I'd really have something to tell people about in the office on Monday morning.

GET IT RIGHT and you come back from your quick fix feeling like you've been away for a week.

The Classic

CHAMONIX, FRANCE

01

PERCY SHELLEY SAID IT WAS 'as if frost had suddenly bound up the waves and whirlpools of a mighty torrent'.

WE ARE TIRED BUT ELATED at the end of an epic day's skiing when we come to the place where it all began. In a minute we'll take the little red mountain train back down into town but, before we do, we turn back, grip the metal handrail and take in the view.

A vast white glacier, the Mer de Glace, fills the whole valley in front of us, its surface slashed by deep blue crevasses. On the far side is the terrifying granite spire of the Aiguille du Dru and, to the right, the jagged teeth of the Grandes Jorasses. It's beautiful but unnerving, threatening and thrilling in equal measure.

As they clambered up to this exact spot in 1741 after a five-hour hike from Chamonix, William Windham and Richard Pococke felt the same sense of awe. Though they didn't realize it, the two British friends were the very first Alpine tourists, and their trip that day would change the way the world viewed the mountains. When their letters describing the view were published in London, they sparked a fascination with the Alps that spread across Europe. Soon Chamonix was an essential port of call on the aristocratic Grand Tour, and its fame kept growing.

Percy Shelley came to see the same view in 1816, saying it was 'as if frost had suddenly bound up the waves and whirlpools of a mighty torrent', and comparing Mont Blanc to a vast animal with 'frozen blood forever circulating through his stony veins'. His wife was so moved by the scene that she worked it into her new book: it is here that Frankenstein confronts his monster.

Tom skiing on the Vallée Blanche glacier

Frankenstein was a hit, Lord Byron declared Mont Blanc 'the monarch of mountains' and, in Chamonix, more and more hotels were built to cope with the ensuing rush of visitors. By 1821 a guiding service had been set up, and in 1908 the first mountain railway opened, from the town up to Montenvers, this celebrated look-out point over the Mer de Glace. Then, in 1924, the town hosted the first ever Winter Olympics, and its status was confirmed. Chamonix remains, to this day, the capital of the Alps.

'Doods! Let's get this party started!' So says Chris Wurfel in a broad West Coast drawl as he welcomes Robin, the photographer, and me to his hotel, Le Vert. We haven't met him before; he greets all his guests like this.

While the Shelleys might recognize many of the town's historic buildings, they might be a little out of their depth at Le Vert. Today, instead of Romantic poets, Chamonix attracts pilgrimages by ski bums, drawn from around the globe by its reputation for super-steep skiing. Le Vert, about a mile out of town, is their headquarters – and arriving here is like stepping into an extreme-sports video. Everyone is wearing low-slung trousers and caps and communicating with strange hand signals and street slang from south central LA (even if their vowels are mainly from Surrey). In the bar a band is setting up, while a group of young French girls play drinking games and down shots off the counter without using their hands.

Sofia explores an ice tunnel next to the Refuge du Requin

4
POWDER

Cocktail hour at Le Vert

The hotel, owned by a collective of ten friends, hosts regular parties and gigs and DJ sets from the likes of Dreadzone, Utah Saints, Giles Peterson and Basement Jaxx. If you want to hook up with like-minded skiers, boarders and adrenalin junkies, this is the place. Over breakfast two Americans chat about wind conditions for base-jumping, some British skiers pool their money to hire a ski guide, others plan a day's speed-riding (a new sport, developed in Chamonix, that crosses skiing and paragliding, with alarming results).

But though a deep seam of extreme sports runs right through the town, Chamonix is big enough to cater to all tastes and in many ways is the perfect all-round weekend resort. The high street boasts branches of Chanel and Lacoste as well as endless climbing shops and snack bars for penniless skiers. For something a little more stylish than Le Vert, try the Clubhouse, the mountain outpost of the Milk and Honey members clubs in London and New York. Housed in a 1927 art deco mansion, its seven rooms have all the prerequisites of a city boutique hotel – Frette linen, teak-decked rainforest showers, wireless internet, plasma TVs and a saucy suite, this one tucked under the rafters, with a 2.7m-wide bed and a selection of sex toys in the minibar.

For tradition and comfort, there's the ever-so-plush Grand Hôtel des Alpes, built in 1840 and staffed by Italians who manage to be formal and incredibly friendly at the same time. Bang in the centre, many say it's the best hotel in town. And if you're looking for a romantic retreat, go to Les Chalets de Philippe, a hamlet of seven chalets which have been rescued from the surrounding hillsides and rebuilt on a sunny shoulder overlooking the Chamonix valley. It's the pet project of a famous French theatre impresario, Philippe Courtines, and the attention to detail is as good as on any set – there's antique furniture, carved wooden four-posters, plus outdoor hot-tubs and a

The band spell it out, Le Vert

chef who will deliver fine food to your door. 'It is so beautiful it makes me want to cry,' he declares with fitting drama.

The funny thing is that, despite all the superlatives, the luxury hotels and fashion boutiques, Chamonix is actually not too expensive. It's a proper, working town, with a year-round local population, so not every shop and bar can mark up its prices to rip off the tourists. Moreover, while during winter there might be 60,000 tourists in the valley, in the summer it's typically 100,000. This is the opposite to most ski resorts, where hoteliers must make almost all their profits in the four months of the ski season, helped by the fact that every room is in such demand that they can name their price. In the most popular resorts – Courchevel and Meribel, for example – many hotels

Chris and Geoff celebrate an epic day

The cable car rises 2,807m, a European record

will refuse to take bookings just for the weekend, because they know they could otherwise fill the room for the whole week. In Chamonix, by contrast, many room rates actually drop in winter.

If you're really on a budget, Chamonix's cheapest beer is at the bar of the Gîte Vagabond on Avenue Ravanel le Rouge. During happy hour, from 4.30 p.m. to 6.30 p.m., a pint of Amstel is just €3, although the bar is a bit of a dingy room and, when we visit, entirely full of men. On the first floor is a dormitory, costing just €15 a night, but this place's real hidden gem is the Aiguille du Midi room, up on the top floor. It's a sweet double in the eaves, ensuite, and with a cute round window looking up the valley. It costs just €62 per night – €31 per person.

After dinner at Le Vert, we head out to explore the town. We wander past the polished steps and bright lights of the casino, past smart French couples taking an evening stroll and into Rue du Moulin, where everything changes. This narrow pedestrian street, tucked away just off the main centre, is party central, with numerous bars facing each other, wall-to-wall Brits (there even used to be a Queen Vic pub) and a raucous vibe. The coolest bar is called Soul Food, but we squeeze into the Australian-themed Bar'd Up, where big groups of thirtysomethings are powering into pitchers of lager.

Next morning I pull the curtain back nervously and breathe a sigh of relief when I see clear skies. This is our big day, our chance to ski the legendary Vallée Blanche, a 20km off-piste descent that in good snow conditions allows skiers to drop 2,800m in one run, all through unforgettable scenery.

The two-stage Aiguille du Midi cable car, built in 1954 (though since updated), boasts Europe's longest vertical ascent. Chamonix sits at 1,035m, the cable car takes you to 3,777m and, from there, an elevator takes you to the viewing platform at 3,842m.

Suddenly going from the streets of a bustling mid-sized town to this glacial wonderland is a quite gloriously discombobulating experience. On the viewing platform people turn in circles in silent awe. To our right is the summit of Mont Blanc du Tacul, at 4,248m, and, behind it, the summit of Mont Blanc itself, at 4,807m the highest point in

western Europe. In front of us is the wide, open Vallée Blanche glacier and, beyond it, the jagged peaks of the Grandes Jorasses. A tiny red gondola slowly moves away from us, high above the glacier to the rocks at the far side, from where cable cars descend to Courmayeur, in Italy.

For most people, it's worth coming up to the Aiguille du Midi for the view alone, but we need to get down on to the glacier to start skiing. And this is the hardest bit.

From the cable-car station, the only option is to walk down a steep, narrow and icy ridge. Slip to your right and you'll crash several hundred metres down to rocks at the glacier's edge. Slip to your left and you'll fall about 1,500 metres, halfway back to Chamonix. Every winter, people do both.

There's a rope to hang on to but, with skis balancing on your shoulder and ski boots sliding around on the ice, it's a terrifying start. At the bottom, perhaps 150m below the lift station, is a flat area, where we breathe easily once more. The sun is out as we clip into our skis and set off on what quickly becomes one of my favourite ever days on skis.

The skiing isn't really challenging – any good piste skier should be able to cope – but the scenery is

Descending the terrifying ridge to the start of the run

SLIP TO YOUR RIGHT and you'll crash several hundred metres onto rocks. Slip to your left and you'll fall halfway back to Chamonix. Every winter people do both.

mind-blowing. We ski right down the glacier, past vivid blue ice formations and under towering white cliffs. Yes, hundreds of people ski this route every week but, out here, a group of five of us surrounded by hundreds of acres of ice, it's hard not to feel intensely alone.

We ski the classic route, straight down the glacier, but Chris from Le Vert and his friends Justin and Sofia mix things up by jumping off the folds and cracks in the ice. Halfway down, at 2,516m on a rocky outcrop above where the Vallée Blanche glacier turns into the Mer de Glace, is a little stone mountain hut, the Refuge du Requin, which serves lunch on its terrace.

If you are on a budget, bring sandwiches and eat them on a rock near by, because a *croûte* (three types of melted cheese on a piece of garlic bread) costs €16, and a *tartiflette* (chopped potatoes and melted cheese) the same. And yet, sitting on that terrace in the sun, watching ice falls clatter down the glaciers and gazing up at the Dent du Géant, it seems like the best €16 I've ever spent. As we linger, drinking a beer, the *choucas*, black birds which, legend has it, are the lingering spirits of dead mountain guides, hop around beside us. It's such a benign, jolly atmosphere, it's easy to forget the danger that's all around us.

From the Aiguille du Midi to the Montenvers station 20km away, there are no other lifts, piste bashers or skidoos so, if anything does go wrong here, it becomes serious. As we are slugging back shots of Madame's homemade apple schnapps, which comes out of a Grolsch bottle, the police helicopter thunders up the valley and lands at the pad beside the refuge. A skier who's hurt her ankle is loaded in, and the chopper lifts off. We give the pilot a huge cheer and he returns the gesture, turning round and buzzing right past our table.

From here, the glacier levels out until it's almost flat but, in some ways, this is the most dangerous part. There are crevasses all over the glacier, covered over with snow. Stay on the usual path and keep up some speed and you ski straight over these snow bridges. Veer off, or slow too much, and the bridges can collapse. Most at risk are snowboarders, who have to take off their boards and walk. Thankfully, today the bridges hold.

THE INSIDE TRACK

Justin Hawxhurst Professional Skier

'Don't leave town without heading to the MBC – a microbrewery on Route de Bouchet. Try the pale ale, La Granite de Chamonix, and order one of the huge burgers or plates of nachos. But, most importantly, get down there on a night when Gary Bingham is doing one of his shows. That guy is a legend – he moved here from Detroit in 1975 and was involved with shooting all the early ski movies in the valley. In the MBC he shows clips from the films, still on the original reels, and talks about being the original ski bum. Sometimes he plays with his band, too – Gary Bingham and the Crevassholes.'

Micro-Brasserie de Chamonix: +33 (0)4 50 53 61 59; www.mbchx.com

Looking down on Chamonix from the Aiguille du Midi

Eventually, we climb up steel ladders and stairs attached to the rock to get off the glacier, take in Windham's view, then take the slow train back to town, its carriage packed with grinning skiers excitedly swapping tales of their day's exploits. Shortly after 4 p.m. we're back in town, outside the Chambre Neuf bar, toasting a day in which we've done just one run but which has been unforgettable.

So famous is the Vallée Blanche, not to mention scores of other legendary off-piste descents in the area, that you'd be forgiven for forgetting that Chamonix has any piste skiing at all. In fact, there are sixty-two lifts and over 210km of pistes, 90 per cent of them over 2,000m and thus more likely to have good snow.

The pistes are spread into four distinct areas, which is both a blessing and a curse. For intermediate and advanced skiers, it means they can explore the differing personalities of each of the areas. In bad weather they might choose the tree skiing and wide slopes above Vallorcine, or perhaps the lower pistes of Les Houches. If it's cold they might head to the south-facing Brévent-Flégère area, where the sun will melt the ice more quickly. And if they want a challenge, they'll head to the Grands Montets, a famous high, steep, north-facing area with lifts rising to 3,275m.

For families and beginners, though, this is all a major hassle. Free buses run between the ski areas, but the distances are significant: Les Houches is 8km west of Chamonix, Vallorcine 18km to the east. It couldn't be more different to a purpose-built resort where all the lifts start, and the runs end, right in the main square.

Inconvenience aside, however, there is some good easy skiing on offer. Head to Le Tour, just beyond the Grands Montets lifts in Argentière, and you find a big area of gentle cruising runs that rarely gets crowded. From the top of the Plan des Reines lift, at 2,770m, you can take red piste 16, then blue 17 and 19, snaking through the forest all the way down to the village of Vallorcine at 1,264m.

The other best spot for inspiring confidence is the wide runs of Les Houches. The slopes here are much lower than in the other sectors so are spurned by expert skiers and hence usually quiet. You can ski from the highest point all the way back to the village on blue runs.

Intermediates will get most out of the sunny Brévent-Flégère sector on the north side of town. Build up confidence on a wide choice of red runs before tackling some very steep and very long blacks – pistes 3 and 14 in Flégère, and the famous piste 10, which clings to the mountainside all the way down to the town centre.

Chamonix isn't convenient, it's not a relaxing, rural village, but for choice of accommodation, extraordinary scenery and advanced skiing terrain, it's very hard to beat. Oh yes, and getting here for the weekend is fantastically easy. When William Windham travelled to Chamonix from Geneva, it took three days. Today it's just over an hour's drive, straight up the motorway. Dragging yourself away will be far harder.

1 *The summit of the Aiguille du Midi*
2 *Chris toasts our run, with the guardian of the Refuge du Requin*
3 *Swapping stories on the Montenvers train back into town*
4 *Skiers arrive at Chamonix's central station*
5 *Tired legs? Your carriage awaits*
6 *The historic casino*

1|2
3
CENTRE VILLE CHAMONIX
4
5
6
CASINO

The Knowledge
Chamonix, France

STATS **Town altitude:** 1,035m **Highest lift:** 3,842m; **Lifts:** 62 **Pistes:** 210km (Chamonix Valley) **Lift pass:** €37–47 per day **Closest airport:** Geneva – 88km

WHY? Famous, long, taxing descents; a 'real' town with huge choice of hotels, restaurants and bars; views of Mont Blanc, western Europe's highest mountain; ski season that runs at least till the end of April; quick and easy transfer **GETTING THERE** You can now fly to Geneva from at least 20 British airports (see flight directory on page 287). By rail, Eurostar from London to Paris takes as little as 2 hours 15 minutes; TGV from Paris to Geneva takes 3 hours 22 minutes **TRANSFERS** From Geneva to Chamonix by train takes at least 3 hours – better to go by road. There is a conventional coach service from Geneva (run by SAT Montblanc, +33 (0)4 50 53 01 15; www.sat-montblanc.com), but this takes just over 2 hours. Instead, use one of the numerous private minibus operators who will do the journey in an hour and a quarter and charge as little as €25 per person each way, depending on group size. Try Mountain Drop-offs (0871 5754810; www.mountaindropoffs.com), Cham-van (0208 144 6347; www.cham-van.com) or AlpyBus (01509 213696; www.alpybus.com) **LIFT PASS** There are two types of pass available. The Chamonix Le Pass covers 38 lifts and 105km of pistes and costs €37 per day. If you want to go up to the top of the Grands Montets area or the Aiguille du Midi, you need the Mont Blanc Unlimited pass, which costs €47 per day and also covers Courmayeur, giving a total of 83 lifts and 270km of piste **WHERE TO STAY** Party animals should head for Le Vert (+33 (0)4 50 53 13 58; www.leverthotel.com), which has double rooms, including breakfast, from €92. Style seekers head to the Clubhouse (+33 (0)4 50 90 96 56; www.clubhouse.fr), which has doubles from €198, half board (4-night minimum stay over weekends). Honeymooners head for Les Chalets de Philippe (+33 (0)6 07 23 17 26; www.chaletsphilippe.com), where a chalet for two costs from €200 per night. Traditionalists will like the Grand Hôtel des Alpes (+33 (0)4 50 55 37 80; www.grandhoteldesalpes.com), where doubles cost from €190, room only. If you're broke, head to the Vagabond (+33 (0)4 50 53 15 43; www.gitevagabond.com), where dorm rooms cost €15 per person per night **WHERE TO SKI** The 20km-long Vallée Blanche is the most famous off-piste run in the world, but there are numerous other classics which experts will want to test themselves against, including Pas de Chèvre, Glacier Rond and Col du Plan. But there is stunning piste skiing too. The Brévent area is most convenient, with lifts rising directly from Chamonix, and has a famous black run that runs back into town. Don't leave without taking the (free) bus up to the Grands Montets, where there are some fabulous wide carving pistes as well as off-piste terrain reminiscent of Jackson Hole, Wyoming

WHERE TO EAT There's the full range, from bargain takeaways (loved by ski bums) such as Midnight Express and Poco Loco (both on Rue Dr Paccard) to the two-Michelin-starred Albert Premier (Route du Bouchet, +33 (0)4 50 53 05 09; www.hameaualbert.fr). For fine food without the Michelin fuss or price tag, locals tip Le Panier des Quatre Saisons (Galerie Blanc-Neige, +33 (0)4 50 53 98 77). Others recommend Elevation, the snack bar opposite the Chambre Neuf bar (*see below*) **WHERE TO PARTY** Start off with après-ski drinks at the Monkey Bar (Place Edmond Desailloud) or the Swedish-owned Chambre Neuf (Av. Michel Croz), then head to the Rue du Moulin, a narrow street lined with bars. After working your way through those, it's time for a club – Les Garages, Choucas, No Escape and Cantina are the favourites

HELP! If you'd like someone to arrange your trip for you, Ski Weekend (01392 878353; www.skiweekend.com) offers a 3-night package from £479, including transfers but not flights

TOURIST OFFICE +33 (0)4 50 53 00 24; www.chamonix.com

The cable car across the Vallée Blanche glacier to Hellbronner in Italy

Five More... Classics

ZERMATT, SWITZERLAND

STATS: Town altitude: 1,620m; **Highest lift:** 3,820m; **Lifts:** 57; **Pistes:** 313km; **Closest airport:** Sion – 80km

WHY? Sitting in the shadow of what is probably the world's most photographed mountain, Zermatt combines a charming centre, great restaurants and sensational skiing

GETTING THERE Limited flights into Sion mean most people use Zurich airport (248km) or Geneva (244km). The best route option is to fly to Geneva then transfer by train – it takes 3 hours 30 minutes, but you only have to change once (at Visp) and it's a stunning ride

WHERE TO STAY The Style Hotel Biner (+41 (0)27 966 56 66; www.hotel-biner-zermatt.ch; doubles from €140, including breakfast) is a traditional alpine-style building given a funky makeover, and has hammocks swinging in the lounge

WHERE TO PARTY Youngsters pack into the sweaty North Wall bar to watch live bands, but the Broken Bar disco, in a vaulted cellar under the Hotel Post on Bahnhofstrasse, is a classic. Take care when dancing on the barrels

TOURIST OFFICE +41 (0)27 966 81 00; www.zermatt.ch

KITZBÜHEL, AUSTRIA

STATS: Town altitude: 760m; **Highest lift:** 2,000m; **Lifts:** 53; **Pistes:** 170km; **Closest airport:** Salzburg – 80km

WHY? Home of the Hahnenkamm, perhaps the most famous of all the World Cup downhills, Kitzbühel has a medieval centre so attractive that many visitors don't even bother to ski

GETTING THERE Andi's Taxi (+43 (0)535 666222; www.andis-taxi.com) operates the Kitzbühel Alpine Shuttle – costing just €30 per person each way, minimum 2 passengers. Alternatively, hire a car at Salzburg for the 1-hour drive

WHERE TO STAY The Golfhotel Rasmushof (+43 (0)535 665252; www.rasmushof.at; doubles from €270, including breakfast) is close to the end of the Hahnenkamm course and is smart but friendly

WHERE TO PARTY Après ski is taken seriously here – start at the Streifalm right at the bottom of the piste. The 2 British pubs – the Londoner and Brass Monkeys – are good fun and, for clubbing, head to the Python or Take Five

TOURIST OFFICE +43 (0)535 6777; www.kitzbuehel.com

The view from the Aiguille du Midi

CORTINA D'AMPEZZO, ITALY

STATS: **Town altitude:** 1,224m; **Highest lift:** 2,939m; **Lifts:** 51; **Pistes:** 140km; **Closest airport:** Treviso – 132km

WHY? The Dolomites' equivalent of Chamonix – a classic mountain resort known for climbing in summer as much as skiing in winter. This is less a place for skiing hard all day long, more somewhere for soaking up the atmosphere, admiring the fabulous views of the craggy cliffs, and enjoying long Italian lunches
GETTING THERE Treviso, a lovely town just outside Venice, is served by Ryanair. Hire a car for the 1 hour 45 minute drive up to Cortina, or take the Terravision coach (+39 331 7814916; www.terravision.eu) which meets Ryanair flights, costs €29 return and takes 3 hours. Taxi for up to four will cost €200 each way (+39 335 6371419; www.taxicortina.com)
WHERE TO STAY Hotel de la Poste (+39 0436 4271; www.delaposte.it; doubles from €240, half board) dates from 1835 and is a focal point of the pedestrianized town centre
WHERE TO PARTY Nightlife here is less dancing on tables, more sipping Prosecco and people watching. Geri's Enoteca is apparently the oldest wine bar in Italy, and Villa Sandi and Brio Divino are also popular. There are six nightclubs in town – the VIP Club in the Hotel Europa is smart and civilized; the Disco Belvedere gets a younger crowd
TOURIST OFFICE +39 0436 3231; www.cortina.dolimiti.com

DAVOS, SWITZERLAND

STATS: **Town altitude:** 1,560m; **Highest lift:** 2,844m; **Lifts:** 51; **Pistes:** 305km; **Closest airport:** St Gallen – 119km

WHY? To be honest, Davos itself is a bit ugly, but the mountains around it are stunning, the ski area large and good for intermediates, and there's great off-piste potential. This was one of the earliest resorts of all – with skiing here tracing its roots back to 1880 – and so coming here is a bit of a pilgrimage for serious snowheads
GETTING THERE Unfortunately, St Gallen is served only by some small domestic flights and private jets. Instead, everyone uses Zurich, 161km away. Train transfers are best – it takes 2 hours 30 minutes from the airport, changing at Zurich main station and Landquart. A taxi will take about the same time and cost around CHF550/£255 (+41 (0)81 410 11 11; www.expresstaxi.ch)
WHERE TO STAY Davos is quite spread out but the three-star Hotel Parsenn (+41 (0)81 416 32 32; www.hotelparsenn.ch; doubles from CHF260/£121, including breakfast) is right opposite the Parsenn mountain railway, a key access point for the slopes
WHERE TO PARTY Après ski starts on the terrace of Scala's in Davos Platz. Chami and Ex-Bar are the key places for evening drinking, then head to the Cabanna Club or the Rotliechtli Bar
TOURIST OFFICE +41 (0)81 415 21 21; www.davos.ch

WENGEN, SWITZERLAND

STATS: **Town altitude:** 1,274m; **Highest lift:** 2,971m; **Lifts:** 45; **Pistes:** 213km; **Closest airport:** Bern – 80km

WHY? This charming car-free village perched on a ledge above the Lauterbrunnen valley was a hit with Edwardian Brits, who started experimenting on skis and did more than anyone else to popularize skiing as a sport for tourists and not a means of transport for farmers. The Jungfraubahn railway, completed in 1912, takes you through a tunnel in the Eiger to the highest station in Europe, at 3,454m
GETTING THERE From Bern, it's a 70-minute drive, and a taxi will cost CHF200/£93 for up to 3 people (+41 (0)33 855 18 19; www.jungfrautaxi.ch). The train will take at least 2 hours 15 minutes, but the views are unforgettable. Take a bus/taxi from the airport to Rubigen station (20 minutes) then a train to Interlaken, then Lauterbrunnen, where you pick up the mountain railway to Wengen
WHERE TO STAY The Hotel Falken (+41 (0)33 856 51 21; www.hotelfalken.com; doubles from CHF270/£125, including breakfast) dates from 1895 and is full of authentic atmosphere
WHERE TO PARTY 'Not in Wengen' is the short answer. But don't miss an afternoon beer outside the Wengenalp Hotel, on the mountain above the village. The Tanne Bar and Sina's Pub are the liveliest watering holes, and there is a disco, Tiffany, underneath the Hotel Silberhorn
TOURIST OFFICE +41 (0)33 855 14 14; www.wengen-muerren.ch

02

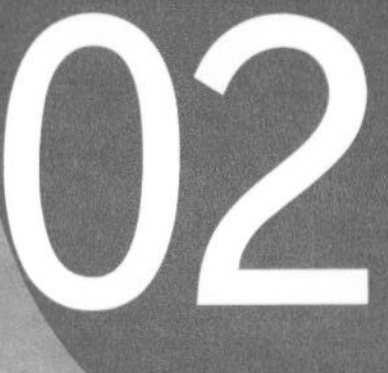

Away from It All

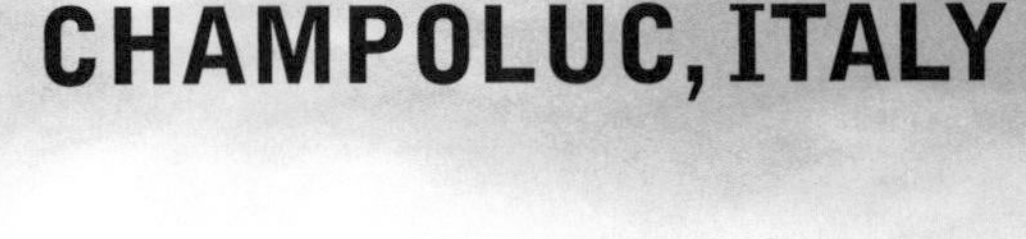

CHAMPOLUC, ITALY

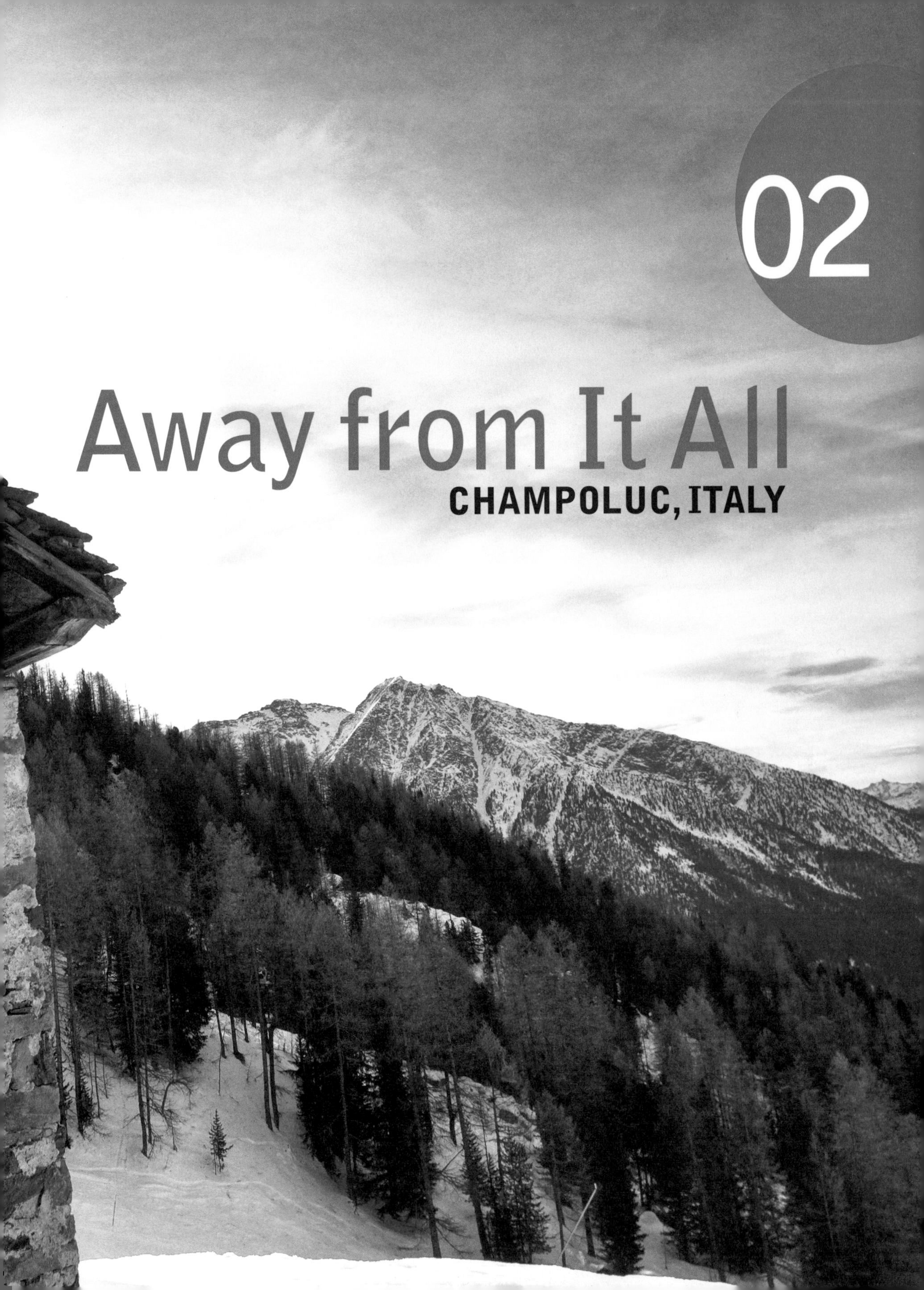

Champoluc's village church

IT HAS BEEN A QUICK and easy journey, but the village square of Champoluc seems a world away from home. We arrive as the last rays of the afternoon sun are warming the cream and pink stucco of the church tower and the locals are coming out for the evening *passagiato*.

There's a smell of woodsmoke and pine trees. Children play on the steps of the shop beside the church, peering through the windows at the elaborate displays of biscuits and cakes. Champoluc is how I imagine skiing was in the 1960s – based around venerable family hotels set in a traditional village, which necessitates a walk to and from the lifts but pays back the effort with endless peace and quiet, and bags of character.

'This isn't Chamonix – there are no clubs, no casino and no swimming pool, and the most exciting shop in town is the butcher's,' says Simon Brown, who moved here with his family nine years ago to run Ski2, one of the very few tour operators that bring people to the village.

Champoluc sits at one side of the Monterosa ski area, which covers three valleys. Beyond it is tiny Gressoney-la-Trinité, and over the ridge from that is beautiful Alagna, a resort revered for its extreme off-piste terrain. Though Turin airport is only ninety minutes away, few Brits could point to Monterosa on a map. Little wonder it's often called 'Europe's best kept secret'.

The main lift is a ten-minute walk from the village square so, though Robin and I have just arrived, we wander up to sample the après ski. In Le Galion pub, opposite the lift, the atmosphere couldn't be any more Italian and any less like the rowdy bars of Val

Fine food at the Relais des Glaciers, but the pizza's great too

d'Isère or St Anton. A group of hardcore male skiers sits drinking beer at the curved pewter bar while, beside them, an amorous couple play with their stylish little white cups of *macchiato*. A television is showing football in the corner and, at the table in front, a big extended family with children ranging from a couple of months to a couple of years old are drinking hot chocolate and talking animatedly. Outside, older children are burying their faces in big slices of pizza from the Dolce e Salato Bar, where they cost €2. We follow suit – they are delicious, piping hot and with a thin crust that melts in your mouth.

We're staying in the Relais des Glaciers, a comfortable, traditional four-star hotel just off the main square, with a roaring fire to lounge in front of with a pre-dinner drink and lavish four-course meals each night. But finding somewhere good to stay should never be a problem here. Unlike some of the more famous and more British-dominated resorts where the majority of accommodation is catered chalets and self-catering apartments, both only let for full weeks, here hotels are dominant.

The five-star Breithorn is probably the pick of the bunch. Built in 2002, it blends traditional and modern – the weathered wooden front door opens to reveal a snazzy glass one, which silently swishes open. Near by is the three-star Hotel Castor, its dark-wood exterior brightened by red and white shutters. Inside, it doesn't look as if much has changed for thirty years, but in a good way, and it seems relaxed and friendly when I drop in to use the internet.

Normally, I would always advise contacting the hotel and booking direct but, in Champoluc, I've arranged it all through Ski2. Realizing how close this

Chefs at the piste-side Belvedere restaurant

gem of a resort is to no fewer than five airports, Simon and his partner, Roger Walker, set up the company specifically to cater for the booming market in short, flexible breaks. They offer packages for however many nights you want, and their prices include private transfers, lift passes, ski guiding, breakfast, supper and even vouchers to exchange for your lunch on the mountain. Three nights at the Relais des Glaciers starts at around £400, which, given everything that's included, is not significantly more than you'd pay doing it yourself. And whereas some short-break ski companies are effectively UK-based middlemen who just make the bookings and add their cut, Ski2 have a huge operation in the village, with reps, shuttle buses and even their own ski school and hire shop. Simon is totally plugged in to village life, and his three children even go to school here.

The next morning, our first on skis, dawns clear but windy, and the link lift to Gressoney is closed. The good news is that it seems the wind has put most people off going out at all, and we have some wonderful pistes all to ourselves. From the top of the Alpe Mandria chair lift there is the long, rolling blue run, Del Lago (C10), and the fast red run Pian de la Sal (C16), flat, wide and perfect for high-speed carving.

Though we're looking up at the back of the Matterhorn, the atmosphere on the slopes is far more low key and relaxed than in Zermatt, the world-famous resort on the mountain's northern side. Lunch takes us even further away from it all. We turn left from the Del Lago piste and swoop through some trees to a little hidden valley. Perched at 2,000m in a clearing below us is Stadel Soussun, an ancient wooden hamlet. There are a couple of old houses sitting on stone mushrooms, a communal oven, and we peer through the door of a tiny chapel devoted to Madonna del Carmine, just big enough for a congregation of four.

The main house in the hamlet is now a restaurant with rooms, and we creak open the heavy door to find a big antique table set and waiting for us. The walls and vaulted ceiling are rough stone and hung with brass pots and old climbers' rucksacks. At one end, a dresser groans under the weight of red-wine bottles.

There's no menu, so Stephania, the curly-haired waitress, just reads out what they have. There's steak with juniper berries and goulash, but we opt for Moretti beers and a huge plate of cheese, dried meats and sausage. It's rounded off in proper Italian fashion with shots of homemade Genepy, made with the

Looking down on Stadel Soussun

1|2
|3
|4
5
6

artemisia flower that grows near by – on the house.

Upstairs are seven beautiful double rooms in what used to be the grain store (staying here half board costs €80 per person per night). As she shows us around, Stephania explains that the house has always been in the current owner, Sergio's, family. When I ask how old it is, she points to a coat of arms carved into a rafter, alongside the date it was built – 1518.

From the piste map it looks as if it's impossible to get back to the slopes from here without a long walk uphill. But in fact it's a cinch. Genepy shots downed, the boss fires up his piste basher, we jump in the back and he drives up a snowy track to the nearest lift.

Stadel Soussun is a memorable and unique place to stay but not the only one in the valley. That night we check out the Hotel California, on the outskirts of the village. From the outside it looks like a fairly ordinary wooden Alpine hotel but, as the owner, Guido, enthusiastically shows us around, it's clear it's anything but. He is a big fan of rock music from the 60s and 70s, and the hotel, which he designed and built himself, is a tribute to his obsession. A huge Wurlitzer dominates the lobby and the corridors are decorated like those of a Western saloon, with dark wallpaper and heavy wood panelling. Each of the twelve rooms is named after a different singer or rock group – Elvis, the Byrds, the Doors, Janis Joplin, the Grateful Dead and so on.

We check out Bob Dylan and, as Guido proudly flips the light switch, the stereo automatically cranks up: 'How many roads must a man walk down . . . ' Each room has music recorded by its namesake, which continues for ninety seconds after turning on the light. Neat, but it could get annoying, especially if you are just getting up for the loo in the night.

The walls are decorated with framed album covers, and we pause to chat by a Gram Parsons album which still has its Our Price sticker. 'I bought that in the King's Road in 1974,' says Guido. '£4.99.' Bizarre . . .

On Sunday, the winds have dropped and so we take the lifts over the pass and sweep down the pistes to Gressoney. It's a peaceful village but lacks the character of Champoluc. Alone, none of the three Monterosa valleys has enough piste skiing to keep you busy for more than a day or two but, together, they can muster 37 lifts and 180km of runs.

Beyond Gressoney, two seemingly endless gondola rides take you up to the Passo Salati at 2,971m, from where you look down towards Alagna, lost in a deep fold in the valley below. Champoluc is getting away from it all but, if you really want to escape the modern world, come up to this ridge then traverse right, following the wooden signpost to one of the two high mountain refuges clinging on to the ridge at 2,880m.

As we skitter down the track towards them, we round a rocky corner to come upon a helicopter loading up with skiers. That's the other surprise of this apparently sleepy, family-friendly area – some of the best heliskiing in the Alps.

The classic route is the Porta Nera, a full day's itinerary that requires just one lift in the helicopter. You're dropped

1 *Peace at last: the view over Champoluc*

2-6 *Dougie bites off more than he can chew*

Preceding page *Rhona, a British snowboarder who spends the whole winter in Champoluc*

CHAMPOLUC IS GETTING away from it all, but if you really want to escape the modern world, come up to this ridge.

The crumbling façade of the Rifugio Vigevano

Alberto shows off his high-altitude wine cellar

Traversing across to the Rifugio Guglielmina

at 4,200m on the Monte Rosa glacier, from where you ski 20km off piste down to Zermatt for lunch. After that you take the lifts up to the top of Klein Matterhorn at 3,883m, walk for half an hour up to the back of Breithorn, then ski all the way back to Champoluc. It costs €260, including the helicopter, guide and Zermatt lift ticket.

Behind the clattering helicopter we see the beautiful walls of the Rifugio Città di Vigevano, half stone, half crumbling yellow plaster. Red paint is peeling off the window frames, revealing the brown wood below. It was built in 1900 and is run by a club, but anyone can come, either for lunch or to stay – there are seventeen charming, basic bedrooms, although only four have hot water; the others have to share the communal bathroom. Dinner, bed and breakfast costs €45 per night. You'll need to bring a sheet sleeping bag, and a torch, because when the generator is off, there are no lights.

Walking around, it is like being inside an eighteenth-century warship. Everything is made of

wood – the sloping floors, the ceiling and the walls. At the end of a dark corridor, double doors swing open to reveal the dining room, which has windows on three sides revealing stunning views, a wood-burning stove in the centre and old wooden chairs and tables.

Fifty metres away, Alberto Calaba is making the final preparations for lunch at his refuge, Refugio Guglielmina. It's more well known, and older than its neighbour, having been built by Alberto's family in 1878, although today it's all far slicker, after a major renovation in 2007. As well as a new roof and exterior rendering, there's heat and light in every room, plus Alberto's pride and joy – the extensive wine cellar, which he drags me behind the bar to see. 'I have 7,000 bottles from Aosta, Piemonte, Tuscany and Sicily – all Italian, of course!' he beams. 'We have wine from €10 to €200. The best is a Gaja Sperss 2001, which is a famous Barolo, or try a 1997 Gattinara Riserva, which is a strong local mountain wine.'

ALAGNA IS REVERED for its extreme off-piste terrain.

We may be in a remote setting atop a mountain but these days the world is a small place. As diners start to take their seats on the large, sun-drenched terrace, Massimo, one of the waiters, shows me around the bedrooms (dinner, bed and breakfast here is €50 per night). He casually mentions he's just moved back to Italy after twelve years living in Brixton. Until two weeks ago he was working as a barber in Tooting Bec. Talk about getting away from it all …

From the refuges, it's a thigh-busting 1,680m non-stop descent all the way to Alagna. There are only four lifts and a couple of pistes here, but this place is all about the off piste – the tiny village markets itself as 'freeride paradise'. Basically, the entire mountainside above Alagna is covered in possible lines, with each descent racking up a vertical drop of close to 2,000m.

Whichever route you take, Alagna doesn't reveal itself until the very last minute but, when you finally come upon it, it's breathtaking, probably the prettiest village in the Alps. While most villages are built on flat ground, Alagna sits in the cleft of a deep valley, its chalets clustered around a church spire and rising up on either side of the valley.

Almost every chalet looks like a museum piece. All are made of the most delicious, chocolate-brown wood, aged by the sun over countless summers. Around their balconies are horizontal wooden struts once used for hanging hay out to dry. Roofs are made with rough slate tiles. The whole place feels more like a Sherpa village in Nepal than somewhere in Italy, and the toothy peak rising sharply on the far side of the village adds a Himalayan touch to the landscape itself.

That night, back in Champoluc, we head out after dinner to meet Simon for a quiet drink in the Favre bar. A few skiers sit in huddles drinking beer, a few villagers read the paper. Through the window we look past a frozen stream to the church, and the deserted village square. All is quiet. Simon is explaining what happens here in spring. 'When the snow melts, everyone just goes back to making cheese.'

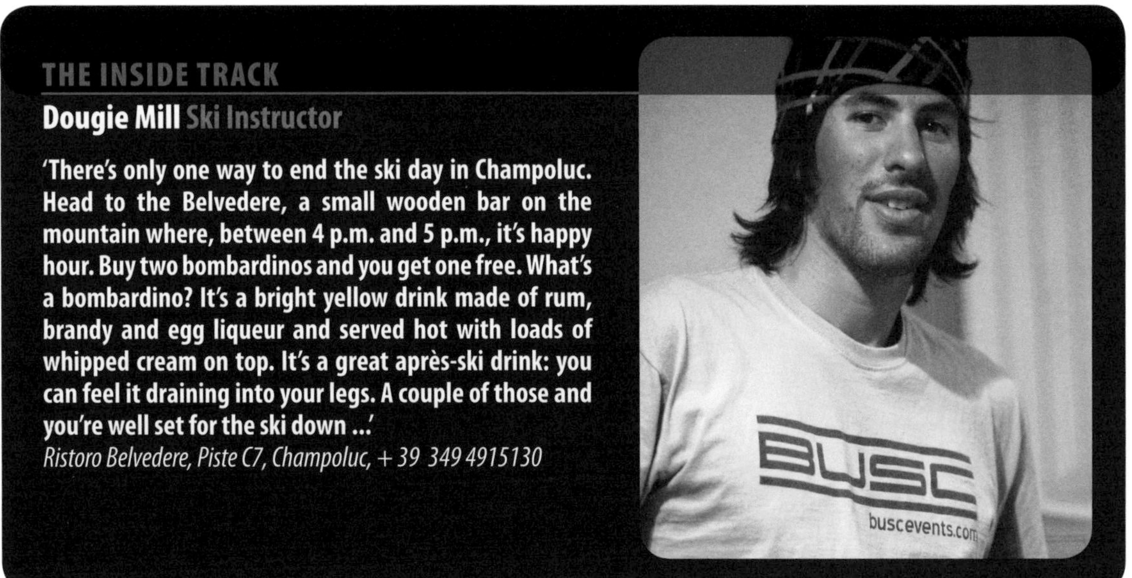

THE INSIDE TRACK

Dougie Mill Ski Instructor

'There's only one way to end the ski day in Champoluc. Head to the Belvedere, a small wooden bar on the mountain where, between 4 p.m. and 5 p.m., it's happy hour. Buy two bombardinos and you get one free. What's a bombardino? It's a bright yellow drink made of rum, brandy and egg liqueur and served hot with loads of whipped cream on top. It's a great après-ski drink: you can feel it draining into your legs. A couple of those and you're well set for the ski down …'

Ristoro Belvedere, Piste C7, Champoluc, + 39 349 4915130

Tom skiing down towards Alagna

The Knowledge
Champoluc, Italy

STATS **Town altitude:** 1,580m **Highest lift:** 2,970m; **Lifts:** 37 **Pistes:** 180km **Lift pass:** €36 per day **Closest airport:** Turin – 100km

WHY? The Monterosa ski area is often called 'one of Europe's best-kept secrets' because of the lack of crowds and stunning scenery. Of the three unspoilled villages that make up the area, charming Champoluc is the best base **GETTING THERE** Ideally, fly to Turin (with British Airways or Ryanair), but other possibilities include Milan (Milan Malpensa, 160km away, is better than Milan Linate, at 190km) and Geneva, 200km away **TRANSFERS** Buses require a change at Verres, where the Valle d'Ayas (which contains Champoluc) meets the Valle d'Aosta, so hiring a car is by far the best option. The drive should take an hour and a quarter from Turin, 2 hours from Malpensa and 3 from Linate or Geneva. Taxis are available, but will be much more expensive than hire cars, at around €170 each way (+ 39 339 7113050; www.taxivalledaosta.com). Ski2 (*see details below*) can organize helicopter transfers, which from Turin cost €1,100 for up to four people, each way **WHERE TO STAY** Pick of the bunch is the four-star Breithorn (+39 0125 308734; www.breithornhotel.com; doubles from €180, including breakfast). The Relais des Glaciers (+39 0125 308182; www.hotelrelaisdesglaciers.com; doubles from €160, half board) is friendly, does excellent food and is right on the village square. Eccentric but lovable is the Hotel California (+39 0125 307977), 2km outside the village centre; doubles from €80, including breakfast. If you really want to get away from it all and stay on the mountain, the options are: Stadel Soussun (+39 348 6527222; www.stadelsoussun.com; from €80pp, half board), Rifugio Città di Vigevano (+39 0163 922993; €45pp, half board); Rifugio Guglielmina (+39 0163 91444; www.rifugioguglielmina.com; €50pp, half board)

Prayer flags flutter over the Val d'Ayas, with Champoluc in the distance

➔ WHERE TO SKI Of the three valleys that make up Monterosa, Champoluc itself has the most piste skiing. The best, and quietest, is further up the valley in the Frachey sector. Rather than ride the lifts up to Frachey in the morning, it's a good idea to drive the few minutes up the valley to the bottom of the Frachey chairlift. Parking is free. The most famous off-piste runs are from the Salati ridge down into Alagna. A new lift to Punta Indren, a rocky outcrop on the ridge at 3,260m, is currently under construction and will open up many more options **➔ WHERE TO EAT** Many people eat in their hotels, but there are some excellent restaurants too. Le Petit Coq (+39 0125 307997), run by Lorenza and Sarro, is a typical alpine chalet near Hotel California serving rustic local dishes, including *bagna calda* – literally, 'hot stone'. La Grange (+39 0125 307835), next to the Frachey lift, serves Valdostani food and is renowned locally for steaks and wild boar **➔ WHERE TO PARTY** The terrace of the Atelier Gourmand at the bottom of the main Champoluc lift is a popular spot for après-ski beers, as is the Galion pub opposite, but this really isn't the place to come for a party. The only real action is in Lo Bistro (below the Galion pub), a restaurant with a dance floor, which can get wild on Saturday nights **➔ HELP!** Ski2 (01962 713330; www.ski-2.com) is the unrivalled expert on the area and offers a 3-night package from €389, including transfers, half board, snack lunches and lift pass, but not flights
➔ TOURIST OFFICE +39 0125 307113; www.monterosa-ski.com

Five More... Away from It All

GARGELLEN, AUSTRIA

➲ STATS: **Town altitude:** 1,423m; **Highest lift:** 2,398m; **Lifts:** 61; **Pistes:** 220km; **Closest airport:** Friedrichshafen – 100km

➲ WHY? A blissful rural backwater hidden away at the end of a valley, it looks as if little has changed since Ernest Hemingway skied here in the 1920s. It's part of the Montafon ski area, which covers 11 nearby villages on one ski pass, although you'll need to take the free buses to travel between them
➲ GETTING THERE Hire a car or book a taxi, which, from Friedrichshafen, will cost around €170 for up to 3 people and take about 1 hour and 15 minutes (+43 (0)555 67808; www.filzmaier-taxi.at)
➲ WHERE TO STAY The Hotel Heimspitze (+43 (0)555 76319; www.heimspitze.com; doubles from €166, half board) is a friendly family-run property with an excellent restaurant. The Madrisa (+43 (0)555 76331; www.madrisahotel.com) is also recommended
➲ WHERE TO PARTY You must be joking. But there is après ski in the little Schirm bar, close to the bottom of the cable car. The Chaverna bar in the Madrisa hotel is the liveliest later on
➲ TOURIST OFFICE +43 (0)555 76303; www.gargellen.at. Montafon area: +43 (0)555 6722530; www.montafon.at

ALPBACH, AUSTRIA

➲ STATS: **Town altitude:** 1,000m; **Highest lift:** 2,025m; **Lifts:** 20; **Pistes:** 46km; **Closest airport:** Innsbruck – 60km

➲ WHY? Once voted Austria's most beautiful village, Alpbach's wooden chalets cluster round a traditional church. The skiing is not that extensive, but this is the perfect place for a family of beginners, or those simply looking for total peace
➲ GETTING THERE Taxi from Innsbruck airport will take 50 minutes and cost about €95 each way (+43 (0)533 65616; www.autoreisen-moser.at). A taxi from Munich, 130km away, will cost €190 each way and take about 90 minutes
➲ WHERE TO STAY The Hotel Post (+43 (0)533 65203; www.hotel-post.cc; doubles from €106, half board) is a comfortable, chalet-style property with big balconies, close to the heart of the village
➲ WHERE TO PARTY Carousing is limited to après ski. For that, head to the bar of the Jakober and Böglerhof hotels, or the Waschkuchl
➲ TOURIST OFFICE +43 (0)533 6200941; www.alpbach.at

BETTMERALP, SWITZERLAND

➲ STATS: **Town altitude:** 2,000m; **Highest lift:** 2,869m; **Lifts:** 35; **Pistes:** 99km; **Closest airport:** Sion – 60km

➲ WHY? It's a pretty, traffic-free village (you arrive by cable car) on a plateau which looks across to the distant Matterhorn. From the highest lift, you get one of the most stunning views in the Alps, down to the huge Aletsch glacier, a Unesco World Heritage Site. The skiing is excellent for intermediates and, at this height, should offer good snow conditions
➲ GETTING THERE Train from Sion to Betten Talstation (from where you get the cable car up to the village) will take about 90 minutes. Zurich (200km) has many more flights and is 3 hours by train, but it's a simple and beautiful journey with just one change from the airport station (at Brig)
➲ WHERE TO STAY Hotel Restaurant Panorama (+41 (0)27 927 13 75; www.tiscover.ch/hotelpanorama; doubles from CHF160/£74 B&B) is a small, traditional Alpine hotel run by Fredy Schmidhalter and family. Simple but stylish
➲ WHERE TO PARTY Scappatina, die Bar is the place for drinks and impromptu dancing, or there's a nightclub and disco at the Hotel Alpfrieden
➲ TOURIST OFFICE +41 (0)27 928 60 60; www.bettmeralp.ch

VAUJANY, FRANCE

➲ STATS: **Town altitude:** 1,250m; **Highest lift:** 3,330m; **Lifts:** 87; **Pistes:** 249km; **Closest airport:** Grenoble – 50km

➲ WHY? A perfect example of the 'secret satellite', that is, a pretty little village that has a lift linking into the ski area of a hulking great mega-resort. Vaujany, a humble farming hamlet, suddenly got rich after a big hydro-electric project was built on its land. It used the proceeds

Lunch in the sun at the Rifugio Guglielmina

to build a huge 160-person cable car linking it to Alpe d'Huez, a resort known for its sensational pistes and hideous architecture

➜ **GETTING THERE** Hiring a car is probably best – the drive takes about 50 minutes. A taxi for up to 3 will cost about €170 each way (+33 (0)6 74 53 13 56; email: alptaxiesposito@yahoo.fr)

➜ **WHERE TO STAY** There's not a lot of choice – most accommodation is tied up by tour operators for full-week skiers. Try the Hotel Les Cimes (+33 (0)4 76 79 86 50; hotellescimes.monsite.wanadoo.fr; doubles from €80, including breakfast); it's simple but comfortable

➜ **WHERE TO PARTY** There's nothing like a nightclub here, but the Swallow Bar is a lively enough place, or try Stieff's pub

➜ **TOURIST OFFICE** +33 (0)4 76 80 72 37; www.vaujany.com

ADELBODEN, SWITZERLAND

➜ **STATS:** **Town altitude:** 1,353m; **Highest lift:** 2,362m; **Lifts:** 56; **Pistes:** 185km; **Closest airport:** Bern – 65km

➜ **WHY?** Sir Henry Lunn organized the first package tours to Adelboden in 1903. Thankfully, they never seem to have caught on, and this remains a traditional village, all but ignored by international visitors. There's a surprisingly extensive ski area too, best suited to intermediates, although a guide will be able to open up some memorable off-piste options

➜ **GETTING THERE** If you can't get a flight to Bern, try Zurich 190km away. From Bern you can travel by train to Frutigen, the station a few minutes' drive down the valley, in under 1 hour 30 minutes – bus or taxi from the airport to Rubigen station, then change at Thun and Spiez. A taxi will cost CHF220/£102 (+41 (0)33 673 28 48; www.taxi-bergmann.ch) and take about an hour

➜ **WHERE TO STAY** Try the atmospheric, wood-panelled Hotel Bären (+41 (0)3 36732151; www.baeren-adelboden.ch; doubles from CHF210/£98, including breakfast). Alternatively, the central, three-star Adler Sporthotel (+41 (0)33 673 41 41; www.adleradelboden.ch; doubles from CHF236/£110, including breakfast) has its own wellness centre

➜ **WHERE TO PARTY** The Berna Bar, within the Hotel Bernerhof, is the only club in town, with DJs on till 3.30 a.m. at weekends. Otherwise, it's more about the tearooms – Tearoom Schmid and Café Haueter, both on Dorfstrasse, are the favourites

➜ **TOURIST OFFICE** +41 (0)33 673 80 80; www.adelboden.ch

SALOMON

03 City
GRANADA, SPAIN

Spring blossom in the valley, snow on the hills

'A VECES LA VIDA ES PERFECTA,' says the advert for Alhambra Reserve beer in the middle of the luggage carousel at Granada airport – 'Sometimes life is perfect.'

At this very moment, as we stand wearily in the baggage-reclaim hall, life seems anything but, and yet I'm excited. We're about to have what looks, on paper at least, like the weekend with everything.

Of course, Granada is an amazing historic city, with everything that encompasses: restaurants, bars, nightlife, cathedrals, culture and a huge choice of fabulous hotels. Less well known is that it has its own ski resort, just thirty minutes' drive up the hill. And we're not just talking about a couple of lowly blue runs – there are 86km of slopes and the top lift rises to an impressive 3,300m.

Better still, you don't need to take a single day off work. If you live anywhere near Stansted airport, you can take Ryanair's Friday-night flight direct to Granada then fly home, after two full days' skiing, on Sunday night.

If you come here during the ski season you get to see the city when it's far quieter than in the peak summer months, and room rates, even at the grandest historic hotels, come crashing down. Oh, and if you fancy easing off the muscles after your day on the piste, you can head down to the seaside – the beach is only an hour down the road.

Thankfully, we don't have to stare at the Alhambra beer advert too long. Ours is the only plane on the tarmac, the terminal is delightfully deserted and our skis and bags come out almost immediately. Picking up our car takes five minutes and, after twenty minutes' drive, we're pulling up to our hotel in the town centre. Just over an hour after landing, we're in our first tapas bar, glasses in hand and, if not perfect, life is looking very rosy indeed.

Perhaps because it's so full of impecunious students, Granada is one of the few cities in Spain where the tradition of giving out free tapas with every drink ordered is still alive and strong. We're told both that the tradition stems from the practice of resting pieces of bread on the rim of the glass to stop flies getting in ('*tapa*' means cover), and that it's simply to keep people eating so they don't get too drunk.

After wandering about the backstreets for a while we chance upon the bar I'd been told to look out for – Bodegas Castañeda, on Almireceros. It's actually one of the most famous tapas bars in the city, but we are the only foreigners here, no one speaks English, and the charming barman, Javier, seems genuinely delighted when we get out the camera and start taking pictures.

It's an utterly classic scene – we stand at the long wooden bar, beneath hundreds of legs of jamón serrano, air-dried ham made just on the other side of the ski slopes in the Alpujarras. Beside the hams, a huge black bull's head peers down at us. Old guns hang from the tiled walls and behind the bar is a stack of ancient wine barrels.

Jamón Serrano hangs in every bar

Even the crowd couldn't be more classically Spanish, though they range from old men with beards sitting smoking quietly to youngsters in designer clothes rowdily downing *chupitos de chocolate con nata,* little chocolate cups filled with cream and alcohol.

Calicasas: approach with caution

Despite being an institution, it's cheap, particularly when you are used to ski resorts. Two beers, two nice glasses of manzanilla plus a *tapa* of ham, cheese and olives comes to €6.80. Javier's eyes light up when I order the house speciality – the Calicasas. Into a tall glass he pours four types of spirit, then goes from barrel to barrel opening the wooden taps to top up the glass with vermouth and different types of wine. It's utterly delicious, especially as it only costs €1.90, but it's absolute rocket fuel.

Next day I feel terrible as we swing up the mountain roads to the resort. There are regular buses, but it's far better to hire a car and drive yourself, thus also avoiding the need for airport taxis. The journey is only 31km and shouldn't take longer than thirty minutes, but only if you leave early – no later than 8.30 a.m. – to beat the crowds, which can cause traffic jams. Despite the lingering taste of vermouth in my mouth, it's a fabulous morning – the sun is just rising behind the peaks, throwing down dramatic shafts of light on to the contour-hugging road.

In lay-bys, old men are opening up stalls selling locally made honey and nuts. We drive past olive and cherry trees, and rows of almond trees covered in delicate pink blossom. It's so warm and spring-like that it seems astonishing we're actually going skiing but, as we pass 2,000m, we finally hit the snowline and at 2,100m we come to the Sierra Nevada ski resort.

At the bottom lift station, there's a huge queue. High winds mean the lifts have remained closed this morning, and an anxious line of skiers snakes around the main plaza. The resort itself is hideously ugly – which is why you'd be mad to stay here instead of retreating to gorgeous Granada. There was never an original village to give focus and charm and, instead of creating a purpose-built resort with coherent styles and themes, the Spanish have thrown up all manner of modern blocks, jumbled together at random. On the up side, the centre is completely pedestrianized and the main square is lined with coffee shops and bars.

At 10.30 a.m. the lifts open at last and we head out to explore. Carlos, our instructor, tells us we're lucky – the previous day wind closed the lifts all day. 'I just drove down to the beach instead,' he says with a grin.

Carlos explains that the snow conditions are unrelated to those in the Alps. This year the Alps have done well, the Sierra Nevada less so, but it can be vice versa, making this a clever alternative. Because of the altitude – most of the skiing is above 2,600m – the season is long, running for five months, from the start of December to the end of April, and the lifts run long hours too – from 9 a.m. until a staggered closing between 4.45 p.m. and 5.30 p.m.

The snow isn't great, but it's clear there's lots of good skiing here, if few off-piste challenges for real experts. At Borreguiles, there's a super-wide area for beginners, with the terraces of a number of cafés directly beneath it, in case there's need for a comforting drink. On a ridge above is a huge radio telescope (sited here on account of the clear skies), beneath which is the resort's steepest black. The best runs of all are hidden away in the secluded Laguna bowl, on the far side of the telescope. Though the bowl has only two lifts, there are a dozen pistes, and many more off-piste options, spreading out across it.

Carlos, our guide, takes a break

FROM THE HIGHEST LIFT we can look down to the olive groves of Cazorla, the city of Granada, and the distant sparkle of the Mediterranean. The piste map even marks Morocco's Rif mountains.

The mountains here feel very different to the Alps. Rather than craning our necks to look at the jagged peaks around us, we're standing on top of the highest mountains for hundreds of kilometres (hence the occasional wind problem), looking down to the grey hills far below. From the highest lift, which stops just short of the peak of Veleta, we can see the olive groves of Cazorla in the north, the city of Granada to the west and, to the south, the plastic tunnels of Almería's fruit farms and the distant sparkle of the Mediterranean.

The piste map even marks the Rif mountains of Morocco in the distance. This must be the only resort in the world that can show the mountains of two continents on its map.

Unfortunately, there is a drawback. The slopes of Sierra Nevada are so convenient for Granada city centre that it gets busy at weekends. We're here on a Saturday, though – the busiest day of all, since Sunday is the usual changeover day for those coming for a full week – and the slopes are certainly crowded, but not nightmarishly so.

A new main gondola from the resort, which is due to open by Christmas 2008, should dramatically reduce queues. Still, it would make sense to come here

during the quieter periods – December, mid-January, then late March and April, when the Spaniards have lost interest and are heading for the beach.

Bar Genil, a wooden chalet close to the top of the Genil chair lift, is a good spot for lunch, but most of the mountain restaurants here are fast-food places owned by Cetursa, the resort's central management company. Better to picnic sitting in the sun in the shelter of the old observatory (just along the ridge from the new radio telescope), or at the statue of the Virgin of the Snows (on the opposite side of the mountain, just above the resort), or to ski down the cracking red Sabina piste back to the village, where there's a range of independent restaurants and bars.

For tapas, locals head to Bar Cartujano, owned by a family from Monachil, just down the valley, which is tucked away in a commercial arcade to the right of Mont Blanco hotel. Though it's in a purpose-built modern block, inside, the bar looks as traditional as anything in the city itself, and Juan, the barman, dishes out delicious fried squid with our beers. For fuller meals, head to the other side of the Mont Blanco, where La Carreta does impressive steaks and Tito Luigi, next door, specializes in Italian food. Carlos

EVEN AS DUSK SETTLES on the city, we can just make out the red run we'd skied a few hours earlier, right at the top of the mountain.

also raves about Crescendo, beside the bottom of the Genil chairlift: 'The best burger in the Sierra Nevada!' he beams.

The other key selling point of this ski area, the southernmost in Europe by a very long way, is the sun. By the time we finish skiing, it's baking hot, and crowds of people are soaking up the rays in the strip of bars at the bottom of the pistes. These bars – Cuna, Tía María and Parallell – are pretty much identical, and don't serve tapas with the drinks, but their terraces face into the afternoon sun and straight towards the mountains, so your view isn't blotted by the resort itself.

On Saturdays you can relax in a deck chair for a few hours in the afternoon then head back up for more skiing. From 7 p.m. to 9 p.m., the gondola is reopened and the long, sweeping El Río piste is floodlit for night skiing. But, for us, the pull of Granada is too great.

Back in town, we are spoilt for choice for spots to sit and watch the sunset over the mountain we've just been skiing on. One excellent vantage point is the terrace bar of the Alhambra Palace Hotel, a grand five-star property right next to the Alhambra, one of the world's most visited historic monuments. The Alhambra was built between 900 and 1238, the hotel in 1920, but this didn't stop the latter aping the grand Moorish style of its elder neighbour. The lobby is covered in finely detailed patterned tiles, the plasterwork beautifully carved. It's also in an ideal location for the ski slopes – just over a kilometre off the main road out to the mountains.

We have a quick drink on the terrace then rush over to the Albaicín, the higgledly-piggledy jumble of whitewashed Moorish houses on the hill opposite the Alhambra. We're walking through the winding cobbled lanes when a woman comes out and empties her bucket of washing water down the open gutter in the middle of the alleyway. It feels more as if we're in Marrakech than Europe.

The Albaicín has some of the most interesting hotels in town. Old Moorish houses, mostly seventeenth century or older, have been converted into wonderful boutique hotels. Hidden off the cobbled streets that run alongside the River Darro, many have gorgeous courtyards and the feel of North African riads. Try the Palacio Santa Inés, Casa Morisca, Casa Capitel Nazarí, Hotel Los Migueletes and Ladrón de Agua. Room rates are reasonable, and the only down side is that you'll have to park a little way off.

Eventually, we emerge at the Mirador San Nicolás, a church square and famous viewpoint, where a crowd of hippyish young people have gathered to watch the sunset. Some are playing the drums, others strumming flamenco guitars, clapping and singing. A dreadlocked couple sell incense; other groups just sit in circles chatting earnestly.

In front of the square, the roofs of the Albaicín tumble away to the River Darro and, beyond it, the hillside rises steeply up to the Alhambra itself, its ancient walls turning a deep purple as the sun dies. Above the Alhambra are the snows of the Sierra Nevada and the shark-fin-like peak of Veleta. Even as dusk settles, we can just make out the red run we'd skied down from the top a few hours earlier.

That night, we eat at Tendido 1, a fashionable

1 | *The Virgin of the Snows*

2 | *Singing at sunset at the Mirador San Nicolás, with the ski area in the background*

3 | *The staff of Tendido 1*

4 | Chupitos de chocolate con nata, *at Bodegas Castañeda*

5 | *Slicing the prized ham*

6 | *The all-female clientele of La Hacienda*

3
4

1
2

5
6

Soaking up the afternoon sun in Plaza Aliatar

restaurant under the seats of the bullring, where old wine barrels and bullfighting posters from the 20s line the walls. The speciality is the *rabo de toro estofado* – bull's tail, which is prized for its tenderness. Rosa, who has just taken us on a walking tour through the Albaicín, explains that if a bullfighter is good, he's rewarded with one of the animal's ears; if he's very good, he gets both; and if his performance has been exceptional, the tail is his, too, and he'll then wave all three at the crowd.

We squeamishly avoid the tail, but the Pata Negra (black foot) ham is sensational, as is the mixed grill done over oak charcoal. Afterwards, we try a couple of new-school tapas bars, which are the latest thing in the city. First is the ultra-sleek Oleum on Calle St Antón, which looks like a minimalist West End fashion boutique, except for a couple of hanging hams. Then it's on to La Hacienda, on Plaza Nueva, where a dressed-up crowd which, for some reason, is almost entirely female, drinks cocktails under the Rococo chandeliers. Rosa had warned me this place was renowned for being expensive, but I still get change from €10 for four beers.

On Sunday we spend the morning on the slopes then shoot off to the beach. The coast is 70km away, an easy hour's drive almost entirely on motorway, descending through a dramatic river gorge. We hit the coast at Salobrenas, once a whitewashed village clustered around a church on top of a small seaside hill. Today, the hill is surrounded by lots of ordinary apartment blocks, as if the tide has come in around it, but persevere, drive through the shabby surrounds and you reach a nice beach, backed by rocks and sheltered from the wind. It's probably horrific in summer, but it's February, and it's deserted but for the odd strolling local. The sea is actually not that cold either.

Our flight home isn't till 9.20 p.m., so we head back to town for some late-afternoon bar hopping in the Albaicín. This time, we stumble across the nicest square of all, Plaza Aliatar. It gets the afternoon sun and its cobbles are covered with tables, at which couples and families are eating and drinking. Buskers play flamenco while a masked dancer performs a strange routine in front of the fountain.

Après ski Granada style at Bar Chiringuito

Beyond the Albaicín, we enter the Sacromonte district, famous for its gypsy population and troglodyte houses. The further we walk away from the centre of town, pressing further up the increasingly steep-sided, narrow river gorge, the more bucolic the atmosphere. At Bar Pibe (41 Camino del Sacromonte), we sit and have a beer under an orange tree as an old man regales us with tales of his travels and his favourite ski resorts. Outside, it looks like a normal bar, but go inside and you find it has simply been hollowed out of the hillside. A rough-walled corridor runs to the bar, with little burrowed-out snugs to the side. A few doors up is El Camborio (number 47) which has a huge chill-out terrace at the top, a big dance floor and is playing some laid-back trance.

We double back towards the Albaicín, heading up Verea de Enmedio, a winding cobbled lane no more than two foot wide. Halfway back, just before we pass back inside the old Arab city wall, the path turns a corner and widens slightly, leaving enough space for a couple of trees to grow. Outside a cave doorway, a little metal table has been set up, from which sangría is being served. A few people sit drinking on a collection of mismatched chairs. Two old gypsy women peel oranges, their skin dark and lined, their eyes dramatically made up. Two kittens play at their feet. Other people straddle the wall, looking past the Alhambra to where the entire city stretches out before them and, beyond, to the setting sun.

There's no sign, but the barman later tells me it's called Bar Chiringuito. I think I've discovered the world's most romantic après-ski bar. Sometimes, life is perfect after all.

THE INSIDE TRACK

Rosa Terrones Walking-Tour Guide

'Lots of people don't know about the hammams of Granada – perfect for relaxing in after a day on the pistes. There's a long tradition of them here, because of our links with Morocco. There is one called Aljibe, on Calle San Miguel alta, which is new but decorated in Arabic style. Or there's one on Calle Santa Ana, behind the church on Plaza Nueva. It's a copy of the Royal Hammam in the Alhambra. All the tiling is hand painted and totally unique, and it's open until midnight.'

Aljibe: + 34 (0)958 522867; www.aljibesanmiguel.es.
Hammam Santa Ana: +34 (0)958 229978; www.hammamspain.com

The Knowledge
Granada, Spain

STATS **Town altitude:** Granada – 680m; Ski resort – 2,100m **Highest lift:** 3,300m; **Lifts:** 23 **Pistes:** 86km **Lift pass:** €37 per day **Closest airport:** Granada – 16km

WHY? Exotic Granada is the perfect destination for a weekend city break, known for its history, food and wine, and architecture that ranges from grand palaces to cave dwellings. Less well known is that there's a ski resort on the doorstep. And you can even go for a swim in the sea **GETTING THERE** Granada airport is currently served by Ryanair from Stansted, East Midlands and Liverpool. Malaga, 130km and nearly 2 hours' drive away, is much less convenient but is served by a wide range of airlines **TRANSFERS** The issue isn't getting from airport to city (taxis cost less than €20) but from the city up to the ski resort, which is 32km away. For this there are buses (run by Autocares Bonal, +34 (0)958 465022, departing 8 a.m. and 10 a.m.), but it makes more sense to hire a car at the airport, which you can then use to get into the city, up and down to the ski resort, and to head to the beach if you want. We hired through Holiday Autos (see car hire directory, page 286), who contract to Auriga Crown – we'd never heard of them either, but they turned out to be excellent **WHERE TO STAY** The Alhambra Palace (+34 (0)958 221468; www.h-alhambrapalace.es; doubles from €197; special offers may be available) wins because of its location, right by the Alhambra but also very close to the road up to the ski resort. There are great views over the city and to the mountains. Alternatively, try one of the converted Moorish houses in the Albaicín, like the Palacio Santa Inés (+34 (0)958 222362; www.palaciosantaines.com; doubles from €86) or Casa Morisca (+34 (0)958 221100; www.hotelcasamorisca.com; doubles from €107). Finally, for something totally different, La Almunia del Valle (+34 (0)958 308010; www.laalmuniadelvalle.com; doubles from €106, including breakfast) is a 'rustic chic' boutique hotel in the hills 10 minutes outside the city towards the ski resort **WHERE TO SKI** Head to the Laguna bowl on the far side of the ridge on which the radio telescopes sit. Here, there's a wide choice of easy red runs, it's high, so the snow should be good and, crucially, you can't see the ugly resort. If the resort is very busy, head for the Parador and Virgen de las Nieves lifts, to the extreme left of the area. These are always quiet, and there's an excellent red piste, Aguila, which returns to the resort

WHERE TO EAT Tendido 1 (+34 (0)958 272302; www.tendido1.com) is a fashionable restaurant beneath the bullring but, really, Granada is all about tapas. Wander down Calle Elvira, which is lined with tapas bars (including La Antigualla, a student favourite on account of the large portions), or seek out the classic Bodegas Castañeda (Calle Almireceros; +34 (0)958 215464). La Hacienda is a stylish place on Plaza Nueva or, for one of the 'new tapas' establishments, check out the funky Oleum (+34 (0)958 295357) on Calle San Antón **WHERE TO PARTY** Take in a flamenco show in one of the cave dwellings of Sacromonte – try Los Tarantos (Camino Sacromonte; +34 (0)958 222492; www.cuevaslostarantos.com). Further up the same road is El Camborio, a small club with great terraces and vaulted rooms hewn from the rock. Much of the nightlife centres around the tapas bars but, when these close, you can head to Mae West (Centro Comercial Neptuno; www.MaeWestGranada.com) or, for a really full-on night, take a taxi to Industrial Copera (+34 (0)958 258449; www.industrialcopera.net), a warehouse in Armilla, a suburb to the south of the main city, where the house music goes on all night **HELP!** Kirker Holidays (0870 1123333; www.kirkerholidays.com) offers a three-night package, staying at the Alhambra Palace, from £611 per person including flights, transfers, breakfasts and a ticket to the Alhambra. For walking tours, contact Cicerone, +34 (0)670 541669; www.ciceronegranada.com **TOURIST OFFICE** City: +34 (0)958 247146; www.turgranada.com. Ski resort: +34 (0)902 708090; www.cetursa.es

Five More... City and Ski

INNSBRUCK, AUSTRIA

STATS: Town altitude: 575m; **Highest lift:** 2,255m; **Lifts:** 15; **Pistes:** 45km; **Closest airport:** Innsbruck – 5km

WHY? Mountains rise up on all sides around Innsbruck and there are numerous local ski areas. You can reach the closest, the Nordpark-Seegrube area, by hopping on the Nordkettenbahn mountain railway right in the city centre. Its 4 stations have recently been redesigned by the architect Zaha Hadid and are now strange, amorphous shapes worth the journey just to see. On the other side of town, trams run to the suburb of Igls, from where a cable car takes you up to the piste used for the Olympic downhill in 1976. Almost as close is the village of Mutters, with 3 lifts and some long runs
GETTING THERE Taxi or shuttle bus from the airport
WHERE TO STAY The Penz Hotel (+43 (0)512 5756570; www.the-penz.com; doubles from €140, including breakfast) in the old town is a stylish option, with a fifth-floor terrace where you can watch the sunset with a cocktail
WHERE TO PARTY Start by sampling the glühwein at the Fischerhäusl bar (on Herrengasse), then head to Jimmy's (on Wilhelm-Greil-Strasse), the favourite nightspot for the city's student population
TOURIST OFFICE +43 (0)512 59850; www.innsbruck.info

OSLO, NORWAY

STATS: Town altitude: 50m; **Highest lift:** 525m; **Lifts:** 7; **Pistes:** 6km; **Closest airport:** Oslo International – 26km

WHY? A fascinating city reinventing itself as Scandinavia's leading centre of design and architecture, Oslo is also one of the few cities in which you see people getting on the underground to go skiing. The biggest ski area is the Tryvann Winter Park, which has 7 lifts and some reasonable slopes – the longest is 1.4km with a vertical drop of 381m
GETTING THERE Sterling, Ryanair and Norwegian Air Shuttle fly from the UK to Oslo. From the city centre, take underground line 1 to Voksenkollen station, where a shuttle bus takes you to the slopes of Tryvann Winter Park (www.tryvann.no)– the journey from the city centre should only take 20 minutes
WHERE TO STAY Thon Hotel Gyldenløve (+47 (0) 23 33 23 00; www.thonhotels.com; doubles from £110) is a minimalist affair in shades of white, mocha and grey. Design ground zero, though, is the new Grims Grenka Hotel (+47 (0) 23 10 72 00; www.grimsgrenka.no; doubles from £200), which boasts a rooftop lounge and hip nightclub
WHERE TO PARTY The best cocktails are at Bar Boca, an intimate, 50s-style place on Thorvald Meyersgate. For a full-on night, head to Bla, a club in a warehouse beside the Akerselva river
TOURIST OFFICE +47 (0) 81 53 05 55; www.visitoslo.com.

MARRAKECH, MOROCCO

STATS: Town altitude: 450m; **Highest lift:** 3,258m; **Lifts:** 8; **Pistes:** 20km; **Closest airport:** Marrakech – 3km

WHY? This isn't a joke – a ski weekend in Africa is perfectly possible (if slightly mad). The resort of Oukaimeden is 76km and an hour's taxi ride from Marrakech. It's currently a ramshackle affair, with lifts that often don't work and donkeys being used to drag skiers up instead. However, all that could change, as Dubai's largest property developer, Emaar, is currently planning to transform it into a swanky golf and ski resort
GETTING THERE Easyjet, Ryanair, Atlas Blue (www.atlas-blue.com) and Royal Air Maroc (0207 439 4361; www.royalairmaroc.com) fly from the UK to Marrakech. Taxis to Oukaimeden can be arranged via your hotel and will cost about £25 each way
WHERE TO STAY The Sultana (+212 (0)24 388008; www.lasultanamarrakech.com; doubles from 3000 dirhams/£200, including breakfast) is an opulent oasis amidst the bustle of the city, with a fabulous roof terrace and pool. There are lots of cheap and chic choices too – boutique-hotel booking service I-Escape is a good place to find them (www.i-escape.com). Alternatively, stay in the mountains at Sir Richard Branson's Kasbah Tamadot (0800 716919; www.kasbahtamadot.virgin.com; doubles from €320, including breakfast), a stunning hilltop retreat with great views and all the luxury trimmings
WHERE TO PARTY Après-ski drinks should be taken on the roof terrace of your riad then, for some proper nightlife, head to Pacha (+212 (0)24 388400; www.pachamarrakech.com), an African outpost of the Ibiza superclub that's out in the desert just outside town. As well as a sleek white-leather-clad main room, there are gardens, terraces and chill-out areas
TOURIST OFFICE 0207 437 0073; www.visitmorocco.com

SALZBURG, AUSTRIA

STATS: Town altitude: 424m; **Highest lift:** 3,029m; **Lifts:** 570 (in the Salzburg region); **Pistes:** 1,700km; **Closest airport:** Salzburg – 3km

WHY? Mozart's birthplace is a romantic mix of medieval cobbled lanes and baroque spires, at its best when under a blanket of snow. Better still, there are at least 15 resorts within an hour's drive – and the closest, the small beginner areas of Dürrnberg and Gaißau, are just 20km from the city centre. Go in December and mix skiing with shopping and drinking at the famous Christmas markets

GETTING THERE Getting out to the numerous nearby ski resorts is easy too, thanks to the Salzburg Snow Shuttle, a coach service that leaves the Mirabell Square at 8.30 every morning (€13 return) and takes skiers to a different resort each day, returning at 5 p.m. Resorts to be visited include Saalbach, Zell am See and Obertauern

WHERE TO STAY The Blaue Gans (+43 (0)662 84249150; www.blauegans.at; doubles from €115, including breakfast) claims to be the oldest inn in town, but has had a striking makeover, and the interiors are now swish and minimalist

WHERE TO PARTY Have dinner at Hangar 7 (www.hangar-7.com), the brainchild of the billionaire behind Red Bull. You eat surrounded by planes, and celebrity chefs are brought in from around the world to cook for just one month each. For something more earthy, try one of the city's many bierkellers – a favourite is the Bräustübl Tavern at the Augustiner Brewery on Lindhofstrasse, a cavernous place that has been serving good cheer since 1621

TOURIST OFFICE +43 (0)662 889870; www.salzburg.info

REYKJAVÍK, ICELAND

STATS: Town altitude: 0m; **Highest lift:** 700m; **Lifts:** 15; **Pistes:** 20km; **Closest airport:** Reykjavík – 37km

WHY? Reykjavík is known as a great place for a party-filled weekend break, but few know you can ski nearby. The Bláfjöll ski area, Iceland's largest, is just 30 minutes outside town. Reykjavík is also known for ruinous prices, but hotels are much cheaper in the winter

GETTING THERE Iceland Express (0870 2405600; www.icelandexpress.com) flies from Stansted and Gatwick; Icelandair (0870 7874020; www.icelandair.co.uk) flies from Heathrow, Glasgow and Manchester. Regular buses run from the airport into the city, and from Reykjavík's Mjódd Bus Terminal to Bláfjöll – or just hire a car at the airport

WHERE TO STAY The Hótel Borg (+354 (0)551 1440, www.hotelborg.is; doubles from 21,900 kronor/£141) dates from 1930; Marlene Dietrich once enjoyed cocktails here. It has recently been restored to all its art deco glory, with just a touch of the new millennium to keep things hip. CenterHotel Thingholt (+354 (0)595 8530; www.centerhotels.com; doubles from 17,000 kronor/£110) is a smart new place close to the waterfront

WHERE TO PARTY Reykjavík's centre is so tiny you can easily hang out on Laugavegur, the main street, and follow the crowds to the party. Try Café Oliver, Pravda, Organ and old favourite Kaffibarinn. Note: people tend to drink at home until midnight to save money, so things don't get lively till late

TOURIST OFFICE Reykjavík: +354 (0)590 1550; www.visitreykjavik.is. Bláfjöll ski area: +354 (0)530 3000; www.skidasvaedi.is

Two and a Half Days' Skiing – Zero Days off Work

LA CLUSAZ, FRANCE

04

ONCE A MONTH, the resort takes inspiration from the beaches of Thailand and hosts a full-moon party.

IT SOUNDS TOO GOOD TO BE TRUE. More than two days' skiing, without a single day off work? Why doesn't everyone do it every weekend?

Well, lean in and listen carefully because, if you know the secret, the time-bending ski weekend becomes perfectly possible. You just need the two magic words: 'La Clusaz'.

Now, La Clusaz isn't the biggest resort in France, it's not the highest, nor the most fashionable, nor the prettiest, but it does have one crucial advantage over the others: stand at the top of its ski area, look north, and you're staring straight down at Geneva, home of the busiest airport in the Alps.

During the winter, Geneva is skiing's biggest hub by far. At weekends there are up to forty-two flights a day, from twenty different UK airports. Geneva is the most common gateway to a huge range of French and Swiss resorts, but the first proper mountains you get to, separated from the flat plains around the city by just a single line of wooded hills, are the Massif des

Previous pages: Tom skiing at the Balme, high above La Clusaz Below: The lifts – and the bars – stay open till 1 a.m.

Aravis, at the foot of which sits La Clusaz. Driving from the airport to the resort takes us fifty-two minutes.

Still, you say, how does that mean you get more time skiing than there are days in the weekend?

Well, the other advantage of La Clusaz is that it likes to promote itself as a young, funky place, particularly as it's home to a string of champion freestyle skiers and boarders. And so, once a month, the resort takes inspiration from the beaches of Thailand and Goa and hosts a 'full-moon party', normally on the Friday night nearest the full moon. The mountain restaurants stay open at night, there are bands and DJs playing outside, the colossal superpipe is floodlit and, crucially, the lifts stay open from 9 p.m. until 1 a.m. Now you're getting it.

So, you catch a 6 p.m. flight (OK, you have to skive off the last few hours of Friday afternoon, but what are 'migraines' for?), landing at 8.15 p.m. local time. You jump in a cab and, by 9.30 p.m., you're in La Clusaz, heading up the lifts with three and a half

hours' riding ahead of you. Even if you don't come for the full-moon party, the ratio of skiing to travel time is exceptional here, since every day the lifts run from 9 a.m. to 5 p.m. or 5.20 p.m., a good hour longer than those in many Austrian and Swiss resorts.

On Sunday evening, you can easily ski till 5 p.m., stop off for a few beers in the sun – even an early dinner – before heading back to the airport for your evening flight home. Could this be the perfect weekend-ski bolt-hole?

We arrive on a cold January evening, dump bags in our hotel and head straight up the lifts. We start in the Bercail restaurant, a traditional chalet in the middle of the Merle piste, where we gorge on Savoyard specialities – soup with bacon and a melting dollop of cheese in it, all sorts of fat sausages in wine, something to do with pig's testicles, and lashings of *tartiflette*, that extravaganza of potatoes, bacon and yet more melted cheese. Outside on the terrace, somewhat incongruously, a rapper and DJ stand in

Lashings of melted cheese at the Bercail

front of a huge Rastafarian flag belting out a heavy dub in a strange mixture of French and Caribbean patois. The growing crowd is loving it.

Full of cheese, at 10.30 p.m. we set off to ski. The snow is silvery blue in the moonlight but, on our first cautious run, I can only really navigate using the dark outlines of trees at the edge of the piste and the cheery shouts of other skiers. Thankfully, my eyes slowly begin to adjust, normal skiing becomes possible and I start to enjoy the new experience.

Really, though, the night is more about the party than the skiing. On the terraces outside all the restaurants and bars that dot the three or four pistes open for night skiing, there are bonfires, DJs and, at one, a full-scale rock band playing AC/DC covers even as the snow starts to fall. We follow the locals as they ski from one bar to the next, stopping at each for warming snifters and a boogie round the fire.

The biggest crowd is gathered around the flood-lit superpipe. We watch the skiers and boarders doing

Late-afternoon sun on the Aravis chain

huge flips off one side then the other, flying several metres clear of the pipe, then gasp as they come back down to the bottom, remove their goggles and reveal themselves to be about twelve years old.

Anyone can jump into the pipe and, fuelled by cheese, schnapps and the watching crowd, I decide to give it a go. I manage a little jump at one side, then a slightly bigger one at the other, and soon I'm starting to imagine myself in a freestyle-ski film. Then, halfway down, it strikes me that I'm not really a superfly ski teen at all and, though it feels like another life, a few hours earlier I was sitting behind my desk in London wearing a suit. The spell thus broken, I also suddenly remember I have absolutely no idea what I'm doing. I slam on the brakes, snowplough humiliatingly down the gutter to the bottom and retreat to the hotel for a consoling nightcap.

We're staying at the Beauregard, a three-star hotel with a huge indoor swimming pool, sauna and jacuzzi which, like the resort as a whole, is friendly rather than fashionable. The rooms are spacious and clean but no one's wasted any time bothering about matching scatter cushions, funky light fittings or flower arrangements. Instead, in classic French style, all the effort goes on the food. Symphonie, the sensational restaurant on the ground floor, is so good it attracts skiers away from the slopes to linger over three wonderful courses at lunchtime.

Best of all, there's a drag lift right outside the front door, which connects up into the main ski area above La Clusaz. Here, there are lots of good cruising blue and red runs, and the slopes gradually get quieter as you head out away from the village and on to L'Étale, a second mountainside. From there, you can ski further away still, towards the wide, gentle and sunny slopes above Manigod, a tiny, satellite hamlet.

There are very few other Brits around. Despite its proximity to the airport, La Clusaz is ignored by most of the mainstream British tour operators, probably because of the lack of big hotels and chalets for them to take over.

We spend the morning in gentle exploration, then stop for lunch on the sun-trap terrace of the Relais de l'Aiguille, at the top of the Crêt du Loup chairlift. Booking is essential here, the wooden tables are packed and, behind them, two chefs in full whites are working away at an outside grill. Order the '*pièce du*

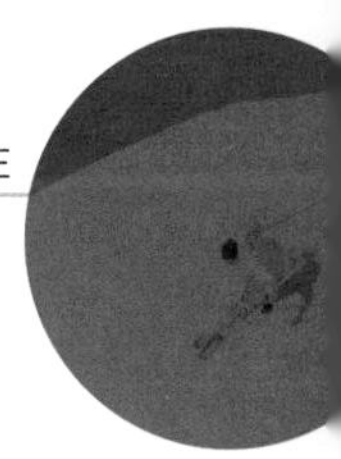

boucher', a thick steak for two people, which comes sliced up (so you can see the charred brown exterior and rich pink middle) on a big wooden board, with just fries, some lamb's lettuce and little pots of mustard. It's not cheap, at €30 per person, but the view is staggering, the food fantastic and the wine list superb (and surprisingly reasonable).

After lunch, we head off to the other end of the valley to ski La Clusaz's highest, steepest and most celebrated area of pistes, the Balme, of which the locals are fiercely proud.

'This is a good family resort, like many others in France, but then we have the Balme, too, which is like something else altogether,' enthuses Olivier, a former professional snowboarder and now an instructor here.

Getting there takes a little while. First there's a gondola, then a slow chair lift. The cloud has come in and, as we inch up towards the Col de Balme, at 2,477m, we can't see more than two chairs hanging from the cable in front of us. Gradually, though, holes start appearing in the cloud and we get momentary tunnel-vision glimpses of jagged peaks lent halos of gold by the sun behind them. Then, suddenly, we've risen above the cloud altogether and are in glorious sunlight.

The slow chairlift up to the Col de Balme

SUDDENLY, we've risen above the cloud altogether and are in glorious sunlight.

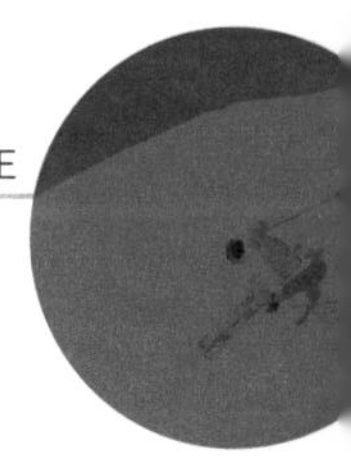

The lift takes us to the top of the ridge, where we are rewarded with a truly astonishing view to the south-east. Below us is a valley which stretches for miles in either direction and is filled with thick cloud like a billion balls of cotton wool. Hidden beneath it is the resort of Megève and, to our far left, we can see the peaks of the Dents du Midi, to the far right, the Vanoise glacier above Courchevel and, directly opposite, the towering bulk of Mont Blanc.

Turning back towards La Clusaz, the Balme is pretty impressive too – a huge bowl, with endless options for skiing off piste. It's here that local boy Candide Thovex, three times X-Games winner and probably the most famous freestyle skier of them all, hosts the Candide Invitational, the biggest freestyle event in Europe. But this, whispers Olivier, is just the start of it.

The Aravis, he explains, is actually a chain of mountains that forms a wall running north-east to south-west and catches snow from all the prevailing storms. Better still, between each of the peaks jutting up along the length of the wall is a snowy bowl – the Balme is one of these, but there are no fewer than eleven more along the chain, none of which can be accessed by ski lifts.

'So hire a guide, hike for twenty minutes from the top ski lift into the next bowl, and you have an entire untouched valley, all to yourself,' he says, beaming.

So far, so idyllic, but it has to be said that there can be a down side to being so easy to reach. The more accessible a ski resort, the more likely it is to suffer from crowds at weekends.

Here, Saturdays aren't a problem – the residents of Geneva and Annecy (also close by) seem to spend the day shopping and putting the washing on, so the slopes are all but deserted – but on Sundays the pistes are at least three times busier.

However, it still never becomes oppressive, and those used to skiing resorts such as Verbier during half-term would probably still consider the slopes pretty quiet, but I would definitely think twice about coming here over Christmas, New Year or Easter.

THE INSIDE TRACK

Olivier Mermillod Ski Instructor

'For a night out in La Clusaz, start in Le Bachal, where they have excellent live jazz, or Les Caves du Paccalye, a classy bar serving tapas. Then head for either Club 18, which is full of young people who've come up from Annecy, or L'Écluse, which has a slightly older, more dressed-up crowd and a glass dance floor with a stream running beneath it.

Up on the mountain try the Telemark Café, at 1,580m on the slopes of L'Étale. There's an outside bar in an Airstream caravan, they do fabulous buffets and people dance on the tables. From the café you can ski right back to the village – and it's a green run all the way.'

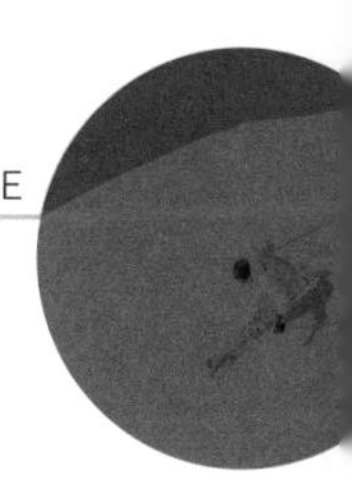

And yet, though within spitting distance of two cities, there's nothing urban about La Clusaz. People have been coming here to ski for a hundred years but it remains a genuine farming village, not a purpose-built concrete-heavy resort like so many in the region. There are twenty farms and 550 cows in La Clusaz alone, making the famous mountain cheeses Reblochon and Tomme Blanche. The tourist office can arrange for you to drop into a farm to see the cheese being made; or go to La Crémerie des Aravis in the village to buy some to take home. La Maison du Jambon, where hundreds of smoked hams and sausages hang on display, should also not be missed.

It's not all about freestylers spinning in the superpipe either. After we finish skiing, we head to the churchyard, where Julian is getting his ponies ready to take us 'skijoring'. Basically, this is how farmers used to get about when in a hurry, and simply involves being dragged along on skis as the horse trots away in front of you. It looks gentle enough but, when the horses get excited, kick up their hind legs and gallop off through the bushes, this sport delivers an adrenalin rush to rival any other. It's definitely worth spending an hour, and €20, to give it a try.

On our second night, we take the bus round to Manigod, pick up snowshoes and poles and set off for a forty-five-minute walk to the Ve la Marie a Nore, a 200-year-old farmhouse on the mountainside. The chalet is rustic perfection – low ceilings, floors that have bowed over the centuries to crazy angles, long benches, a wood-burning stove, lots of cups of kir and more bowls of hearty meat stews and melted cheese.

Walking back through the woods, the trees' branches laden with snow, I realize I'm exhausted. It's our second late night in the high mountains and we've another day on the slopes to go. And yet already it feels like I've been on holiday for a week, if not more – and that is what a white weekend is all about.

The Knowledge
La Clusaz, France

STATS Town altitude: 1,100m **Highest lift:** 2,477m; **Lifts:** 96 (including Le Grand Bornand) **Pistes:** 220km **Lift pass:** €30 per day **Closest airport:** Geneva – 55km

WHY? For convenience, La Clusaz is hard to beat – this is the closest proper resort to Geneva airport. Plus, there are full-moon parties with skiing till 1 a.m. and, even though it's so close to the city, this remains a farming village with bags of charm **GETTING THERE** Geneva airport is just 55km from the resort. Much of the drive is on a motorway, so it takes less than an hour. You can go direct by TGV from Paris to Annecy (in 3 hours 42 minutes), which is 32km from La Clusaz **TRANSFERS** Of course there are all the main car-hire companies at Geneva, but La Clusaz is one of the few cases where a taxi is a sensible option, especially if you are in a small group. A taxi carrying up to four should cost around €112 each way, or €150 on Sundays. Book it through your hotel or try Allo Taxi (+33 (0)6 08 83 08 45; www.allotaxi74.com); Taxi Beauregard (+33 (0)6 63 51 32 58); Taxi Lacroix (+33 (0)6 87 63 28 33). There are also buses from the airport, which run three times a day on Friday, Saturday and Sunday, cost €54 return, but take an hour and 45 minutes (the coach company is called Ballanfat; to book call the Geneva Airport bus station on +41 (0)22 732 02 30 or see www.mouv-aravis.com; note: you need to reconfirm your return ticket at the tourist office) **WHERE TO STAY** The Hôtel Beauregard (+33 (0)4 50 02 43 75; www.hotel-beauregard.fr; doubles from €180, half board) is a friendly three-star, right by the bottom of Le Bossonnet lift, so you can ski straight from your door. Alternatively, try the Alpen Roc (+33 (0)4 50 02 58 96; www.hotel-alpenroc.fr; doubles from €176, half board), which is 150m from the lifts. The Alp'Hôtel (+33 (0)4 50 02 40 06; www.clusaz.com; doubles from €186, half board) and Carlina (+33 (0)4 50 02 43 48; www.hotel-carlina.com; doubles from €170, half board) are also popular **WHERE TO SKI** La Clusaz (with 72 pistes covering 130km) is linked by a free 10-minute ski bus to its neighbouring resort of Le Grand Bornand (with 43 pistes over 90km). In La Clusaz, the highest and longest runs are in the Balme area, a wide bowl where there's great potential for exploring the deep snow between the pistes. Beginners will enjoy the wide, quiet slopes above Manigod on the Massif de L'Étale, which catch the sun in the afternoon. In Le Grand Bornand, the long blue from the Tête des Annes gives beautiful views, while experts will enjoy the 'Espace Freeride,' an unpisted, extremely steep but avalanche-controlled slope down the back of Mont Lachat **WHERE TO EAT** On the mountain, the Relais de l'Aiguille (+33 (0)6 19 50 60 68) at the top of the Crêt du Loup

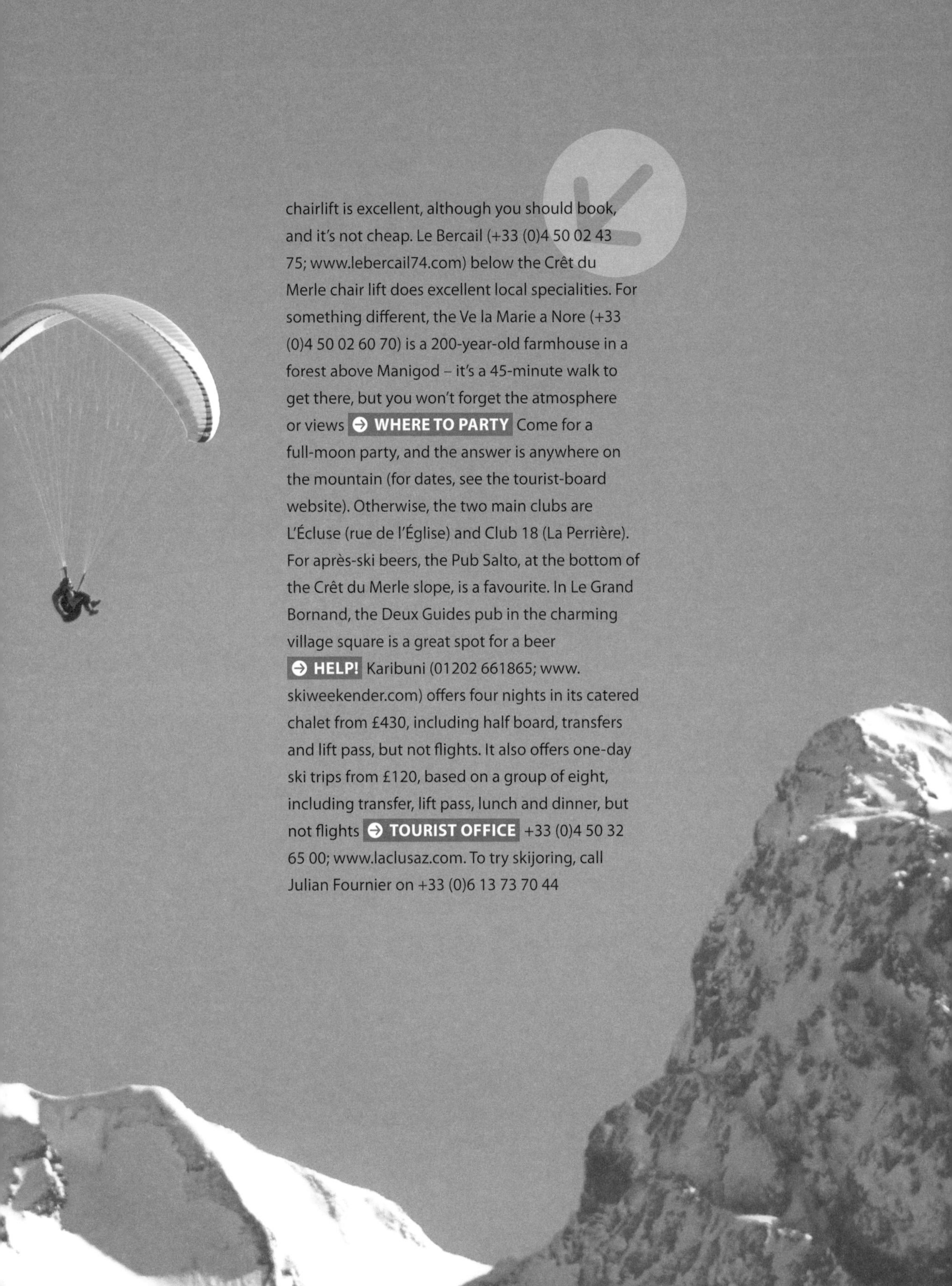

chairlift is excellent, although you should book, and it's not cheap. Le Bercail (+33 (0)4 50 02 43 75; www.lebercail74.com) below the Crêt du Merle chair lift does excellent local specialities. For something different, the Ve la Marie a Nore (+33 (0)4 50 02 60 70) is a 200-year-old farmhouse in a forest above Manigod – it's a 45-minute walk to get there, but you won't forget the atmosphere or views **➔ WHERE TO PARTY** Come for a full-moon party, and the answer is anywhere on the mountain (for dates, see the tourist-board website). Otherwise, the two main clubs are L'Écluse (rue de l'Église) and Club 18 (La Perrière). For après-ski beers, the Pub Salto, at the bottom of the Crêt du Merle slope, is a favourite. In Le Grand Bornand, the Deux Guides pub in the charming village square is a great spot for a beer **➔ HELP!** Karibuni (01202 661865; www.skiweekender.com) offers four nights in its catered chalet from £430, including half board, transfers and lift pass, but not flights. It also offers one-day ski trips from £120, based on a group of eight, including transfer, lift pass, lunch and dinner, but not flights **➔ TOURIST OFFICE** +33 (0)4 50 32 65 00; www.laclusaz.com. To try skijoring, call Julian Fournier on +33 (0)6 13 73 70 44

Five More... Zero Days off Work

SEEFELD, AUSTRIA

➔ **STATS: Town altitude:** 1,200m; **Highest lift:** 2,100m; **Lifts:** 32; **Pistes:** 48km; **Closest airport:** Innsbruck – 21km

➔ **WHY?** An almost comically short airport transfer makes this ideal for a snatched weekend. It's known as Austria's cross-country capital (with 266km of trails), but there are just about enough downhill pistes to keep you busy for two days, especially for beginners and intermediates

➔ **GETTING THERE** Innsbruck airport is only 20 minutes' drive away. A taxi should cost around €40 (+43 (0)512 5311; www.taxi-innsbruck.com)

➔ **WHERE TO STAY** The five-star Hotel Klosterbräu (+43 (0)521 226210; www.klosterbraeu.com; doubles from €270, half board) is a grand former monastery dating back to 1516, with an indoor pool and extensive spa facilities

➔ **WHERE TO PARTY** Surprisingly for a smallish town, there are six discos. Most popular are the cheerily named Fun Disco Jeep, the cowboy-themed Buffalo Westernsaloon and Le Dôme, close to the Hotel Klosterbräu

➔ **TOURIST OFFICE** +43 (0)508 8010; www.seefeld.com

FLAINE, FRANCE

➔ **STATS: Town altitude:** 1,600m; **Highest lift:** 2,561m; **Lifts:** 78; **Pistes:** 265km; **Closest airport:** Geneva – 70km

➔ **WHY?** Flaine isn't just convenient for the airport – in many ways it's the classic ski-in ski-out purpose-built resort. Families have long appreciated the relaxed atmosphere, but the resort has been spurned by the fashionable set on account of its utterly uncompromising1960s 'space station' architecture (lots of concrete blocks). Now, it's coming back into vogue – style buffs are fawning over the Bauhaus-style buildings and sculptures by Picasso and Dubuffet, and serious skiers are waking up to an area that rivals the big names but gets far fewer visitors

➔ **GETTING THERE** The drive from the airport takes 75 minutes. Hire a car, or book a taxi, which will cost around €160 each way for up to 3 (Mont Blanc Taxi: +33 (0)8 05 80 00 01; www.flainetaxi.com). There are 3 daily buses too, operated by SAT, costing €74 return and taking 1 hour and 40 minutes (details: +33 (0)4 50 37 22 13; www.coach-station.com)

➔ **WHERE TO STAY** Keen to encourage weekenders, the tourist office has put details of hotels offering short breaks on their website – see www.flaine.com/en/short-ski-break-france.php. La Cascade (+33 (0)4 50 90 87 66; www.lacascade-flaine.fr) and the Hôtel Club Aujon (+33 (0)4 92 12 62 12; www.mmv.fr) offer 3-night weekends from as little as €152 full board, but only at off-peak times. There are lots of self-catering apartments in Flaine, and Flaine Reservation (+33 (0)4 50 90 89 09; www.flaine-reservation.com) acts as a booking service for short breaks

➔ **WHERE TO PARTY** Not the liveliest, but the White Pub and Flying Dutchman have some atmosphere and the Diamont Noir has been going strong since the 1980s. La Perdrix Noire, a restaurant specializing in Savoyard food, shouldn't be missed

➔ **TOURIST OFFICE** +33 (0)4 50 90 80 01; www.flaine.com

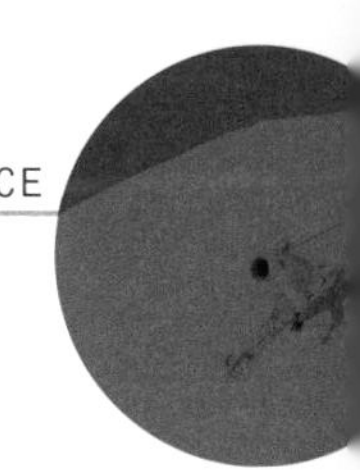

SCHLADMING, AUSTRIA

STATS: Town altitude: 745m; **Highest lift:** 2,015m; **Lifts:** 90; **Pistes:** 167km; **Closest airport:** Salzburg – 90km

WHY? Just an hour from Salzburg, Schladming has outstanding piste skiing on 4 interconnected, north-facing mountains which hold their snow well. The medieval town, sitting on the valley floor, is lively, attractive and friendly too

GETTING THERE A shuttle bus costs €41 return (+43 (0)368 723005; www.reisen-habersatter.at), but taxis are reasonable – about €120 each way for a minibus for up to 8 (Taxi Maxi: +43 (0)368 722222; www.taxi-maxi.at)

WHERE TO STAY The Alte Post (+43 (0)368 722571; www.posthotel-schladming.at; doubles from €230, half board) is a characterful four-star right on the 18th-century main square, with its own spa

WHERE TO PARTY Most partying goes on in the afternoon straight after skiing, especially at the bottom of the Planai pistes. Charlys Treff is great fun, serves local beer and is (they say) a favourite of Arnold Schwarzenegger. Siglu is a glass igloo full of Jägermeister-downing skiers. For late-night drinking, head to the Hanglbar or Sonderbar

TOURIST OFFICE +43 (0)368 723310; www.schladming.at

CHÂTEL, FRANCE

STATS: Town altitude: 1,200m; **Highest lift:** 2,466m; **Lifts:** 208; **Pistes:** 650km; **Closest airport:** Geneva – 75 km

WHY? This French farming village, just south of Lake Geneva, has 83km of piste in its own ski area, but also links into the vast Portes du Soleil area (12 interconnected resorts straddling France and Switzerland). The slopes aren't particularly challenging, but intermediates will love notching up the miles on offer. The centre is a little spread out, but a free shuttle bus runs between the lifts, which are at opposite ends of the village

GETTING THERE A taxi will take 90 minutes and cost around €150 for up to 3 (+33 (0)4 50 73 32 83; www.joelrubin.com). Public buses from the airport only run on Saturdays

WHERE TO STAY The Fleur de Neige (+33 (0)4 50 73 20 10; www.hotel-fleurdeneige.fr; doubles from €88) is a pretty wooden chalet and has a good restaurant. The Hôtel Rhododendrons (+33 (0)4 50 73 24 04; www.hotel-rhododendrons.com; doubles from €65) is very central but has a 3-night minimum. If you want peace and quiet, stay in La Chapelle d'Abondance, a tiny village 6km up the valley with its own ski lifts. There, book into the highly praised two-star Hôtel Cornettes (+33 (0)4 50 73 50 24; www.lescornettes.com; doubles from €170, half board)

WHERE TO PARTY The Tunnel and L'Avalanche are the two liveliest bars, often featuring DJs or live bands. Down the road in La Chapelle, check out Le Fer Rouge, a microbrewery

TOURIST OFFICE +33 (0)4 50 73 22 44; www.chatel.com. See also www.portesdusoleil.com

OBERTAUERN, AUSTRIA

STATS: Town altitude: 1,740m; **Highest lift:** 2,315m; **Lifts:** 26; **Pistes:** 100km; **Closest airport:** Salzburg – 90km

WHY? Obertauern is an oddity in Austria, where resorts are usually low-lying farming villages. This is a high-altitude, purpose-built resort with superior snow conditions and a long season. The pistes, which are best for intermediates, run in a circle right around the village, and you can make the circuit in either direction. Best of all, it's only an hour from the airport

GETTING THERE The tourist office arranges shuttle buses, which cost €42.50 return and meet Ryanair and Thomsonfly flights into Salzburg. Book on the tourist-office website. Taxis are cheap too – from Salzburg it will cost around €140 each way for up to 8 (Taxi Obertauern: +43 (0)645 67777; www.taxi-obertauern.at)

WHERE TO STAY The Sporthotel Edelweiss (+43 (0)645 67245; www.luerzer.at; doubles from €196, half board) is a comfortable four-star close to the nursery slopes. It's also where the Beatles stayed when they came here in 1965 to film *Help!* and there's plenty of memorabilia on display

WHERE TO PARTY Après ski gets lively at the Edelweissalm and Lasch'n Alm by early afternoon. In the evening, the key spots are Monkey's Heaven in the Hotel Rigele Royal, and the Lurzer Alm

TOURIST OFFICE +43 (0)645 67252; www.obertauern.com

05

Green

WHITEPOD, SWITZERLAND

A chalet in Les Cerniers and, far below, the river Rhône

Mountain guide Eric, and Adou, a Hungarian Vizsla

ABOUT A YEAR AGO, I received my first anonymous hatemail. 'You are killing the planet,' said the letter. Inside was a meticulously produced collage showing a picture of a mountain with hundreds of aeroplanes above it blocking out the sky. Underneath, in block capitals, was scrawled: 'Get a new job!'

Today, in some quarters at least, the travel industry is viewed with the same disgust as the tobacco business and the fur trade. In tempting people to indulge themselves with holidays abroad, travel firms (and the journalists who write about them) are encouraging the gratuitous emission of more carbon into the atmosphere, accelerating climate change.

And skiing attracts more anger than anything else. It is, in the words of French conservation group Mountain Wilderness, 'the cancer of the Alps'. The WWF makes a similarly thunderous pronouncement: 'the most ecologically devastating form of leisure industry is the one connected with winter ski tourism.' And Sergio Savoia, director of the WWF's Alpine Programme, adds: 'Artificial snow is not the root of all evil, but it is very close.'

There is a horrible irony in all this. Skiers and snowboarders are passionately in love with the mountains. We spend all year looking forward to a few precious days in the fresh air and the natural, unspoilt Alps. And now we're told that we're killing the very thing we love? It's an idea that seems so absurd, most skiers prefer to ignore it altogether.

But sticking your head in the snow is becoming harder and harder. In Tignes, you might notice that it is no longer possible to complete that off-piste route you skied a decade ago, because the Grande Motte glacier has retreated so far. Above Grindelwald, you might realize that the charming old Bäregg mountain restaurant is no longer there: the ground literally fell away beneath it when a big chunk of the Eiger collapsed thanks to melting of the glacier and permafrost. You might have heard about the authorities in Andermatt being forced to wrap their glacier in protective sheeting. And you may well have been kept up at night by the constant drone of hundreds of snow cannons, making the silent Alpine night a thing of the past.

So is the outlook really that bleak? Should we all give up skiing?

Waking up at Whitepod, the outlook doesn't seem bleak at all. In many ways, this place is a blueprint for a new kind of eco-friendly ski holiday, but it's also incredibly beautiful, romantic and fun. Staying here certainly isn't about hardship and hair shirts.

I'm lying in a wide double bed, under a heavy duvet, inside a 'Pavilion Pod' – a big, domed tent. Beside me, a few embers are still glowing in the wood-burning stove. In front of me, through a semicircular window three metres across, I have a widescreen view of the sun rising up from behind the snow-laden branches of the forest, throwing shafts of light down into the Rhone Valley far beneath me and slowly turning the Massif des Diablerets, on the valley's far side, from inky purple, to blue, to gold.

I throw on clothes, walk out and head down the hillside, following a path surrounded on either side by high banks of snow and dotted every few metres by a little lantern. The path weaves its way past eight other pods, each sitting on a stilted wooden platform. Snow is piled up a foot high on their domed roofs, and their little chimneys each have a precarious white hat. It looks like some kind of Antarctic research station but, inside, they are toasty, kept warm by a thick, insulating layer of wool and natural fibres and made homely with cowhide and sheepskin rugs.

Typically, there would be between ten and twenty people in the camp, but we're here in early December, at the very start of the season, and the only guests are Robin and me.

1 | 2

| 3

| 4

| 5
6

At the bottom of the hillside, on the edge of the hamlet of Les Cerniers, is the Lodge, an old chalet where guests take meals and use the toilets and showers; it even has a sauna. Inside, Sofia de Meyer, Whitepod's founder, is waiting to serve breakfast. She's Swiss but spent six years working as a lawyer in London before dreaming up this place.

'I wanted to prove to people that ecology could be comfortable and hip,' she says. 'The idea is for you to be snug and warm, but still feel as if you're sleeping close to nature.'

The room we're sitting in sums up the concept. On one hand, it's ecologically blameless, having been refurbished using only local materials, recycled wood or that sourced from sustainable Swiss forests. Under the bar are rows of recycling boxes, one for batteries, one for bulbs, one for the little metal bits on the bottom of tea lights, and many more besides.

On the other hand, such is the attention to detail that the room looks like a set from the pages of a Habitat or Boden catalogue. On the windowsills are wooden boxes filled with flowers or fir cones, and painted twigs tied in beautiful lace. In the centre, chairs are arranged around a free-standing fireplace and artfully discarded on sidetables beside them are old Swiss cookery books and historic Baedeker and Ward Lock guidebooks to the Alps.

The homemade jam, *confiture de lait* and spiced apple jelly that arrive with breakfast (alongside toast, yoghurt, organic muesli and slices of apple and pear) come in cute little jars with hand-written labels. It's wonderfully homely and, as Sofia runs me through Whitepod's eco-credentials, Adou and Pouillac, her two brown Hungarian Vizslas, saunter up and rest their chins on our thighs, hoping we'll stroke their heads.

The idea is that the Pods are 'zero-impact' accommodation, the opposite of building a new hotel or apartment block. At any time they can be taken away and the land returned to its natural state (in fact, plans are currently underway to move them to a slightly more isolated location not far away). Energy use is kept to a minimum: only the two bigger Pavilion Pods have any power, and even then it's just two bulbs each; the others rely on oil lamps. Water use is kept low, with showers only available in the Lodge and guests politely asked to take quick 'sports showers'. Washing products are all biodegradable. Food is bought from local suppliers who source it from the surrounding area. To support the community, whose only shop and restaurant had closed down, the Lodge also acts as a small grocery store, while local people are employed as staff.

To be honest, though, probably more important than all of these combined is Whitepod's policy of encouraging visitors to travel by train. It doesn't ram this down their throats but does offer free shuttles up from Aigle station and discounts of 15 per cent for train passengers. The reasoning is simple: travelling by train from the UK to the Alps results in about 24kg of carbon per person; flying, just under 200kg.

Getting to Whitepod by rail is pretty straight-forward too: St Pancras to Paris (two hours twenty minutes), change from the Gare du Nord to Gare de Lyon (two stops on RER line D), then take the TGV direct to Aigle (four hours forty-eight minutes). Carrying your skis between stations in Paris isn't much fun, but lounging around on a TGV – reading the papers, drinking wine and watching Lake Geneva slip past the window – beats air travel any day. If this is being an eco-warrior, sign me up.

1 | *Sofia de Meyer, Whitepod's founder*

2 | *Inside the Lodge, where residents of the Pod come to eat, drink and wash*

3 | *The view from a Pavilion Pod*

4-6 | *Gourmet food and stylish interiors in the Lodge*

WE HAVE OUR OWN private ski resort, covered in completely untouched powder.

But as well as train travel, recycling and supporting the local economy, there's a bigger idea behind Whitepod. Again, it's subtly suggested rather than enforced on guests, but driving the project is the belief that tourists should enjoy the mountains without harming them. And, in practice, that means weaning people off conventional downhill skiing in favour of less damaging activities.

'When they started making artificial snow, I realized things were getting absurd,' says Sofia. 'These days there is such demand for skiing but the season is so short that the resorts are trying to capitalize by building more pistes and more accommodation, which leads to deforestation, harms wildlife and uses huge amounts of energy. When they've invested so much, they want to remove the only variable factor, the snow, so they add snow cannons, which use even more power and disturb the wildlife even more.'

There *is* downhill skiing at Whitepod, but just two short drag lifts and two runs, and the idea is that it's just one in a range of activities, including snow-shoeing, dogsledding, ski touring, hiking, wildlife

Skiing is just one of the activities on offer

watching and paragliding. 'I'm a skier, I love the sport,' says Sofia, 'but it just isn't sustainable any more and we need to find an alternative.'

I think she might be slightly aggrieved that, during our visit, though it's so early in the season, there is over a metre of fresh snow and so we decide the wildlife watching will have to wait. Alain, Sofia's business partner, starts the two lifts running, and we have our own private ski resort covered in completely untouched powder. I know this really isn't what it's all about, but I do lap after lap, jumping off the pod's wooden platforms and slaloming through the trees. Adou and Pouillac come chasing down after us, bounding deliriously through the deep snow. It's the most peaceful ski day I've ever had.

That night, over a fabulous dinner of baked-apple salad, grilled baby chicken stuffed with thyme and alpine herbs and bitter chocolate fondant with ginger, we talk further about whether we should be hanging up our downhill skis for good.

There is an argument that skiing is being unfairly singled out, possibly because the effects of climate

READING THE PAPERS, drinking wine and watching Lake Geneva slip past the window beats air travel any day. If this is being an eco-warrior, sign me up.

change are most readily seen in the mountains. Yes, going skiing is worse for the environment than going cycling in the West Country, but is it as bad as going on a fly-drive to California or a shopping break in Dubai?

I used to enjoy looking up at the lights of the piste bashers working away at night. These days, it always makes me feel guilty. Each one uses 25–30 litres of diesel per hour. A resort like Courchevel has twenty-one of them, working through the night – which adds up to about 6,800 litres of fuel. Shocking.

But possibly not as shocking as the fact that today's biggest cruise ships easily use over 300,000 litres of fuel per day. And though there might be three thousand guests on the ship, that's a lot fewer than in a resort like Courchevel. Of course, the skiers will also use lifts, which require a huge amount of electricity to run (though, it being France, it's largely nuclear so not directly contributing to carbon emissions, and other alpine resorts rely to a great extent on hydro-electricity).

Another argument is that the carbon from skiing and the tourism industry is dwarfed by other sources (the 2006 UK-Government-commissioned Stern report found the carbon emissions from deforestation were nine times greater than those from global aviation).

Ultimately, though, pointing the finger at other types of holiday or sources of pollution isn't going to help. And while all the existing resorts aren't going to knock down their hotels and erect tents, in a few years, failing snowfalls might start forcing some to start looking at Whitepod's example so they too can promote winter mountain holidays that aren't solely about downhill skiing. Sofia lets on that actually this is already happening – she won't say which, but admits that several big Swiss resorts have made noises about setting up their own Whitepod camps.

After dinner, we wander off for a night-time snow-shoe through the forest. The stars are out, the peace is absolute, the air icy and pine-scented. Compared with this, giving up on massive lift-systems, busy pistes and luxury hotels doesn't seem like a sacrifice at all.

THE INSIDE TRACK

Richard Hammond Founder Greentraveller.co.uk

'If you want to keep enjoying the snow with a clear conscience, by far the best single thing you can do is take the train to the slopes instead of the plane. You'll slash your carbon footprint, and it needn't limit where you can go – there are plenty of resorts that are easily accessible by train in a day or overnight on the sleeper via Paris. Also, look for low-impact alternatives to lift-based holidays. One of my favourite resorts is Luchon in the French Pyrenees (on the train line from Toulouse), from where you can go snow-shoeing over rivers, valleys and mountains into Spain. In the Alps, I recommend the car-free Swiss resort of Saas-Fee – it's a great place for cross-country skiing through larch forests and along the frozen river Vispa.'

The Knowledge
Whitepod, Switzerland

STATS **Camp altitude:** 1,292m **Highest lift:** 1,700m; **Lifts:** 2
Pistes: 3km (approx) **Lift pass:** €40 per day **Closest airport:** Geneva – 105km

WHY? An utterly different mountain experience, tranquil, relaxing and romantic. It could also be the blueprint for less environmentally damaging winter holidays of the future **GETTING THERE** Rail travel is encouraged – so much so that those who travel from the UK by train are offered discounts of up to 15 per cent. Whitepod is located on the edge of the hamlet of Les Cerniers. The closest station is Aigle, served by direct TGV from Paris Gare de Lyon, or change in Lausanne. Both journeys take the same time – just under 5 hours. For tickets and information, contact Rail Europe (see page 286) **TRANSFERS** Whitepod organizes two complimentary daily transfers from Aigle station, at 1.15 p.m. and 5.15 p.m. The drive up to the camp takes about 25 minutes. If you fly to Geneva, take the escalator down to the on-site railway station – from here there are direct trains to Aigle, taking 1 hour and 20 minutes (see www.sbb.ch for timetable information) **WHERE TO STAY** Whitepod (+41 (0)24 471 38 38; www.whitepod.com) offers two types of tent. There are Pavilion Pods, which have a toilet, shower, basin and a couple of lightbulbs, sleep up to 4 and cost from CHF585/£270 per night. Expedition Pods, which are lit by lamp, sleep two and cost from CHF325/£150. Both rates include morning coffee and afternoon tea and cake. Another option is the Refuge, a mountain hotel beside the piste at 1,604m, which is owned by Whitepod and has had a stylish makeover. It sleeps up to 60 in dormitory beds. It's often used for corporate events but can be booked individually from CHF85/£40 **WHERE TO SKI** With only two drag lifts, you'll have fully explored the area pretty quickly. As well as the slopes beside the lifts, there's a third piste beyond the forest, which gets a glorious blast of morning sun. The bigger decision is whether you want to use the lifts at all or whether you'd rather try ski touring, snowshoeing or dogsledding. All must be paid for separately – a full day snowshoeing with a guide costs £100 per person, 90 minutes' dogsledding is £95 per person, an hour paragliding is £78, a day's guided ski touring is £105 each for the first two guests, £35 for any additional participants. If you think you don't need a guide, you can just borrow snowshoes and follow the paths on your own. Whether by snowshoe or ski touring, you should aim to get up to the Dent de Valerette, at 2,058m. This is the top of the hill behind Les Cerniers and, on reaching the top, you'll get an amazing view of the mountain range beyond it, the Dents du Midi **➔ WHERE TO EAT** There's only one option – the Whitepod Lodge at the bottom of the hill, which also acts as a lounge and bar for those staying in the pods. Thankfully, the food is excellent

➔ WHERE TO PARTY Forget it – just enjoy sitting reading beside your wood-burning stove or watching the stars from the terrace outside your tent

➔ HELP! Original Travel (0207 978 7333; www.originaltravel.co.uk) offers a 3-night package, including flights, from £840

➔ TOURIST OFFICE +41 (0)84 876 53 45; www.chablais.info

Five More... For Green Skiing

WERFENWENG, AUSTRIA

➡ STATS: **Town altitude:** 1,000m; **Highest lift:** 1,836m; **Lifts:** 11; **Pistes:** 25km; **Closest airport:** Salzburg – 45km

➡ WHY? This tiny village has been pursuing some of the most ambitious green policies of any tourist resort, winter or summer. The central policy is the promotion of 'Soft Mobility', i.e. car-free holidays. Guests are encouraged to leave their cars at home, or in a car park for the duration of their stay. Free shuttle buses run up from the station 12km away (details: +43 (0)646 233030; www.mobilito.at), and in summer visitors are allowed to drive a variety of electric cars and scooters around the village. The tourist office will also arrange a pick-up from Salzburg airport for the bargain flat-fee of €25 return. The resort uses some solar power and promotes alternatives to downhill skiing, including cross-country, snowshoeing, paragliding, sleigh rides, and trekking through the snow with kids. This makes a great destination for families or beginners, but the lack of serious skiing means it won't appeal to all
➡ GETTING THERE Unfortunately, taking the train is a long haul – it's nearly 17 hours overnight from London to Salzburg (see www.seat61.com for routing advice). The €25 taxi from the airport can be booked through the tourist office or any Soft Mobility hotel. The drive takes 40 minutes
➡ WHERE TO STAY The Alpenhof Wenger (+43 (0)646 620034; www.wenger-alpenhof.at; doubles from €96, half board) is a traditional wooden chalet with big balconies for soaking up the views
➡ WHERE TO PARTY Bring a book
➡ TOURIST OFFICE +43 (0)646 64200; www.werfenweng.org

SAAS FEE, SWITZERLAND

➡ STATS: **Town altitude:** 1,800m; **Highest lift:** 3,600m; **Lifts:** 26; **Pistes:** 140km; **Closest airport:** Sion – 70km

➡ WHY? Saas Fee is famous for its glacier skiing, which goes on all year round and makes it a key training base for many top teams. What's less well known is that this charming farming village, full of old wooden chalets, was an early adopter of environmental policies. Cars were banned in 1951, the resort is ISO14001 approved (this is an international standard for environmental management applicable to any organization), and a designated 'Energy Town', a label granted in recognition of its energy-reduction policies. In fact, the town's traditional appearance isn't a coincidence – it has some of the country's most restrictive building and development regulations, down to the minimum amount of wood in every building's façade
➡ GETTING THERE Given the current lack of flights to Sion, choose Bern (125km away) instead. From Bern, a combination of bus and train will take 2 hours 20 minutes to Saas Fee – bus to Rubigen station, train to Thun, then Visp, then bus to the resort (see www.sbb.ch). Direct trains run to Visp from both Zurich (245km) and Geneva airports, taking about 2 hours and 30 minutes, the bus to the resort adding another 35 minutes
➡ WHERE TO STAY The three-star Unique Hotel Dom (+41 (0)27 958 77 00; www.uniquedom.com; doubles from CHF180/£88, including breakfast) is indeed pretty unique – communal spaces are a mix of bold colours and traditional chalet design, with the odd dash of Americana or a fake leopardskin. Bedrooms are far more sober. Unfortunately, like most hotels in the village, it only rents rooms by the week during peak times. At those times, weekenders should contact the tourist office, who can help with short and last-minute bookings
➡ WHERE TO PARTY The Popcorn bar, part of the Dom, is famous among the snowboarding community, and has 1950s jukeboxes, pool tables and DJs. It organizes some massive parties too
➡ TOURIST OFFICE +41 (0)27 958 18 58; www.saas-fee.ch

ZÜRS, AUSTRIA

➡ STATS: **Town altitude:** 1,716m; **Highest lift:** 2,811m; **Lifts:** 85; **Pistes:** 280km; **Closest airport:** Innsbruck – 115km

➡ WHY? One of the few resorts awarded a five-star rating by the Saveoursnow.com website (see below), Zürs has a Biomass communal heating plant, which burns waste at a central point and pipes resultant hot water to over a hundred hotels and two hundred homes. Solar panels contribute energy to some lifts (albeit relatively small amounts), and the resort commits itself to not using chemical additives in artificial snow. Green issues aside, this is a pretty village linked in to the huge St Anton ski area
➡ GETTING THERE From Innsbruck airport, you take a local bus or taxi to the city's station, from where there

are direct trains to Langen am Arlberg, taking 1 hour 21 minutes (timetables at www.oebb.at). A taxi from Langen to Zürs will take 15 minutes and cost €35 (+43 (0)558 325010; www.taxi-lech.at). The same taxi firm will bring you from Innsbruck airport for €225

WHERE TO STAY Zürs is a refined, old-money destination, and the five-star Zürserhof (+43 (0)558 325130; www.zuerserhof.at; doubles from €410, including full board and spa) is a classic. Less expensive is the Schweizerhaus (+43 (0)558 32463; www.schweizerhaus.org; doubles from €178, half board)

WHERE TO PARTY The Kaminstuble in the Hotel Schweizerhaus is a good après-ski spot. The Vernissage in the Alpenrose Hotel and the Zürserl in the Hotel Edelweiss are the two late-night watering holes, although for a wild night you should taxi round the corner to St Anton

TOURIST OFFICE +43 (0)558 32245; www.lech-zuers.at

LES GETS, FRANCE

STATS: **Town altitude:** 1,170m; **Highest lift:** 2,466m; **Lifts:** 208; **Pistes:** 650km; **Closest airport:** Geneva – 65km

WHY? An attractive village that's part of the Portes du Soleil ski area, Les Gets is another five-star resort, according to Saveoursnow.com. It has replaced some diesel generators for ski lifts with solar panels, introduced strict planning controls and a water-management programme, and is working towards banning cars from the village

GETTING THERE A taxi from Geneva airport will cost around €115 for up to 4 (+33 (0)6 09 33 99 44; www.acces-taxi.com) and take an hour. Buses run 3 times a day from the airport, costing €51 return and taking 1 hour and 25 minutes (details: +41 (0)22 732 02 30; www.coach-station.com). If coming by train, take the TGV to Cluses (4 hours 30 minutes from Paris), which is 22km from Les Gets, and take a taxi

WHERE TO STAY The Hôtel Crychar (www.crychar.com; doubles from €300, half board) is right beside the piste in the centre of the village. A cheaper option is the Alpen Sports Hotel (+33 (0)4 50 75 80 55; www.alpensport-hotel.com, doubles from €150, half board)

WHERE TO PARTY Nightlife is quite low key, but the Irish Pub and the Bush Bar are good spots to try before heading to L'Igloo, the only disco

TOURIST OFFICE +33 (0)4 50 75 80 80; www.lesgets.com

FIONNAY, SWITZERLAND

STATS: **Town altitude:** 1,490m; **Highest lift:** n/a; **Lifts:** 0; **Pistes:** 0km; **Closest airport:** Sion – 74 km

WHY? Fionnay is a hamlet of 18 souls, tucked away at the end of the Val de Bagnes, which also contains Verbier. But its one hotel is used as a base for introduction to ski-touring weekends by guide Andy Perkins in cooperation with the Ski Club of Great Britain. By using no lifts at all – you walk up using sticky skins – you avoid all energy use and the need for eyesore infrastructure, so learning to tour is probably one of the greenest things you can do. Tourers tend to stay in remote communities, like Fionnay, thus having a beneficial social as well as ecological impact

GETTING THERE You can come by train – start with Eurostar and TGV to Geneva (6 hours 30 minutes). From there, or if you've flown to Geneva, take the train to Le Châble, via Martigny (just over 2 hours), and take a taxi the final 15 minutes to Fionnay. A taxi all the way from Geneva will cost around CHF570/£260 each way (for listings of taxi firms, see www.verbiertaxi.ch)

WHERE TO STAY Andy Perkins' touring weekends stay at the Hôtel du Grand Combin (www.fionnay.ch) and cost £425 for 4 nights, not including flights (details: 0208 410 2022; www.skifreshtracks.co.uk)

WHERE TO PARTY Sorry, not on this one

TOURIST OFFICE Fionnay is covered by Verbier's tourist office: +41 (0)27 775 38 88; www.verbier.ch

FOR MORE INFORMATION: See www.saveoursnow.com, which gives ski resorts a star rating according to their eco-performance. Also look at the 'Respect the Mountain' pages on the Ski Club of Great Britain site, www.skiclub.co.uk; and see www.alpinepearls.com, an association of ski resorts working towards improved environmental standards.

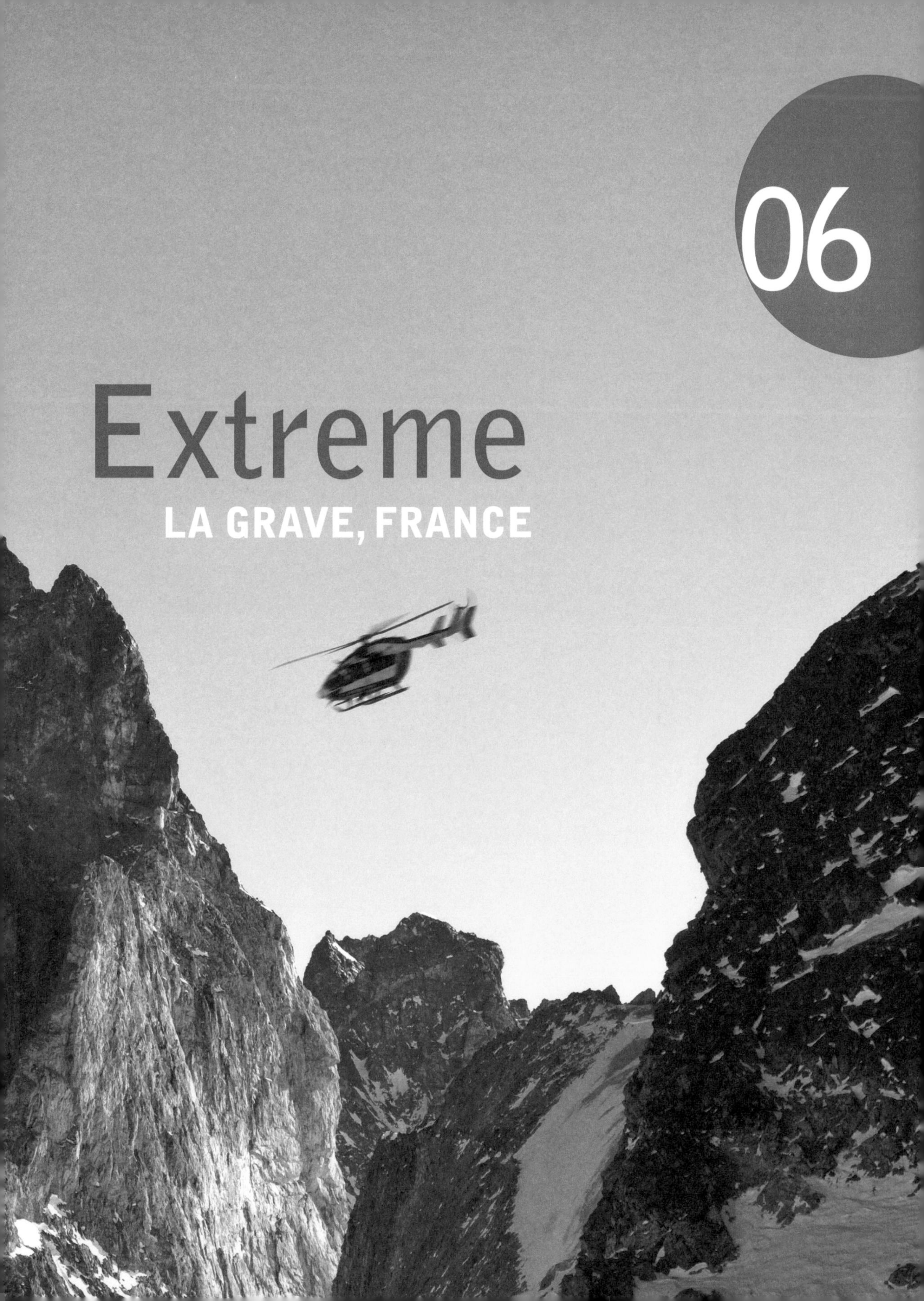

06

Extreme

LA GRAVE, FRANCE

IT'S LIKE TOYING with oblivion, pushing as close as you can to the line while just retaining control.

I'M DANGLING FROM A ROPE, skis tied to my rucksack, boots scrabbling for purchase on the icy rock. I'm being lowered into a couloir, a ribbon of snow falling straight down between rock walls, in which I know at least eight people have died. Bravado has long since given way to anxiety, then simple fear. This is skiing at its most serious.

'How does it look?' calls my mate Paul from above as I reach the end of the rope and kick a step into the icy slope. 'Probably more tombstone than wheelchair,' I shout back. I know it's childish, but scaring him makes me feel ever so slightly better. Still, my head spins and my mouth waters as I bend down to clip into my skis, concentrating furiously on keeping my balance and desperately trying to ignore the slope disappearing beneath me. Drop a ski here and it wouldn't stop.

We're at a side entrance to the couloir known as Triffide, which drops for around 300m. It's steep – 45 degrees in places – and narrow: at one point, the rock walls touch both tail and tip of my skis. The guidebook's advice is clear but not hugely helpful: 'Do not fall.' At the back of my mind is a nagging, if entirely pointless (given there's no other way down) question: Why?

I guess I'd come to see if I was as good a skier as I thought I was, to see if I could handle the slopes that command almost mythic status among hardcore skiers. Mention the name La Grave in an après-ski bar and the hubbub of tall tales and boasts will momentarily be silenced.

It might seem strange that this tiny French village by the side of a quiet road should command more respect among those in the know than the celebrated slopes of Jackson Hole or Chamonix. For a start, there are only three lifts. But it's the resort's statistic for the length of its pistes that really starts to impress – 0km. Here, there are simply no pistes – the whole mountain is given over to off-piste skiing. There are also no safety patrollers or route markers and no one to set off explosives or do anything else to reduce the risk of avalanches. Here, you are on your own.

Add to that the fact that the slopes are all north-facing so rarely get any sun. And that, though there's just the one gondola and two little T-bars, the couloirs and rocky powder fields drop steeply down for a massive 2,150m under the jagged peaks of La Meije.

'This is not a resort,' says Pelle Lang, who moved to La Grave in the 80s and runs the Skierslodge hotel and guiding service. 'In a resort the terrain is adapted to the skier. In La Grave you must adapt to the terrain.'

And then there's the name. It comes from the small pebbles (gravel) on the banks of the river that runs through the village but, given the death toll – at least twenty-five since 1994 – it's hard to avoid the other connotations of the word.

Even with La Grave's fearsome reputation, the skiing world still went into shock when Doug Coombs, the world's best-known extreme skier and twice winner of the World Extreme Ski Championship, was killed here in April 2006. It was, in the words of another guide, 'like Superman dying'.

Doug and a group of friends had been enjoying fabulous conditions and were skiing a couloir called Polichinelle towards the end of the day. Then, Doug's friend and protégé, Chad VanderHam, slipped. Keith Garvey, the American guide I've been skiing with here, knew Coombs and VanderHam well and won't

In La Grave, you're on your own

Deep powder in front of La Meije

forget the day they died. 'Nobody knows exactly what happened, but Chad slipped and went over a cliff. Doug shouted for a rope and then sidestepped right out there on the rock to look down. It's not clear if Doug's skis slipped from under him on the rock or if he tried to jump off the cliff to save his friend.'

Many routes start with an abseil

Doug had pioneered super-steep skiing in Alaska but moved to La Grave in pursuit of its endless challenges: after nearly a decade, he said he was still finding new runs. He always joked that he loved everything about the place apart from the name.

Arriving in such an intimidating place, I was already feeling anxious as we rode the long, brightly coloured gondola up the mountain on the first morning. Things didn't start well. Six turns into our first run, one of our group fell heavily and snapped his femur. While Keith gingerly cut open his salopettes to investigate the wound, the remaining four of us hovered nervously near by, unsure of what to say or do. Twenty minutes later, the rescue helicopter's downdraft was blasting freezing snow into our faces, and neither the thump of the rotors nor liberal doses of morphine could muffle the screams as our friend was lifted from the ground.

Now, as I stand here on Triffide, bouncing slightly in my bindings, all of this streams through my mind. I try to still my thoughts, empty my brain and get ready to commit 100 per cent to the all-important first turn. Any hesitancy will almost certainly lead to a fall. And the problem with a fall is that you don't stop but go sliding down, picking up speed and slamming into one of the rock walls on either side. In La Grave, it goes without saying, you wear a helmet.

I jump around to the left, then stop to test the snow before jumping right again. Soon, the confidence begins to build, the turns start to link together and flow, the speed increases and the sense of euphoria mounts.

My heart pounds in my chest with the effort of the jump turns, I'm sweating heavily beneath my helmet, my teeth are clenched. This isn't the simple sensual thrill of floating through a deep-powder field; it's tense and technical. Jump, get both edges stuck in cleanly across the slope, jump. During each turn there's a moment when your skis are pointing straight forward, down the slope, ready to accelerate away to disaster if you lose concentration for a moment. It's like toying with oblivion, pushing as close as you can to the line while just staying in control.

Eventually, the gradient starts to ease, the rock walls open out and we emerge on an easier exit slope – exhausted, jubilant and feeling utterly alive.

Though the danger is clearly part of the attraction,

La Grave's iconic 'pulse' cable car

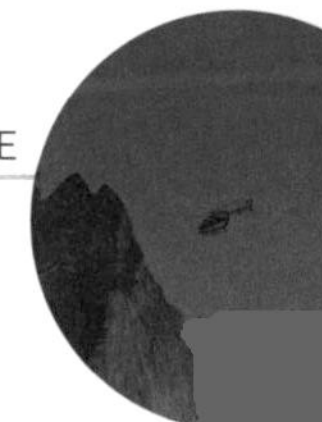

and bookings soared after Coombs's death, the irony is that, in La Grave, there's not a trace of machismo around. In the bars and restaurants, there's no boasting; on the slopes, there's no showing off – it's far too serious for that.

There's none of the pressure-cooker atmosphere of Chamonix, Verbier or St Anton, where every morning is a race to get first tracks in the fresh snow and every bar is showing videos of insane cliff jumps. This is a remote, rural village. As you walk down to the lift station in the morning, you pass a small farmer's market selling the local mountain cheeses and hams.

A busy day in La Grave might see 200 people using the lift, compared to 10,000 in a resort like Tignes. This means that, as soon as you leave the lift station, you're on your own, with just your group for company. A long day might mean three runs – but with the top lift station at 3,550m and the village at 1,400m, each one is like an expedition.

As you've probably inferred, coming here without a guide would be suicidal. The good news is that the Skierslodge – which provides half-board accommodation, with guiding included in the price – makes this far easier and cheaper to arrange than if you had to do so independently.

After an epic day's skiing, my friends and I retire to Le Pub, the bar in the basement of the Skierslodge. The whole hotel is like a clubhouse for ski nuts, and the walls of the bar are covered with old skis and classic adverts for K2, the American ski brand. Beside them are maps of the Alaskan mountains, the stuff of dreams for heliskiers.

Dotted amongst them are signed photos from the most famous skiers in the world, thanks to Pelle's involvement in shooting several classic skiing films. Pelle himself is something of a legend in his native Sweden, so you'll probably find many of the other guests are Swedes. The rooms are basic but comfy, there's a lounge with a log fire, sofas and lots of skiing books from around the world, and the food is great

THE INSIDE TRACK

Katrina Kralova Bar Manager, La Grave

'La Grave is wonderful, but it's a small place and sometimes you want to escape. To get away I walk up the hill to La Chaumine, a tiny hotel in the hamlet of Ventelon. It takes an hour to walk, or it's seven minutes by car. It's run by three Dutch friends, Tom, Joost and Karin. La Grave is in the shade from early afternoon, but La Chaumine is on the south side so gets sun until early evening. It's a small, beautiful chalet and, inside, there are sofas around a little bar and fireplace, and it feels like you're sitting in a friend's house. The food is great too.'

La Chaumine: +33 (0)4 76 79 90 28; www.hotel-lachaumine.com

Tom in a couloir above the Vallon de la Selle

THOUGH DANGER IS part of the attraction, the irony is that in La Grave there's not a trace of machismo around. In the bars, there's no boasting; on the slopes, there's no showing off.

– on our first night we have warm goat's cheese salad, oven-baked turbot with gnocchi and vermouth, cheese, then pineapple confit with pistachio ice cream. Breakfast has a delightfully Swedish flavour: as well as porridge and cereal, there's a hard, nutty cheese, hard-boiled eggs, and peppers and tomatoes.

Early the next day, Pelle and his wife, Ayse, Robin and I ride the gondola up to its top station at 3,200m under beautiful clear skies. We take a warm-up run down, pausing to look at the glacier hanging to the side of La Meije. Pelle explains that we're standing in an area known as the '*zone interdite*', the forbidden zone. 'The seracs, the big ice walls in the glacier, can break off and fall down, starting avalanches,' he says. 'If that happens, the avalanche will sweep over where we're standing. Let's keep moving.'

Back up at the top of the lift, we stop for an early lunch. The restaurant is actually called Le Chalet Haut-Dessus, but Pelle calls it 3,200 (its altitude) and everyone else knows it as Daniel's, after the owner. From the terrace there's a wonderful view over the glacier and, looking north, we can see Pic Blanc, the highest point of Alpe d'Huez. Inside, though there are a lot of guys with impressive beards, ropes, harnesses and technical gear, the chat is all about which band will be playing in Le Pub tonight. Daniel himself is more concerned with the wine – he spends the summer touring around vineyards choosing the wines he'll serve here. The food is excellent, too.

Pelle is constantly looking at his watch. Not, I think, because my conversation is that bad, but because skiing safely in La Grave involves a lot more than being good at jump turns. Timing is everything.

Our objective is to reach St Christoph, a little hamlet on the far side of the mountain, but there are various ways of getting there. One is to take La Rama, a couloir that drops 1,000m in a straight line from the top of the mountain, the Dôme de la Lauze. The other is the Classique route, down more open slopes. We're planning to do La Rama but, at the last minute, Pelle, who keeps disappearing to get updates on temperature from the lift operators or to check snow texture in different locations, decides we should revert to the Classique.

I'm slightly disappointed, but this soon fades as we push off from 3,550m, side-slipping through a rocky corridor, then begin to relax, putting down turn after turn as we drop further and further into the empty valley, surrounded by towering peaks and hanging glaciers on all sides. It reminds me of Chamonix's Vallée Blanche, except here there are just the four of us in the entire valley. There are twists and turns through rocky outcrops, and your skis occasionally glance off buried rocks, reminding you that this is '*ski sauvage*', but it doesn't feel so steep.

At the valley floor, with the sun starting to fall behind the rocky spires above, we start an 8km meander alongside a half-frozen stream, sometimes taking our skis off to ford the water, sometimes pushing through bushes, occasionally having to carry skis to walk sections where the snow has melted.

Halfway down we get to a point where we can look up into La Rama. It's in full sunshine, has been for several hours, and looks pretty inviting. But Pelle

1 *Technical gear is de rigueur here*
2 *Pelle Lang leads the morning guides' meeting at Skierslodge*
3 *Psyched-up and ready to go*
4 *A café in St Christoph*
5-6 *K2 logos at the Skierslodge, 'like a clubhouse for ski nuts'*

1 2
Skiers Lodge
3
CAFE RESTAURANT
4
K2 SPORTS
5
6

Walking back through La Grave after a hard day

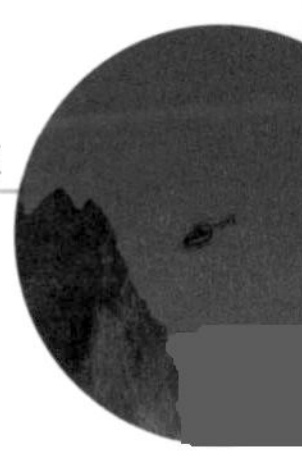

Marie Claude Turc shows Ayse one of her legendary tarts

explains that, while we were at lunch, the temperature at the summit dropped well below freezing. The snow in the couloir would have melted in the morning sun, then frozen hard, making it almost impossible to grip with our skis' edges in the tight couloir.

'Everyone thinks about the danger from avalanches, but not many people consider the freeze-thaw effect,' he says. 'In La Grave, it's all about timing – half an hour can make the difference between a fatality and a fantastic run.'

Eventually, we ski through the trees and gardens and into St Christoph, which in winter has just ten residents. It's a cluster of close-packed houses, a church, and La Cordée, the village's bar, shop, restaurant, hotel and social centre, all rolled into the space of one tiny house. It's been open since 1907 and it doesn't look as if anything much has changed since then. Ricard-branded porcelain jugs sit on the wooden bar, hundreds of bottles of liqueurs line the shelves behind. The owner is Marie Claude Turc, whose ancestor Gaspard was the first man to climb the Meije and whose surname adorns almost all of the gravestones in the pretty churchyard opposite. Marie Claude is justifiably proud of her tarts – pear and myrtille are on today, but she also makes fabulous pistachio and walnut ones.

As we sit at the bar, chatting, drinking beer, eating charcuterie and *tarte aux myrtilles*, it's as if we've found a whole different type of après ski. You come to La Grave for the challenge and adrenalin; you end up falling in love with the peace and the beauty.

On our final morning, we ski over the top of the Dôme de la Lauze, connecting into the big neighbouring resort of Les Deux Alpes, and get a shock. Hundreds of people are careering down the piste, there's a huge queue for the chairlift and in the big, soulless self-service cafeteria grumpy staff sell microwaved food and 50 cent tickets to use the toilet. We long to be back in La Grave. Steep, deadly and serene – there's nowhere else like it.

STATS **Town altitude:** 1,450m **Highest lift:** 3,550m; **Lifts:** 3 **Pistes:** 0km
Lift pass: €34 per day **Closest airport:** Grenoble – 77km

The Knowledge
La Grave, France

WHY? It's a unique place – a wild mountain rather than a conventional ski resort, with some of the most extreme skiing in the Alps. The whole mountainside is off piste, and from the top to the bottom is an astounding vertical drop of 2,150m **GETTING THERE** Fly to Grenoble. If that's not possible, other options are Lyon (193km) or Turin (134km). Grenoble is also served by TGV (direct) from Paris, taking 2 hours 55 minutes (so a journey time of about 6 hours 30 minutes from London) **TRANSFERS** It's probably best to hire a car at the airport. The drive to La Grave takes an hour and a half. Taxis (+33 (0)4 76 79 92 87; www.taxidelameije.com) will cost about €200 each way. There are also buses, but these are much slower, because you need to take the shuttle from the airport to Grenoble bus station before making a connection with the bus to La Grave. The bus is line 35 from Grenoble to Briançon, run by VFD (+33 (0)4 76 60 47 08; www.vfd.fr); a return ticket costs €32

WHERE TO STAY The Skierslodge (+33 (0)4 76 11 03 18; www.skierslodge.com) is an essential part of a visit to La Grave – it combines good food, great atmosphere and top-notch guiding in one package. The guides are all UIAGM qualified, the highest international standard. A full week's package, including six days' guiding and half board, costs €960. Four-night packages, half board, with three days' guiding, but without flights or transfers, cost €600. In St Christoph, La Cordée (+33 (0)4 76 79 52 37; www.la-cordee.com; doubles from €94, half board) is the hotel, restaurant and bar rolled into one – and it's utterly charming

WHERE TO SKI The descent down the Vallon de la Selle to the hamlet of St Christoph is beautiful and sublimely peaceful. The Classique route is actually not that difficult but, if conditions are right, you can descend La Rama, a couloir that drops 1,000m straight into the valley. Other famous couloirs include Triffide, Banane, Patou and the extremely exposed Pan de Rideau

WHERE TO EAT The four-course evening meals in the Skierslodge are excellent. On the mountain there is Daniel's place, Le Chalet Haut-Dessus, at the top of the cable car, but the restaurant beside the lift's mid-station, at 2,400m, is also very good. Le Vieux Guide (+33 (0)4 76 79 90 75) in the village centre is also recommended

WHERE TO PARTY La Grave isn't really a party town. For après ski, the terrace outside the Hôtel Castillan, opposite the lift, is open from 2 p.m. In the evenings, the only place with any action is Le Pub, the bar beneath the Skierslodge. On Fridays and some other days, there is live music, and it can get wild **HELP!** Skierslodge can arrange transfers for you, but if you want the full package, including flights, the Ski Club of Great Britain (0845 4580784; www.skifreshtracks.co.uk) organizes weekends staying at the Hotel Edelweiss and using local guides. Four nights with three days' guiding cost from £695

TOURIST OFFICE +33 (0)4 76 79 90 05; www.lagrave-lameije.com

On the Classique route to St Christoph

Five More... Extreme

KRIPPENSTEIN, AUSTRIA

➲ STATS: **Town altitude:** 514m; **Highest lift:** 2,100m; **Lifts:** 3; **Pistes:** 14km; **Closest airport:** Salzburg – 90km

➲ WHY? Talk about a secret stash – I've never met anyone who has heard of Krippenstein, a small ski area above the village of Obertraun. Its low altitude and lack of lifts means it gets very few skiers, but word is spreading among the freeride community that this is the place to come for a taste of beautiful, steep and empty mountains. American ski bible *Powder* magazine asked, 'Is this the best snow in Europe?' while German mag *Planet Snow* put it at number one in a list of Europe's best freeride spots. Realistically, though, it is a small place – perfect for a tough weekend rather than a week. For guides, contact Outdoor Leadership (+43 (0)613 56058; www.outdoor-leadership.com)

➲ GETTING THERE Hire car or taxi is easiest. A taxi will cost around €120 for up to 8 and take about 1 hour (Taxi Rastl: +43 (0)613 1542; www.taxi-rastl.at). You can also fly to Linz (130km away) with Ryanair (from where a taxi will cost €160 and take 90 minutes)

➲ WHERE TO STAY The Hotel Haus am See (+43 (0)613 126777; www.hotel-hausamsee.at; doubles from €72, including breakfast) in Obertraun looks out over the Hallstättersee lake. Alternatively, stay on the mountain in the Lodge (+43 (0)613 58808; www.lodge.at; doubles from €90, half board)

➲ WHERE TO PARTY The Haifischbar ('shark bar') is the place to go. If you want action, go during the weekend of the Rip the Krip snowboard competition, usually the start of April

➲ TOURIST OFFICE Ski area: +43 (0)613 68854; www.krippenstein.at. Obertraun village: +43 (0)613 1351; www.oberoesterreich.at/obertraun

ANDERMATT, SWITZERLAND

➲ STATS: **Town altitude:** 1,445m; **Highest lift:** 2,965m; **Lifts:** 25; **Pistes:** 130km; **Closest airport:** Zurich – 90km

➲ WHY? A two-stage cable car takes you from the village all the way to the top of the Gemsstock at 2,965m, from where there are only a couple of pistes but a whole mountain of off-piste opportunities. The village can feel deserted at some times but seems reliably to get great powder snow conditions even when other resorts don't

➲ GETTING THERE Most take the train – it's 2 hours 21 minutes from the airport station, changing at Zurich main station and Göschenen. Driving takes about 2 hours; a taxi for up to 7 will cost around CHF375/£184 (Genial Shuttle: +41 (0)41 622 42 22; www.genialshuttle.com)

➲ WHERE TO STAY The River House (+41 (0)41 887 00 25; www.theriverhouse.ch; doubles from CHF240/£118, including breakfast) is a new boutique hotel in a renovated 250-year-old house. There's a good restaurant and excellent bar for après ski too

➲ WHERE TO PARTY For a drink, try Bar La Curva in the Hotel Monopol, and the Baroko Music Bar in the Hotel Schweizerhof, but the key nightclub in town is Dancing Gotthard

➲ TOURIST OFFICE +41 (0)41 887 14 54; www.andermatt.ch

ENGELBERG, SWITZERLAND

➲ STATS: **Town altitude:** 1,050m; **Highest lift:** 3,028m; **Lifts:** 24; **Pistes:** 82km; **Closest airport:** Zurich – 90km

➲ WHY? A popular resort in Victorian days, Engelberg faded into obscurity, only to be rediscovered in recent years by serious powder hounds. There are two main reasons. First is the massive vertical drop of just under 2,000m, from the highest lift close to the summit of the mighty Titlis back to the town. Second is the north-facing Titlis glacier, which helps keep temperatures cool and preserve powder conditions. Classic routes include the Laub and the Galtiberg

➲ GETTING THERE Most people take the train – from Zurich airport station it takes 2 hours 25 minutes with just one change, in Luzern. Train the whole way is possible: Paris–Basel–Luzern–Engelberg. The drive from the airport takes 90 minutes – hire a car, or a taxi for up to 3 will cost CHF240/£118 (+41 (0)41 637 33 88; www.taxi-haecki.ch)

➲ WHERE TO STAY The Hotel Terrace (+41 (0)41 639 66 66; www.terrace.ch; doubles from CHF280/£138) dates from 1904 and, though it may not be quite as grand as it once was, still has plenty of character, plus its own spa and nightclub. The ancient mini-funicular railway that connects it to the town was replaced by a modern lift system in 2008

➲ WHERE TO PARTY The Yucatan, in the Bellevue Hotel, is probably the liveliest place, great for après ski

and with happy hours and TexMex food. Later, hit the Spindle Disco Bar and the Eden Bar and Lounge
➲ **TOURIST OFFICE** +41 (0)41 639 77 77; www.engelberg.ch

SAINTE FOY, FRANCE

➲ **STATS: Town altitude:** 1,550m; **Highest lift:** 2,620m; **Lifts:** 4; **Pistes:** 30km; **Closest airport:** Chambéry – 120km

➲ **WHY?** For many years this place was a secret known only to ski instructors from Val d'Isère and Tignes, the big resorts just up the road, who came to play in the powder on their days off. Now the word is out, and the small village is being slowly developed, but for the moment the slopes above still remain deserted compared to its famous neighbours, and offer sensational off-piste routes which remain untracked days after a storm. Conversely, the quiet centre and gentle lower pistes also make this a great spot for families
➲ **GETTING THERE** A taxi from Chambéry airport will cost around €225 for up to 3 (+33 (0)6 09 44 35 75; www.tonictaxi.fr). The drive takes about 90 minutes. There are also infrequent buses – check the timetable at www.altibus.com
➲ **WHERE TO STAY** Hôtel Le Monal (+33 (0)4 79 06 90 07; www.le-monal.com ; doubles from €105, including breakfast) is simple but comfortable, and in the old part of the village rather than the modern development
➲ **WHERE TO PARTY** La Pitchouli is the liveliest bar, has a pool table and does good pizzas too
➲ **TOURIST OFFICE** +33 (0)4 79 06 95 19; www.saintefoy.net

ALAGNA, ITALY

➲ **STATS: Town altitude:** 1,212m; **Highest lift:** 2,971m; **Lifts:** 37; **Pistes:** 180km; **Closest airport:** Milan Malpensa – 120km

➲ **WHY?** The hardcore heart of the Monterosa area (see chapter 2), Alagna is like that other extreme mecca La Grave in being a very traditional, quiet village and having only a couple of lifts (discounting the link to Monterosa's other resorts, Alagna can muster just 3 lifts and 24km of piste). However, there's a whole mountainside for exploring off piste, and the options will grow even more when the new lift to Punta Indren at 3,275m (replacing an old one that stopped working several years back) is completed
➲ **GETTING THERE** Hire a car or, if there are a few of you, take a taxi. Alagna's tourist agency Lyskamm Viaggi (+39 0163 922993; www.alagna.it) offers a minibus for up to seven people for €180 each way. The drive takes about 2 hours
➲ **WHERE TO STAY** Built in 1865, the Hotel Monterosa (+39 0163 923209; www.hotelmonterosa-alagna.it; doubles from €140, half board, 3 nights minimum) was the village's first hotel and is opposite the church in the centre. The smartest option is the four-star Cristallo (+39 0163 922822; www.hotelcristalloalagna.com; doubles from €200, including breakfast)
➲ **WHERE TO PARTY** Café delle Guide in the Hotel Monterosa is the busiest spot, but also try Bar Cà Nostra, and the wood-panelled wine bar An Bacher, where you can try 400 different wines and nibble local cheese and salami
➲ **TOURIST OFFICE** +39 0163 922988; www.atlvalsesiavercelli.it

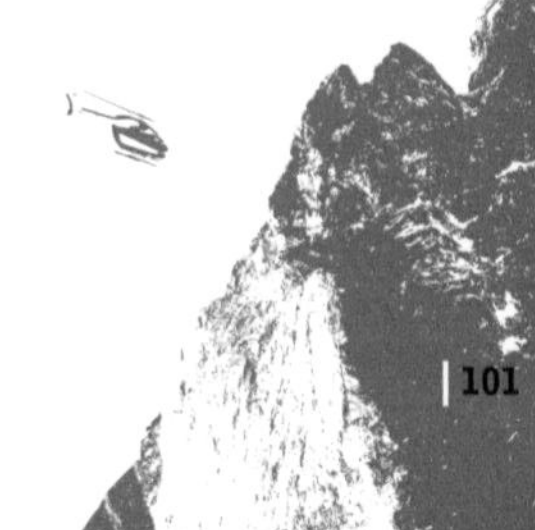

07

Kids

NEUSTIFT, AUSTRIA

WE WATCH THE KIDS slaloming along, throwing up their arms and waving as they crest each bump.

The village of Neustift in the Stubai Valley

HIGH UP IN THE AUSTRIAN ALPS, in the middle of a vast glacier, a heated debate is raging.

'I hate it when the instructors say you have to turn,' says Jake. 'I just want to go straight.'

Alex interrupts: 'I like it best when I trip people up when they come off the chair lift.'

'No, the best bit is when you go down backwards, especially on red runs,' insists Gabriel, before Alex breathlessly fires back his trump card: 'I nearly knocked myself out on a black run – it was brilliant!'

We're sitting on small red plastic chairs eating chicken and chips while the boys – all eight years old – discuss the finer points of skiing and I take down the most rapid shorthand of my life. Behind the table is a glass wall through which we can see the Stubai glacier, and a 6m-high inflatable dog. Welcome to the Mickey Mouse Ski Club, probably the best place in Europe for children to learn to ski.

We're all staying in Neustift, a village down in the valley far below us, and in many ways a perfect

Kids having the time of their lives at the Mickey Mouse Ski Club

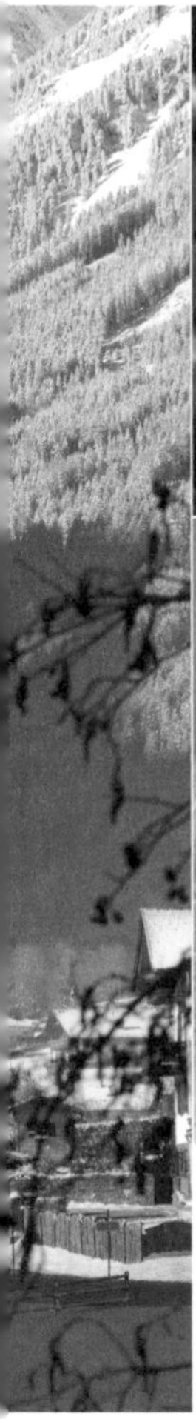

weekend destination, kids or no. For a start, there's the location – turn south from Innsbruck on the main route towards Italy, then take a right, leave the motorway behind and head into the gloriously peaceful, dead-end Stubai Valley. Follow the river along the bottom of the valley as startling mountains rear up on either side and, 16km later, you're there. The drive from airport to village takes no more than thirty minutes.

Then there's the snow. You might expect a resort so close to a city to be a bit of a compromise – convenient, yes, but with limited, and low, slopes. But the opposite is true. Up here at the end of the valley is the Stubai glacier, with 110km of pistes and one of the country's highest ski lifts, which rises to 3,210m. There's not just one high lift either. Most of the pistes, which fan off in every direction around a huge, high alpine bowl, are above 2,600m, so the snow will usually be as good as any in the Alps. It's also guaranteed: the main season here runs from November to mid-May, but some runs are open all summer.

Slalom champs start early

And then there's the Mickey Mouse Ski Club. Neustift is fiercely proud that it is the only official Disney-franchised resort in Europe. To be honest, at first it all sounded a bit naff to me – do we really want corporate America invading the picturesque valleys of the Tirol? Can't children enjoy the mountains without the help of a cartoon mouse? But having spent the morning here, with Alex, Jake and co., I am completely won over (and utterly exhausted). The first thing I see in the reception is a photo of David Hasselhoff here with his kids – and if it's good enough for the Hoff …

The club caters for pretty much all ages – parents just drop children off at the reception, where they are enrolled and given a Mickey Mouse name badge, then head off to enjoy the slopes. Kids of up to three are looked after by nannies in the SpielParadis kindergarten. It's light, warm and well equipped, and the children are taken outside to play whenever it's not too cold. For those used to childcare prices in the UK, it's also a bargain – a full day's childcare, from 8.45 a.m. up to 4 p.m., costs just €22; half days are €15.

Outside is a large roped-off area where children aged four and over can learn to ski. Adults (other than instructors) are banned. 'We get parents who come and look over at their children from the edges, but we discourage it,' says Verena, the beaming instructor showing us round. 'If they're left alone the kids get on with it and don't even notice their parents aren't there.'

One almost flat corner is reserved for absolute beginners. Here they get used to putting skis on, and green strips of matting allow them to walk up without slipping before skiing back down. After getting to grips with the green mats, children move into the main area, where there are three 'magic-carpet' lifts of differing lengths and three slopes – one smooth, one bumpy and one slalom. The magic carpets – conveyor belts which the kids just have to stand on to be slowly but surely taken uphill – are inside protective Perspex tunnels, so the kids won't get cold if it's windy.

If skiing gets boring, there's a little wooden chalet for drawing, singing or a cup of hot chocolate, and a merry-go-round with inflatable cars pulled slowly round on the snow.

Lessons run from 10 a.m. till midday and 1 p.m. till 3 p.m., and most parents leave their kids to have lunch in the children-only club restaurant in between the two sessions. Two days, including lunches, costs €115, four days €175.

We watch the kids slaloming along, throwing up their arms and waving as they crest each bump. The funny thing is that, while expert skiers will sit for hours talking about types and textures of snow, there's a peculiar assumption that it doesn't really matter with beginners. In 99 per cent of resorts, the nursery slopes are right at the bottom and so beginners end up struggling on the iciest or slushiest runs in the resort. Here, we're at 2,620m and the snow is fabulous.

Once the kids have outgrown the three magic carpets, their instructors will take them on to the surrounding pistes proper. Being on a glacier, these are supremely wide, and many are relaxed, undulating blues, perfectly suited to kids and learners. The lifts are almost all chairlifts, and those close to the Mickey Mouse club are especially slow. Children have a special entrance and are helped on to the chair. Oh, and did I mention that, up to the age of ten, they don't even have to pay for a lift pass?

So, with the kids happily ensconced with Mickey, Goofy et al., parents can guiltlessly answer the call of the high peaks rising all around. Let's face it, anyone who takes children for a weekend ski trip is likely to be a pretty serious skier and so isn't going to be satisfied just with an intermediate-only area. And the good news is that, as well as the easy runs around the Mickey Mouse club, the Stubai glacier also has some top-notch expert skiing.

There are numerous steep off-piste routes off the Rotadlikopf under the four-man Rotadl chair, a

The altitude guarantees great snow for young learners

WITH THE KIDS happily ensconced with Mickey, Goofy et al., parents can guiltlessly answer the call of the high peaks around them.

Tom enjoying the powder on the Stubai glacier

cracking couloir from the top of the Wildspitze down towards the Eisjochferner blue piste (number 1), and then there's the Wilde Grub'n, an incredible 10km run from the top all the way back down to the car park at the bottom of the gondola. It's classed as an 'alpine ski route', but really it's a red-level piste. The run itself is a blast but, if there's powder on the mountain, you can cut alongside the piste and enjoy the kind of descent that would usually be the climax of a week of ski touring.

Of course this is a glacier, so there's the added danger of falling into crevasses and, if heading off-piste, you should take a guide. I ask Verena if they ever lose anyone down them.

'Oh yes, but usually just in the autumn when a little bit of snow has made the crevasses hard to see,' she says with a smile.

At the very top is Austria's highest mountain restaurant, the Jochdole, at 3,150m. It's a cool, modern place, shiny metal on the outside, stripped wood inside, tucked into the lee of a rocky outcrop as shelter from the wind. Here, Robin and I sit outside, eat homemade apple strudel and drink in the view to the south – the Dolomites, the Italian plains, and even Venice (or so they say).

So why don't we all go there? Well, there is a bit of a snag. Neustift is a twenty-five-minute drive from the base of the Stubai glacier lifts and the road can get busy but, for weekenders with their own car, this isn't really too big a deal. Even if you don't hire a car, there are regular buses, the cost of which is included in the lift pass.

Neustift knows it's a family favourite and the hotels go out of their way to look after kids. If money's no object, you can't beat the Hotel Jagdhof, a five-star Relais et Chateaux with one of the country's most famous wine cellars (1934 Mouton Rothschild anyone?). It's also got some lovely family apartments, linked by tunnel to the main hotel, a wonderful indoor/outdoor swimming pool (joined by a space-age sliding underwater door that the children will love), and the on-site nursery where childcare is free for over-fours until 9 p.m. Meals and drinks for kids are free too.

Slightly cheaper are the Stubaierhof and the Tirolerhof, both of which come highly recommended.

Those coming for a week can stay with British family skiing specialist Esprit in their catered chalet right in the village centre.

And, once the kids are in bed and the babysitters on duty, the parents can sneak off for a beer in the Dorf pub on the village square. Downstairs is a rowdy bar with bands; upstairs, where the tables surround the barrels of a micro-brewery, is a lovely, relaxed spot to settle in for the evening.

There is more to skiing in Neustift than just the glacier, and on our second day we head to its other hidden gem – Schlick 2000, a separate ski area altogether, behind the wonderfully named village of Fulpmes, just down the valley from Neustift. Now this really is a homespun little family ski resort. There's not even a normal piste map, just a colour photocopy on a piece of A4. It's far smaller than the glacier – with about 25km of runs – and has a casual, easygoing atmosphere. When people fall over here they don't shout and swear, they say 'Hop là'.

Schlick is known for the standard of its piste grooming, and today there is perfect corduroy all over the mountain. After the children have had a couple of days in the Mickey Mouse club up on the glacier to get their ski legs, and if you're away for a longer weekend, this would be a great place for the family to come to ski together. Head for the blue run 4c, which slowly winds its way right down the edge of the ski area. Halfway down, stop at the Stern family's restaurant, the Schlickeralm, for a coffee and cake, and to watch the resident St Bernard stoically putting up with non-stop petting, then snowballing, from passing children. Here you can swap your skis for a toboggan (it costs €6 for a whole day). From the Schlickeralm you toboggan down a snow-covered road to the gondola middle station. Be careful, though: it's steep towards the bottom so you need to watch your speed.

Schlick is full of nice mountain restaurants. The Sennjochhütte, at 2,230m, the top of the area, is cosy, traditional and excellent value (pint of beer: €3.10, goulash and bread: €4), but there's an even better place, although getting there takes a little more effort.

Halfway down blue piste number 1, between the Schlickeralm and the gondola mid-station, we come across a carved wooden board saying 'Galt Alm

NEUSTIFT KNOWS it's a family favourite and the hotels go out of their way to look after kids.

Express', a seat and a Tirolean flag, and a couple of skiers standing about waiting. It's not immediately clear what they are waiting for until there's a rumble in the trees above and a piste basher emerges on a small track.

Only when Andreas, the driver, unfurls a rope from the back of the machine do I grasp what's happening – every half-hour between 11.30 and 1.30 he tows a line of skiers behind the piste basher, up through the woods to the Galt Alm, a little restaurant just out of reach of the pistes and the lift system. The fifteen-minute ride (which is free) is gentle enough for all but the most hesitant beginners and at the end we find an idyllic scene – an old chalet with a sunny terrace and views all the way down to Innsbruck in one direction and, in the other, up along the valley to Neustift and the glacier. A couple of groups are lounging about eating puddings, a child plays on a swing. Antlers hang above the door, sheep's bells tinkle in a shed around the back, and a sign advertises homemade honey.

This is the spot for your final day. After a big lunch here, ski down the winding path back to the pistes, continue all the way down to Fulpmes, jump in the car and, twenty-five minutes later, you'll be in the departure lounge. The kids will sleep all the way home.

1 *Swap skis for a toboggan at Schlick 2000*
2 *Expert childcare at the Mickey Mouse Club*
3 *Schlick 2000 is renowned for the quality of its pistes*
4 *Coffee and homemade cake at Austria's highest restaurant*
5 *The Sennjochhütte at Schlick 2000*
6 *Under-10s ride the lifts for free*

THE INSIDE TRACK

Lorna Conner Resort Manager for Esprit

'What's the ideal age to take your child on their first ski trip? We take children into our classes from three but, at that age, it's very much about just having fun in the snow rather than being a proper ski lesson. There can be a bit of a mob mentality – if one of them is upset, it sets the next one off, and so on – and they haven't got so much experience of being left with other people. But leave it till age five or six and they are used to being in school classes, they have a bigger vocabulary (so if their boots hurt they can explain where, for example) and they will be able to understand the lessons. At that age they can make real progress in a few days.'

1|2

|3

|4

|5
6

The Knowledge
Neustift, Austria

STATS **Town altitude:** 1,000m **Highest lift:** 3,210m; **Lifts:** 39
Pistes: 149km **Closest airport:** Innsbruck – 32km

WHY? Neustift has the perfect recipe for a family resort: a super-quick transfer; a specialist, Disney-themed kids' club; wide, easy, snow-sure runs; and a picturesque centre with bags of character **GETTING THERE** Fly to Innsbruck with British Airways or Easyjet. Alternatively, Munich airport is about 210km away **TRANSFERS** You can simply jump in a taxi in the rank at the airport for the 30-minute drive or, if you want to take a bus, take the shuttle to Innsbruck train station (line F, every 15 minutes; journey takes 18 minutes) and pick up the STB bus to Neustift (hourly; journey time 50 minutes; details: +43 (0)512 5307303; www.innbus.at). However, remember that it's a 25-minute drive from Neustift to the valley's best skiing, at the Stubai glacier. There are free ski buses on the route (see www.ivb.at) but, if you're only here for a couple of days, hiring a car is always going to be more flexible (and there's a large, free car park at the bottom of the Stubai glacier lifts) **LIFT PASS** The Stubai valley has four separate ski areas: the Stubai glacier (24 lifts, 110km of piste); Schlick 2000 (8 lifts, 25km of piste); Mieders (4 lifts, 7km of piste); and Elfer (3 lifts, 7km of piste). The Stubai Super ski pass covers all four areas but is only available for a minimum of four days. If you're there for less than that, you need to choose your area and buy a day pass – on a short break it probably makes sense to stick to the Glacier (€36 per day; 10- to 14-year-olds €18; under-10s free) and Schlick (€29.50; 10- to 14-year-olds €15; under-10s free) **WHERE TO STAY** If money is no object, it would be hard to beat the Hotel Jagdhof (+43 (0)522 6266111; www.jagdhof-hotel.at), a traditional five-star property on the edge of the village, with meat and game from its own farm and its own on-site nursery. Family apartments cost from €394 per night, half board, based on two adults and two children sharing. Cheaper alternatives that are also popular include the friendly four-star Stubaierhof (+43 (0)522 62450; www.stubaierhof-neustift.at; doubles from €162, half board) and Tirolerhof (+43 (0)522 63278; www.tirolerhof-neustift.at; doubles from €130, half board)

WHERE TO SKI Kids should head straight for the Mickey Mouse Ski Club (+43 (0)522 68108; www.skiclub-mickymaus.com), in the Garmsgarten part of the Stubai glacier ski area. Parents will enjoy the fabulous snow on the glacier near by, and the 10km-long Wilde Grub'n ski route all the way back down to the car park at the bottom of the lifts. Don't ignore Schlick just because of its weaker statistics – there are some excellent, quiet and very well-groomed runs here – perfect for a family day out after a few days of ski school in the Mickey Mouse club **WHERE TO EAT** When up on the glacier, the best option is the Jochdole, which at 3,150m claims to be Austria's highest restaurant but still manages an excellent homemade goulash and apple strudel. In Schlick, make the effort to reach the Galt Alm (www.galtalm.at). In the village, most people eat in their hotel, but the Grillstube (+43 (0)522 63147) does good steaks, while Bellafonte (+43 (0)522 62215) is popular for pizza **WHERE TO PARTY** The liveliest bar is the Dorf pub, which brews its own beer and occupies two floors on the main village square. If you have a good babysitter, you can cross the square and carry on partying at the Rumpl Disco **HELP!** Made to Measure Holidays (01243 533333; www.mtmhols.co.uk) can arrange packages, and offers, for example, four nights at the Jagdhof from £961, including flights and half board **TOURIST OFFICE** +43 (0)522 62228; www.stubai.at

Five More... For Kids

ÅRE, SWEDEN

➜ **STATS: Town altitude:** 380m; **Highest lift:** 1,297m; **Lifts:** 40; **Pistes:** 95km; **Closest airport:** Östersund – 80km

➜ **WHY?** The resort has an area specifically designed for families and learners, Björnen, with easy slopes and lifts and little runs through the trees. The Swedes are friendly, speak perfect English and are expert at easing the way for harassed parents, plus there are lots of fun alternative activities – dog sledding, swimming and moose-spotting trips by snowmobile

➜ **GETTING THERE** You can fly via Stockholm to Östersund (from where buses and trains run to the resort), but from the UK it's easier to take a direct flight with Norwegian (www.norwegian.no) to Trondheim, 135km away over the border in Norway. From there, there is a direct train to Åre station, which takes 2 hours 30 minutes (timetables at www.nsb.no)

➜ **WHERE TO STAY** The best hotel in town is the 100-year-old Diplomat Åregården (+46 (0)647 17800; www.diplomathotel.com; 3-night packages from 7,000 Swedish Kronor/£590 per double room, including breakfast). Alternatively, the Holiday Club (+46 (0)647 12060; www.holidayclub.se; doubles from 2,100 Kronor/£177, including breakfast) has family rooms and apartments and a huge swimming complex with 8 pools and a 67m waterslide

➜ **WHERE TO PARTY** It may be a family favourite, but there's some enthusiastic partying too. For après ski head to the Wersens bar/restaurant or the bar of the Tott Hotel. For late-night action, the Country Club, part of the Diplomat Åregården, and the Bygget, in the Fjallby area, are the key nightclubs

➜ **TOURIST OFFICE** +46 (0)771 840000; www.skistar.com/are

SERFAUS, AUSTRIA

➜ **STATS: Town altitude:** 1,427m; **Highest lift:** 2,828m; **Lifts:** 53; **Pistes:** 185km; **Closest airport:** Innsbruck – 100km

➜ **WHY?** The village of Serfaus is attempting to establish itself as Europe's number-one family resort, with a huge range of activities for children. There's a big children's play area on the mountain, with magic-carpet ski lifts, slides, toboggan runs, a Red Indian camp and a series of interconnected igloos for them to explore. Mürmli the marmot, the resort mascot, is usually on hand to play with the kids too, and the Mürmli trail is a piste with different kids' activities dotted along the way. Kids 1.3m tall and above can try the Fisser Flieger, a sort of cross between a hang-glider and deathslide that zooms above the slopes at up to 80kmph. There's also mini-skidoos for kids, Segway trekking, the huge Skyswing ... the list goes on

➜ **GETTING THERE** Driving takes about 75 minutes, and a taxi will cost €135 (+43 (0)547 66238; www.taxi-serfaus.at)

➜ **WHERE TO STAY** The Hotel Löwe and Hotel Bär (Lion and Bear) are 'kinderhotels' designed specifically for kids. They offer 'children's après ski' (there's a magician's school, plus plenty of dressing-up), crèches, childcare, a huge variety of indoor and outdoor play areas and swimming pools with slides (the waterslide in the Bär is 100m long!). Doubles at the Löwe from €200, full board; at the Bär from €246 (details: +43 (0)547 66058; www.loewebaer.com)

➜ **WHERE TO PARTY** It's not St Anton, but there can be some surprisingly lively après ski – head for the George Pub (not as English as it sounds) and the Patschi

➜ **TOURIST OFFICE** +43 (0)547 66239; www.serfaus-fiss-ladis.at

OBERGURGL, AUSTRIA

➜ **STATS: Town altitude:** 1,930m; **Highest lift:** 3,080m; **Lifts:** 23; **Pistes:** 110km; **Closest airport:** Innsbruck – 85km

➜ **WHY?** A traditional village set around a church at the dead end of a high valley, Obergurgl's gentle atmosphere has long attracted families. The village centre is mostly traffic-free, and there are lots of family-friendly hotels. It's also the highest parish in Austria, so has some of the country's most reliable snow conditions, and lots of easy pistes for group skiing. Kids up to age 9 get free lift passes

➜ **GETTING THERE** Driving from the airport should take a little over an hour. A taxi will cost around €155 for up to 4 (+43 (0)525 66540; www.taxiossi-obergurgl.com). Alternatively, the Ötztal shuttle bus costs €40 each way, but can take up to 2 hours – book a ticket by calling +43 (0)525 43550, or see the tourist-board website

➜ **WHERE TO STAY** The Hotel Alpina (+43 (0)525 66000; www.hotelalpina.com; doubles from €272,

including breakfast and five-course dinner) has a children's playroom, indoor pool and crèche (included in price). Kids will also like the castle-like appearance of the Granat Schlössl (+43 (0)525 66363; www.hotel-obergurgl.at; doubles from €146, half board), close to the bottom of the Festkogel lift

WHERE TO PARTY It's far quieter than other Austrian resorts, but there's still some fun après ski. The best spot is the Nederhütte, on the mountain close to the bottom of the Nederlift. You have to ski blue piste 6 to get back to the village afterwards. Later on, the Krump'n Stadl often has live music

TOURIST OFFICE +43 (0)572 00100; www.obergurgl.com

VALMOREL, FRANCE

STATS: Town altitude: 1,400m; **Highest lift:** 2,550m; **Lifts:** 49; **Pistes:** 150km; **Closest airport:** Chambéry – 90km

WHY? A car-free resort where convenience is king (most accommodation is right on the piste). It's purpose built, but the designers wanted it to look and feel like a pretty, traditional village. They've succeeded – everything is wooden and low rise and the snowy main street has a charming atmosphere. There's a big choice of easy blue runs too

GETTING THERE Hire a car or take a taxi, which will cost around €160 and take about 75 minutes (+33 (0)4 79 24 39 17; www.ajs-taxi-valmorel.com). There are also public buses run by Transavoie (timetables at www.transavoie.com)

WHERE TO STAY The Hôtel du Bourg (+33 (0)4 79 09 86 66; www.hoteldubourg.com; doubles from €140, including breakfast) is right in the centre of the village

WHERE TO PARTY Nightlife is quiet, limited to a few *vins chauds* in bars along the pedestrianized main street – try La Cordée and the Ski Roc. There is one nightclub, Les Nuits Blanches, which stays open every night until 5 a.m.

TOURIST OFFICE +33 (0)4 79 09 85 55; www.valmorel.com

CERVINIA, ITALY

STATS: Town altitude: 2,050m; **Highest lift:** 3,820m; **Lifts:** 57; **Pistes:** 313km; **Closest airport:** Turin – 118km

A break from skiing at the Mickey Mouse Club

WHY? Any parent who's been there knows that Italy has one great advantage as a family destination – Italians adore children. While the maître d's in French restaurants might look askance at little ones being brought into the dining room, in Italy the young ones will be treated like royalty no matter how badly behaved. Plus Cervinia has high, snow-sure, wide and sunny pistes – perfect for family outings – not to mention an excellent nursery slope, and you can make long day trips skiing over the top into Zermatt

GETTING THERE Hiring a car will be cheapest for the hour-and-a-half drive. A taxi will cost around €220 for up to 8 (+39 0166 61330; www.taxilavalle.com)

WHERE TO STAY The four-star Hotel Punta Maquignaz (+39 0166 949145; www.puntamaquignaz.com; doubles from €180, half board) is an attractive wooden chalet-style building, with log fires and antique furniture, close to the lifts. The Sertorelli Sporthotel (+39 0166 949797; www.sertorelli-cervinia.it; doubles from €194, 3 nights minimum) is another recommended four-star, with spa and children's play room

WHERE TO PARTY The Dragon Bar, a Welsh pub at the bottom of the pistes, is by far the most popular drinking spot, and Lo Yeti is another favourite. There's a hip nightclub too – the White Rabbit

TOURIST OFFICE +39 0166 944411; www.cervinia.it

08

Glamour

VERBIER, SWITZERLAND

THE RESORT has suddenly moved up a gear and the serious money, and sophistication, is flooding in.

THINK TWICE BEFORE OFFERING to buy a round at the Coco Club in Verbier. If you do, and someone asks for an Ice Chalet cocktail, just fall down and feign illness before you reach the bar.

For the Coco is the self-styled 'first luxury VIP nightclub in the Alps, and the Ice Chalet is its signature cocktail, a concoction of Krug, Hennessy Paradis Cognac and 'elixirs of love' served in a hand-carved ice-sculpture. The good news is that it serves eight people, through straws sticking out of the chalet roof. The bad news is that it will set you back CHF10,000, or round about £4,500.

We're here on the opening night of the season and, though the club is full of a super-glamorous, diamond-wearing crowd dotted with models such as Jodie Kidd and Astrid Muñoz, there's still a ripple of excitement when an Ice Chalet is brought out to a table. 'So what's it like?' I ask, angling for a slurp.

'Fizzy and a bit sweet,' giggles a girl in a sequin dress. I think I'll stick to the beer.

But even if the Ice Chalet doesn't quite live up to its billing, it's symbolic of the sudden emergence of Verbier as the glitziest resort in the Alps. True, it has always had its share of moneyed skiers, but back in the

A rooftop hot tub at the Nevai and, below, Jodie Kidd

Previous pages: The reception desk at the minimalist Nevai hotel

80s it was all about Sloaney chalet girls larking about in the Farm Club in jeans and pink shirts – collars up, natch – while looking for a husband. Chief among Sloanes, Fergie, even used to live here.

Now, though, the resort has suddenly moved up a gear, and the serious money, and serious sophistication, is flooding in. As if to underline the point, in January 2008 Sir Richard Branson chose Verbier for the launch of his first business foray into skiing, a chalet which sets a new record as the most expensive in the Alps. The Lodge, which is marketed alongside Branson's Necker Island and the Ulusaba private game reserve in South Africa, sleeps up to eighteen adults and costs up to £57,000 a week, not including flights, transfers or even a lift pass …

What St Moritz was to the 50s and Courchevel to the 90s, Verbier is today – the place for the young jet set. Recent visitors have included Posh and Becks, Hugh Grant and Jemima Khan, and Jamie Oliver, while James Blunt has a chalet here (as does, er, Les Dennis). And while Courchevel and St Moritz always existed in a sort of timeless, glitzy but fashion-free bubble, where Spanish princesses and Italian counts danced to generic Europop, Verbier is far more identifiably

A lavish spread laid on by Picnics on the Piste

1|2

|3

|4

|5
|6

British and more self-consciously fashionable. Every weekend DJs and club promoters, as well as hundreds of punters with second homes, fly in from London to lead the party. When Wills and Harry go on a family holiday with their dad, they head for Klosters. When they go away with their London mates, they come to Verbier.

'We wanted Coco to be like a proper London club,' says the wonderfully named Louis de Rohan, its creative director. He's succeeded too – this couldn't be further from the student-night atmosphere of most resort nightclubs. There's the granite bar, hand-painted wallpaper, the fur curtains, the private rooms, the curved red banquettes, and the sparkling wall behind them covered in £30,000 of gold leaf. Order a CHF10,000 cocktail, or even the more reasonable CHF800 Avalanche, which comes in a mountain-shaped glass dotted with Swarovski crystals, and it will be served to your table by one of the Snow Birds – the club's own glamorous hostesses, who have become the stuff of fantasy for every ski bum in town.

Membership of the club for the season costs £1,000, but non-members can come in if they pay on the door – £20 at weekends; £10 during the week. It seems most visitors are unlikely even to notice the charge. The week after we visited, Harvey Sinclair, the British entrepreneur who owns the club, took a booking from a group of Muscovites, who wanted a booth reserved for them for seven consecutive nights, with twenty bottles of Cristal set aside each night. They paid the bill in advance, all £78,000 of it . . .

Of course, this being the most glamorous night of my life, I'm coming down with flu and, while live dance-music band Crazy P rock out and Radio 1 DJ Chris Coco takes to the decks, I snuffle into my hanky. Still, this being Verbier, there's always another party tomorrow.

'The thing about this town is that the people who come here are hardcore skiers, and that keeps the atmosphere young, happy and sporty,' says Gul Coskun, as she shows me round her newly opened art gallery beneath the Rosalp hotel. The idea is that it will attract passing skiers on their way back from the Medran lift and tempt them into an impulse buy. This doesn't seem at all strange, until you take a closer look at the art on offer.

Consider that Picasso originals are confined to a little back room and you start to get the idea. Out front are all bright, boisterous bits of pop art – a Robert Indiana sculpture spelling out the word 'Love' is on offer at £350,000, a photograph of some cowboys by Richard Price is a little over £500,000, and there are numerous Roy Lichtensteins and Andy Warhols.

'I think the pictures come alive here, with the snow and the sunshine,' says Gul, who also has a gallery in Chelsea, 'but I'm not here to make money, I'm here for the skiing and the experience. The gallery's almost like an excuse.'

Though the idea that anyone in salopettes is going to drop £500,000 on a photograph shows you how far Verbier's bubble now soars above ordinary life, it's true that serious skiing remains central to life here

1-4 *Opening night at the Coco Club, and the Ice Chalet cocktail, yours for CHF10,000*

5 *The Coskun gallery*

6 *The Nevai's lounge area*

rather than just being an occasional diversion from the conspicuous consumption.

This morning there's a buzz of anticipation outside the Medran lift, for the famous Tortin run is to be opened for the first time this season. Usually, the number of skiers who tackle this off-piste route mould the slope into moguls the size of small hatchbacks but, when we reach the top at 10 a.m., it's still just a field of virgin, thigh-deep snow.

I'm skiing with Tom Lewis, an instructor with the Warren Smith Ski Academy, which has played a central role in moving Verbier towards the top of serious skiers' to-do lists. Smith, who has starred in ski films as well as being an instructor, organizes the annual Verbier Ride competition, which attracts huge publicity and some of the world's top extreme skiers, who leap cliffs and straight-line couloirs in a bid for glory. Lewis is not impressed by my old-school short powder turns and urges me to ski the next section in just three turns instead of twenty and to increase the speed and aggression in true freeride style.

'Come on, open it up, scare yourself a bit,' he urges, before charging off down the slope in colossal, high-speed arcs, leaving little swirls of white smoke behind him.

The ski area is officially called the Four Valleys and, as the name suggests, it's very spread out. Verbier sits to the far south of the area and, the further you travel, over the ridges and into each successive valley to the north-east, the quieter the runs become. By the time you pass the village of Siviez and take the lifts on Mont Rouge beyond, the bustle and glitz of Verbier seem a long way behind.

Most of the long connecting runs are reds – strong intermediates and above will get the most from the area – but the resort's hardcore reputation is built on the large number of itinerary runs, or ski routes. These runs, marked in a yellow-and-black-dotted line on the map, are a sort of cross between on and off piste. The snow isn't prepared by piste bashers, and there is a risk of avalanche, but they are marked out with poles and, because they are popular routes, if you get into trouble, help shouldn't take too long to arrive. Classics include the Vallon d'Arby, a long descent down a secluded valley, starting on open slopes then plunging through the trees, and Col des Mines, a steeper route above Verbier itself.

Less confident skiers should head to the Savoleyres sector. It's directly above Verbier but is a 'dead end', so you get none of the through traffic heading over to the other valleys. Here you'll find some stunning long blue runs – the Planard back towards Verbier, and the Altiport, on the other side of the ridge, which snakes its way down to the small village of La Tzoumaz.

My favourite spot for lunch is the Cabane de Mont Fort, an old stone-walled refuge perched on an outcrop below the highest peak in the Verbier area. Its sunny terrace has amazing views over the valley to Bruson on the far side and, if the resort's partying is getting too much, you can come up here to stay for the night. The simple double rooms in the eaves of the refuge and the coin-operated showers, which tend to run out when you're still covered in soap, couldn't be further from the Coco Club, but absolute peace, and first tracks in the morning, are guaranteed.

However, another new business in town promises a lunch that will keep up the glamour factor. As Tom and I sweep down towards La Chaux, we see a uniformed butler flanked by two beautiful waitresses clad all in black standing beside the piste. On his tray is a bottle of Bollinger, which is duly popped and poured out into ice-cold flutes. 'Welcome to your Picnic on the Piste,' he says with a flourish, before leading us away from the run to where a table and chairs have been cut from the snow and covered with tablecloth, rugs and cushions.

Launched in Verbier in 2007, British-owned company Picnics on the Piste offers a range of

Great skiing in Verbier's La Chaux sector, with the Grand Combin in the background

THE NEVAI is cool and minimal, a sort of St Martin's Lane hotel for the mountains.

Below and main picture: No salopettes in sight at a Verbier fashion show

A bedroom, and the dining room, at the Nevai

organized picnics – starting at the basic 'green' level with soup, sandwiches and fruit, for €15 per head, and going up to 'black' at €69, which includes foie gras, charcuterie, goat's cheese salad, quiches, patisserie and chocolate truffles. Given the silver service and mountain-top location, the Bollinger, at €45 per bottle, seems pretty reasonable.

Afterwards, Tom and I take the lifts to the Col des Gentaines and spend the next thirty minutes scaling the so-called Stairway to Heaven. We use the frozen footsteps of previous skiers to struggle up to a ridge, where, even though we're bang in the middle of a very busy ski area, an untouched bowl of deep snow awaits us.

For years, après ski in Verbier has started with beers in the Mont Fort Pub or the bar of the Farinet Hotel, just off the Place Centrale. Even here things have taken on a more sophisticated edge since Rob Sawyer, the man behind the UK's PooNaNa chain of clubs, bought it. For

the 2008 season, club legends Hed Kandi were brought in to play nightly warm-up sets in the bar, then more full-on dance in the Casbah nightclub downstairs.

We're staying at the four-star Nevai hotel, opening for the first time this weekend and harbouring ambitions to shake up the staid world of Swiss Alpine hotels.

There are a few glitches but it's clear that, once these are ironed out, the hotel will be rather fabulous. Instead of chintzy soft furnishings and lashings of wood, the Nevai is cool and minimal, a sort of St Martin's Lane hotel for the mountains. *'Nevai'* means snow in the local Swiss dialect, and the colour scheme is predominantly icy white. In the foyer, past acres of sparkling white floor tiles, is a bulbous reception desk resembling a white pebble, a sunken-bar area and ruby-red freeform sofas for lounging on. One wall is taken up with a 3m-long rectangular fireplace and, at the end of the room, behind a lacy black curtain, is an entirely red boudoir area for couples in need of privacy.

The rooms are similarly airy and white, with one wall covered in a funky silver-birch wallpaper, Egyptian cotton bedding, iPod docks, flat-screen TVs and Elemis smellies.

Those who want more traditional comforts should head to Le Chalet d'Adrien, next to the Savoleyres lift. It's Verbier's only five-star hotel and yet manages to do luxury and top-class service in a totally relaxed, unpretentious way which could teach the town's young upstarts a thing or two.

Attached to the Nevai is the legendary Farm Club, still run by the Berardis, the two Italian brothers who founded it thirty-five years ago. Tonight, the German DJ is still plugging away with Abba hits, and things don't seem to have changed since Fergie's day. But this is the rare exception to the rule in the brave new Verbier world and, after a spin round the Farm's dance floor, we head to the Nevai's first-floor bar area, where Groove Armada are DJ-ing at the opening party. The room, with its textured silver wallpaper and cool light fittings like molten lava, is full of fashionable young things, journalists from British style magazines, and Warren Smith boogying away at the back.

Is all this getting out of hand? Certainly some locals are privately voicing fears that the resort's new glamorous persona is getting out of control. 'It's great that the resort is thriving, but we don't want the real skiers to get priced out by the fur-coat brigade,' one mountain guide told me. 'At the moment the ski bums in ripped Gore-Tex still happily co-exist with the millionaires, but it would be a shame if suddenly the place was just full of Russian oligarchs with bodyguards and trophy wives who never set foot on a piste.'

For some people, Verbier today will already be a vision of hell, precisely what they left the city to escape. But for a full-on, diamond-encrusted, champagne-fuelled and celebrity-studded weekend, this is the place.

THE INSIDE TRACK

Warren Smith Professional Freeskier and Coach

'If you're hitting the resort of Verbier, one thing you need to do is hire a qualified pro and ski the back side of Mont Fort. This amazing freeskiing paradise has a variety of different descents and takes you into the wilderness of Verbier's vast back-country terrain. The first section you ski is the steepest, around 40 degrees, and you can go steeper if you wish. En route, you'll normally get to ski three or four really nice faces of freeride terrain before exiting at the village of Siviez. For those in the know, this is definitely the highlight of the holiday.'

STATS Town altitude: 1,500m Highest lift: 3,330m; Lifts: 89 Pistes: 410km
Lift pass: CHF64 (£29) per day Closest airport: Sion – 64km

The Knowledge
Verbier, Switzerland

WHY? A long-time favourite of hardcore skiers, Verbier has suddenly emerged as the millionaire's favourite weekend haunt. But while there is champagne swilling and designer frocks aplenty, the atmosphere is much younger, cooler and more British than old-school Eurotrash favourites like St Moritz or Courchevel **GETTING THERE** Sion is the closest airport, and a 45-minute drive away, but is currently served only by weekly charter flights from Gatwick, Stansted and Edinburgh, operated by Darwin Air and Flybe. Instead, most people fly to Geneva, 160km away (Zurich is doable at a stretch, at 300km away). Taking the train is possible instead of flying – it is 3 hours 22 minutes on a direct TGV from Paris to Geneva, 3 hours 54 to Lausanne **TRANSFERS** Train is probably best, as you won't need a car when in the resort. From Geneva Airport station, it takes 2 hours 12 minutes to reach Le Châble, the station in the valley below Verbier, with one change on the way, at Martigny. From Lausanne, it's 1 hour 20 minutes. From Le Châble, buses run up the hill to the resort (taking 10 minutes), or you can take the gondola. If you hire a car, it will take about 90 minutes from Geneva. Taxis will cost around CHF570 (£260), each way, for up to four people (for listings of taxi firms; see www.verbiertaxi.ch) **WHERE TO STAY** The Nevai (+41 (0)27 775 40 00; www.nevai.ch; doubles from CHF570/£263, including breakfast; full-week rates are cheaper) is the hip new place to stay – central and with minimal décor that's almost unique in the Alps. However, service is far better at Le Chalet d'Adrien (+41 (0)27 771 62 00; www.chalet-adrien.com; doubles from CHF600/£277), the resort's only five-star, which has a beautiful, sunny terrace restaurant, a great swimming pool and is right beside the Savoleyres lift. At the other end of the spectrum, there's the Bunker (+41 (0)27 771 66 01; www.thebunker.ch; dorm beds from CHF30/£14, including breakfast), a converted nuclear shelter underneath the sports centre **WHERE TO SKI** Beware the runs from Les Ruinettes back into town in the afternoon as they can be horrendously busy. To escape the crowds, locals head to the far side of the valley and the village of Bruson, whose slopes are always deserted (because you need to take the cable car down to Le Châble and a shuttle bus up the other side). Plans to build a huge cable car directly across the valley from Verbier are currently on hold, thanks to opposition from environmentalists. After ticking off the various ski routes, expert skiers will want to tackle the more hairy-chested off-piste options, including the Creblet Couloirs; a guide is essential. To book a course with Warren Smith, go to www.warrensmith-skiacademy.com

WHERE TO EAT Picnics on the Piste (+33 (0)6 20 05 36 64) will create a wow factor for a special occasion. The Cabane de Mont Fort (+41 (0)27 778 13 84; www.cabanemontfort.ch), at 2,457m, is a fabulous place for lunch and also has rooms (from CHF80/£40 per night, half board). In town, the Milk Bar, between Place Centrale and the Medran lift, does great tea and cakes. L'Alpage (+41 (0)27 771 61 21), part of the King's Hotel, is popular and homely; L'Écurie (+41 (0)27 771 27 60), just off Place Centrale, is family run and does good local specialities. If money's no object, the best in town is probably Le Restaurant Pierroz within the Rosalp Hotel (+41 (0)27 771 63 23; www.rosalp.ch). If it is, try Le Monde des Crêpes (+41 (0)27 771 72 96) on Rue de la Poste, which has been making every kind of crêpe for 32 years

WHERE TO PARTY Après-ski HQ is the Pub Mont Fort (+41 (0)27 771 48 98; www.pubmontfort.com), near the bottom of the Medran lifts, but it never gets anything like as lairy as in Austria. Instead, people save themselves for going out after dinner. For this, the Coco Club (+41 (0)27 771 66 66; www.cococlub.ch) on Place Centrale is the glitziest option, while the other favourite is Casbah (+41 (0)27 771 66 26; www.hotelfarinet.com) below the Farinet Hotel, also on Place Centrale. The Farm Club (+41 (0)27 771 61 21; www.kingsverbier.ch, attached to the Nevai) is a legend, but doesn't seem to have changed since its 70s heyday **HELP!** Flexiski (01273 244668; www.flexiski.com) offers short breaks in Verbier. Three nights staying at the Hotel Montpelier costs from £982, including flights and taxi transfer

TOURIST OFFICE +41 (0)27 775 38 88; www.verbier.ch

Five More... For Glamour

COURCHEVEL 1850, FRANCE

➔ **STATS: Town altitude:** 1,850m; **Highest lift:** 3,230m; **Lifts:** 183; **Pistes:** 600km; **Closest airport:** Chambéry – 105km

➔ **WHY?** Victoria Beckham's favourite resort, Courchevel has long been the number-one destination for Europe's fur-coat wearing, Cristal-drinking elite. There are more super-luxury hotels than anywhere else – oh, and the skiing's rather good too. Avoid Russian new year (January 13), when Courchevel is taken over by oligarchs and their retinues and prices go through the roof
➔ **GETTING THERE** If you're really going for glamour, take a helicopter straight to Courchevel's Altiport. It takes 25 minutes from Chambéry, 35 from Geneva, and will cost around €1,200 for up to 4 (see www.whitetracks.co.uk). A taxi will cost €250 for up to 4, and the drive from Chambéry takes about 90 minutes (+33 (0)6 09 40 19 10; www.courchevel-prestige.com)
➔ **WHERE TO STAY** Right on the Bellecôte piste, Le Mélézin (+33 (0)4 79 08 01 33; www.amanresorts.com; doubles from €730) is the alpine outpost of Asian über-spa chain Aman, and somehow manages to be understated and opulent at the same time
➔ **WHERE TO PARTY** Les Caves de Courchevel is the glitziest and most expensive spot in town, or try the slick piano bar Mangeoire. If you're sick of champagne and just fancy a knees-up, start by squeezing into Le Jump bar on the Croisette, then head across the road to the Kalico, where the sweaty dancing goes on till 4 a.m.
➔ **TOURIST OFFICE** +33 (0)4 79 08 00 29; www.courchevel.com

ST MORITZ, SWITZERLAND

➔ **STATS: Town altitude:** 1,820m; **Highest lift:** 3,305m; **Lifts:** 56; **Pistes:** 350km; **Closest airport:** Samedan – 5km

➔ **WHY?** Synonymous with the artistocracy, St Moritz is the complete winter resort, with as much going on off the slopes – polo, golf and cricket on the frozen lake, the Cresta run, and numerous festivals – as on them. So many visitors don't bother to ski that the slopes are often delightfully quiet. The streets are lined with designer boutiques and there are even heated pavements
➔ **GETTING THERE** Fly direct to Samedan, the airfield just down the valley. You'll need a private plane, of course – allow around £3,500 per person for a 2-night break, based on 4 sharing a Citation Jet through Jeffersons (0208 746 2496; www.jeffersons.com). Ordinary people fly to Zurich, 200km away, and take the train (3 hours 30 minutes, 2 changes, see www.sbb.ch), or even Ryanair to Verona Brescia, from where they hire a car for the 200km drive
➔ **WHERE TO STAY** Badrutt's Palace Hotel (+41 (0)81 837 10 00; www.badruttspalace.com; doubles from CHF460/£214, including breakfast) is the classic, a sort of gothic castle with great views over the lake. It's so smart it nears self-parody – the car park is literally crammed full of Rolls Royces and Maybachs, and you aren't allowed in without a jacket in the evening. We also like the Carlton (+41 (0)81 836 70 00; www.carlton-stmoritz.ch; doubles from CHF950/£441, including breakfast), with the same owner as the Tschuggen in Arosa. Its newly refurbished interior is a riot of colour
➔ **WHERE TO PARTY** Start with dinner at the Chesa Veglia, a chalet in the centre of St Moritz dating from 1658 which is now the smartest restaurant in town, then head to the Diamond nightclub. If you want to escape the fur and diamonds, head for Bobby's Bar, where the teenage offspring of the millionaire parents hang out in baseball caps and jeans
➔ **TOURIST OFFICE** +41 (0)81 837 33 33; www.stmoritz.ch

DUBAI, UNITED ARAB EMIRATES

➔ **STATS: Town altitude:** 20m; **Highest lift:** 85m; **Lifts:** 2; **Pistes:** 1km; **Closest airport:** Dubai International – 5km

➔ **WHY?** It sounds like an ecological nightmare, but now you can combine staying in Dubai's sumptuous hotels with a ski holiday, thanks to the vast indoor ski centre bang in the middle of the desert. It offers 22,500m^2 of snow-covered slopes year round, runs up to 400m long and even has an indoor chairlift. And after a few runs, you can come back out into the 40-degree heat and go for a swim
➔ **GETTING THERE** Ski Dubai (+971 (0)4 4094000; www.skidxb.com) is in the Mall of the Emirates in the centre of town. The hotels will arrange airport transfers
➔ **WHERE TO STAY** If money's no object, it has to be the Burj Al-Arab (+971 (0)4 3017777; www.burj-al-arab.com; doubles from around 4500AED/£600), the 321m-high tower that looks like a billowing sail. For comedy value, stay in a 'ski chalet' at the Kempinski Hotel (+971 (0)4 3410000; www.kempinski-dubai.com; doubles from 1350AED/£180; chalets from around 2000AED/£265), which has views over the ski slope
➔ **WHERE TO PARTY** Despite a tendency to imprison DJs for possessing minute amounts of drugs, Dubai has a thriving club scene. Start off with a sundowner taking in the view from the top level of Bussola at Le Meridien Mina Seyahi or the Koubba Bar terrace at the Madinat Jumeirah, then head to the Lodge or Chi
➔ **TOURIST OFFICE** +971 (0)4 2230000; www.dubaitourism.ae

LECH, AUSTRIA

➔ **STATS: Town altitude:** 1,450m; **Highest lift:** 2,811m; **Lifts:** 85; **Pistes:** 280km; **Closest airport:** Innsbruck – 120km

➔ **WHY?** At the opposite end of the ski area from rowdy St Anton, Lech is the refined, respectable face of the Arlberg. A favourite of Princess Diana, it's not show-offy like St Moritz or Courchevel, it's more about discreet old-money types holing up in the charming traditional hotels and enjoying the village atmosphere and great, empty slopes
➔ **GETTING THERE** It's about 90 minutes' drive from Innsbruck airport. A taxi will cost around €225 for up to 3, €250 for up to 8 (+43 (0)558 325010; www.taxi-lech.at)
➔ **WHERE TO STAY** Diana favoured the Hotel Arlberg (+43 (0)558 321340; www.arlberghotel.at; doubles from €374, half board) in the centre of town, where you can sit on the terrace and listen to the river flowing past. There's an indoor/outdoor pool and spa too
➔ **WHERE TO PARTY** Nightlife is tame compared to St Anton, but there's some fun après-ski atmosphere in the bars outside the Krone and Tannbergerhof hotels and in the Schneggarei bar. Late-night action centres on the Archiv, Fux and S'Pfefferkorndl
➔ **TOURIST OFFICE** +43 (0)558 321610; www.lech-zuers.at

MÉRIBEL, FRANCE

➔ **STATS: Town altitude:** 1,850m; **Highest lift:** 3,230m; **Lifts:** 183; **Pistes:** 600km; **Closest airport:** Chambéry – 105km

➔ **WHY?** This one is less about the resort, more about the company who takes you there. Descent International (0207 384 3854; www.descent.co.uk) is the smartest chalet company of them all, patronized by royalty, celebrity and aristocracy. Normally, you have to hire an entire chalet for a full week (and this might set you back up to £57,000) but, for one weekend in December, the company runs a ski-test weekend, when you book by the room and see how the other half live at a fraction of the cost. Snow + Rock provide the latest equipment for you to test, while Perrier Jouet champagne is on tap
➔ **GETTING THERE** Transfers in discreetly liveried, leather-upholstered 4x4s are all part of the package
➔ **WHERE TO STAY** Exactly which chalets are offered will change from year to year. A 4-night break, including most meals and drinks, costs around £700pp, excluding flights
➔ **WHERE TO PARTY** It's hard to draw yourself away from the comfort of a fully staffed Descent chalet, but the best après-ski spot is the Rond Point des Pistes, just above the village, before the fun moves down to the Doron Pub, where there are often live bands. All roads eventually lead to Dick's Tea Bar
➔ **TOURIST OFFICE** +33 (0)4 79 08 60 01; www.meribel.net

ROLEX

09

Budget

NASSFELD, AUSTRIA

INSTEAD OF STAIRS, concrete ramps lead from one floor up to the next.

Nassfeld's Cube: 'like a misplaced spaceship'

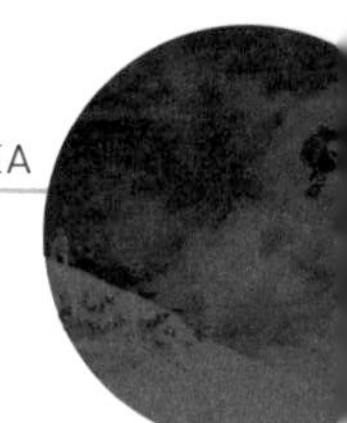

WE ARRIVE AT 10 P.M., but the Cube isn't hard to find. After driving through the dark streets of the quaint southern Austrian villages of Hermagor and Tröpolach, their houses and hotels shuttered for the night, we suddenly come upon a glass box four storeys high, glowing neon orange and green against the night sky.

Inside, the scene couldn't be more different to the standard Alpine hotel. There's no wood panelling, no receptionists in traditional dress, no black-and-white photos of the resort in days gone by. Instead, it's more like some kind of futuristic youth club.

The whole place is open plan, with a big central atrium where an indoor bungee-jumping contraption is currently set up. Instead of stairs, concrete ramps lead from one floor up to the next – the idea being that, in summer, mountain bikes can simply be pushed up to guests' rooms. On the ground floor, groups of beanie-hatted and baggy-trousered teens and twentysomethings are lounging at the bar, which stays open twenty-four hours for drinks and pizzas. Nearby, others are relaxing on rectangular red sofas, watching a film being shown on the big screen.

While your traditional Alpine hotel likes to cover walls, ceilings, furniture and anything else not breathing in wood, here the obsession is concrete. The floor is concrete; the pillars are concrete; even the fireplace in the lounge area is concrete. It's all just about funky enough to make it feel like loft-style industrial chic, not a prison.

A surly girl who looks about thirteen years old gives us key cards, and we head up to our rooms or, in Cube lingo, 'boxes'. The rooms sleep from two to eight, but all follow a similar layout. The door and landing wall are made of green or orange glass. Inside is your 'showroom' – an ante-chamber where you store your skis, board or, in summer, your mountain bike, hang your wet clothes and dry your boots on the drying machine. Behind that is the proper room, which again treads perilously close to the Wormwood Scrubs aesthetic but is saved by a few nice touches. The sink is a funky concrete square; the duvets are soft and white; the shower is powerful. Walls are varnished chipboard and, instead of curtains – far too much like soft furnishing – there's an exterior blind which you wind down. Under the bed are big, lockable boxes (padlocks are sold in reception for €5). There are no TVs – the idea being that you're too busy having fun to watch it.

'We realized that the rooms could be basic, because people don't spend any time in them,' Marc, the manager, explains later, 'but that what they do want are clubs, bars, chill-out areas and entertainment within the hotel. The Cube concept is all about combining sports, entertainment and design.'

And price. A two-night weekend stay in an en suite double room costs as little as €188. Oh yes, and that includes your lift pass, use of the sauna and steam room, plus entry to the nightclub, and breakfast and supper. Since the lift pass alone would cost €72, this is an absolute bargain and, since the Cube has 638 beds, availability is unlikely to be a problem.

Getting here for a weekend is cheap and easy too. The closest airport is Klagenfurt, an hour and a quarter's drive away, to where, if you book ahead, you can get a Ryanair flight from Stansted for a few pounds. If you've left it late and the flights are full, check out Ryanair's flights from Stansted or Birmingham to Trieste, just over the border in Italy (ninety minutes' drive), or Easyjet's to Ljubljana, in Slovenia (an hour and forty-five minutes away). The tourist office will book taxis from all three airports, for €40 per person each way, or just hire a car.

We dump our kit in our cells – sorry, boxes – and head to the bar, then go downstairs, past the sauna and steam room on the basement level to the Cube's other key asset – its on-site club. Tonight, a Friday, the Belgian division of MTV has taken it over to film a

The Cube's industrial interior: concrete, glass and steel

THE MOST IMPORTANT thing to remember about staying here is: do not forget your earplugs.

gig by a rock band and, when we walk in, the crowd surfing has already begun. Soon after, a limbo contest breaks out and, before long, one man is walking round with no trousers on. Belgians, eh?

It might have something to do with the fact that the drinks here are a steal too. To put this in perspective, bear in mind that, in a nightclub in Val d'Isère – or almost any French resort for that matter – you can easily pay €8 or more for a beer. Here it's €3, and that's for a half-litre. Actually, few people are drinking beer; instead, they are all clutching miniature bottles of multicoloured spirits – Kleiner Feigling (a fig vodka), and sour-cherry or sour-apple Klopfer (a type of schnapps, I think, although my notes become a little garbled here). At only €2 a bottle, these seem to be the Austrian equivalent of the alcopop.

At the Cube, pretty much anything goes. That night, the club keeps rocking till at least 5.30 a.m., and the hotel's concrete atrium reverberates to shouts and songs as successive parties stagger back to bed. The most important thing to remember about staying here – even if you are the raddest, most party-hungry bunch of snowboarders – is that you must not forget your earplugs.

Next morning, at 9.30 a.m., the restaurant is deserted. True, breakfast is served till 3 p.m. here, but we have the mountain to see. The Cube sits right beside the piste and the main gondola, looking like a misplaced spaceship. When it landed here in 2004 the locals must have been little less surprised than if it *had* been a spaceship. At the end of the millennium, Tröpolach was a sleepy village of 700 souls. There wasn't even a ski lift, but you could drive 10km up the road to Nassfeld, not a resort at all, but a ski area on the pass into Italy.

Then the Millennium Express gondola, the longest in Europe, opened, connecting the village with the ski area, and the Cube and the Hotel Carinzia, a big four-star spa property, were built close by. Suddenly, Tröpolach had become a major ski destination.

Skiing here feels different to the big, well-known resorts of the Tirol – more relaxed and low key. This is the southernmost ski area of Carinthia, Austria's southernmost province, and somewhere that feels like a pleasant backwater, tucked away on the border and forgotten about. Most of those on the slopes at the weekend are day trippers from nearby towns and, during the week, the pistes are deserted.

With that in mind, you might expect rickety old lifts but, in fact, they are state of the art. Nassfeld is Carinthia's biggest ski area, with thirty lifts and 110km of pistes and three more lifts planned to open for the 2009/10 season. It's relatively low – Tröpolach is down at 610m, the highest lift goes to 2,020m and most runs are between 1,300m and 1,900m – but as well as claiming to be Austria's sunniest ski area, Nassfeld also says it's one of the snowiest, thanks to storms coming up from the Adriatic. Nevertheless, it has invested in snow machines to cover every run.

1 *The glass exterior changes colour at night*

2 *There are chill-out areas on every floor*

3-4 *Wild times in the basement nightclub*

5 *Bedrooms are a bit like prison cells, but sheets and showers are good*

6 *Ramps replace stairs so mountain bikes can be wheeled up in summer*

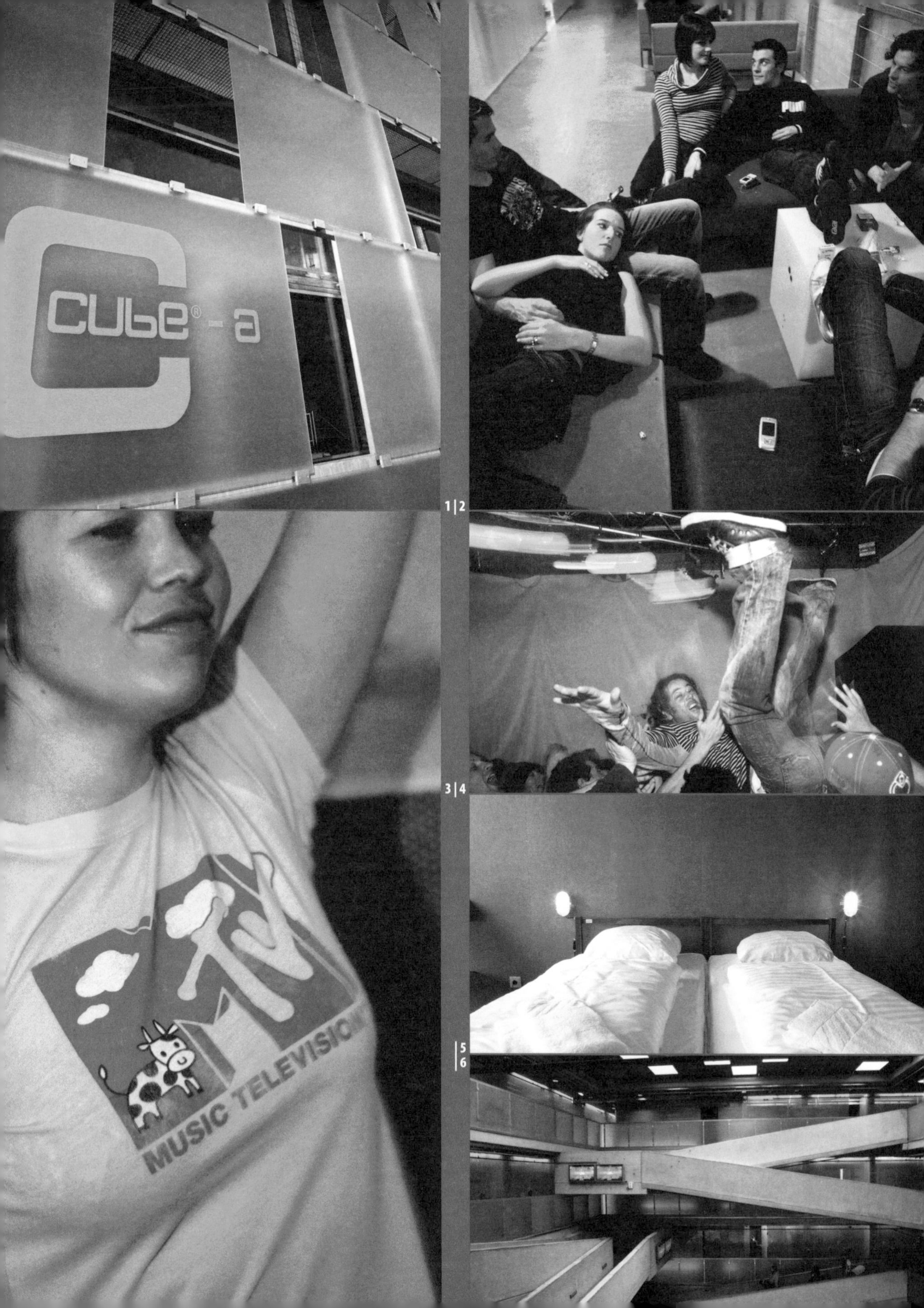

1|2

3|4

5
6

Perhaps because of the low altitude, it's a very beautiful area, with runs spread out across five forested mountainsides. Today the mist is swirling dramatically through the trees, occasionally collecting in the valleys below us, sometimes clearing to give views down to the flat, snow-covered fields of the farms around Tröpolach.

There are some tough pistes here, but really this is a perfect area for intermediate skiers and snowboarders. Quite why there are so many of the latter is a bit of a mystery. True, there's a half-pipe and fun park, and Burton is due to build an even bigger one for the 2009 season, but neither comes close to the scale of those in the big French resorts like Les 2 Alpes or Les Arcs.

Soon though, we hook up with a gang of teenage boarders who are only too keen to explain.

'We love riding the rails and the half-pipe,' says Thomas, sixteen, 'but for us it's really all about freeriding out in the backcountry. Look around – this place is full of natural kickers and jumps, and we know them all. Come on . . . '

With that, Robin and I find ourselves (on skis) tailing a gang of boarders half our age away from the piste towards a succession of little rocky outcrops, where they take it in turns to do ever bigger jumps. Elias, sixteen, gets the most respect, doing a front flip (a mid-air forward roll) as he flies off the small cliff. I start to wonder if we are in loco parentis and will get in trouble if there's an accident. I'm clearly not feeling the rad, snowboard vibe.

Don't be too surprised if you see some odd sights on Nassfeld's slopes. Keen to promote itself as a spawning ground for new-school snowsports, the Cube includes in its room rates the chance to try a whole range of bizarre alternative ways to get down the mountain. There's the Airboard, a kind of reinforced, inflatable Li-Lo on which you lie with your head pointing down the mountain and steer simply by adjusting your body weight. After that, try the

THE INSIDE TRACK

Christoph Winkler Student

'I'm at school in Villach, just down the road, and I come here every weekend to board with my friends. We don't go to any of the restaurants on the mountain because they are way too expensive and we hate that après-ski music – we're more into punk and metal. But, at Sonnleitn, in the middle of the ski area, at the second stop of the three-stage Millennium Express gondola, is a little supermarket. We go there, pick up a sandwich and a drink, then head out into the backcountry to build a kicker and chill while we have a picnic.'

Right, Elias shows some steez

elan
Nassfeld

'FOR US IT'S REALLY all about freeriding out in the backcountry . . .'

Boarding is big in Nassfeld

Snow Scooters, Snow Cycles, Snow Tubes (rubber rings on which you descend a specially prepared course) and, most bizarre of all, the Ski Fox, a sort of wooden stool attached to a single ski . . .

Though the Cube is ultra-modern and utterly international, up on the mountain you are never far from a traditional Austrian mountain hut. A classic, just below the terrain park, is the Watschiger Alm, where *käsespätzle* (cheese dumplings), *almgröstl* (a fry-up of potatoes, bacon, sausage and egg) and *Kaiserschmarren* (chopped-up pancakes) with sultanas and fruit are the order of the day. Prices are far lower than those in the better-known Austrian resorts.

If you want a change, you can ski down to the Albergo Al Gallo Forcello and Albergo Wulfenia Livio Fedrigo – two hotels which are just over the border – where pizzas, pasta and fish dishes are specialities.

At the end the day, there's only one way down, the Carnia red run, piste 80, which drops 1,212m over a length of 7.6km to bring you back to the Cube's front door. You could bomb down to test your calves or, more sensibly, stretch out the run still further by stopping repeatedly along the way at the succession of piste-side huts for a beer. My favourite is Jokls Hütte, on the edge of a farming hamlet, where a slight smell of livestock only adds to the charm.

At the bottom, reflected in the Cube's glass walls, is the Barenhütte – a log cabin with thigh-slapping Alpenpop, accordion music and happy Austrians swinging their steins. The yoofs hurry straight past disapprovingly and head inside the Cube's own après-ski bar, where rap and rock are blaring, but we linger on the Barenhütte's terrace, soaking up the afternoon sun and the fruity *weissbier*.

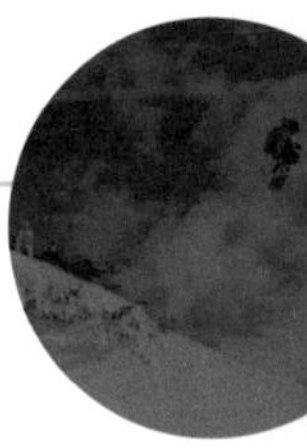

Earning their turns

The traditional Barenhütte couldn't contrast more with the Cube

The ski area is spread across five forested mountains

Back at the Cube, an administrative hiccup means my room has been given away, and I open the door to find two teenage girls in bed. Elsewhere, this might be a cause for serious alarm but, in the anything-goes Cube, the girls take it extremely well and are even vaguely apologetic.

Dinner is in the same open-plan, school-canteen-style area as breakfast. If you can, it's better to book in on bed and breakfast only and eat a few yards away at the Bar Alpin, a sleek pizzeria opposite the gondola where the staff are Italian and pizzas from the stone, wood-fired oven cost under €8.

If, after living so frugally thus far, you feel the need for a treat, head to the Hotel Carinzia, 50 metres or so further into the village. It's worth it just to see the interior design. Like the Cube, there's a four-storey atrium but, while the Cube is all bare concrete, here vertical slats of richly stained wood run from floor to ceiling, creating a startling modernist take on Alpine architecture. The hotel bar is a welcome contrast to the high jinx of the Cube. The floor is slate, the lighting low, and one wall is made from natural rock and has water coursing down it. Here, rather than Feiglings and Klopfers, the crowd are sipping raspberry caipirinhas (€8.50), or sharing bottles of Prosecco (€21.70).

After dinner at the Alpin, we stroll around the quiet village, where the local schoolkids are having a torch-lit procession past the ancient church. Meanwhile, in the glowing spaceship on the edge of the village, the non-stop fun continues. An archery class and a table-tennis tournament are going on and, in the club, the price of a bottle of beer has been slashed to €2. By now, you may be finding it all slightly relentless but, at that price, you've really got no excuse not to join in.

The Knowledge
Nassfeld, Austria

STATS **Town altitude:** 610m **Highest lift:** 2,020m; **Lifts:** 30 **Pistes:** 110km **Lift pass:** €37 per day **Closest airport:** Klagenfurt – 95km

WHY? Ignored by the international ski set, Nassfeld is excellent value. There's a surprisingly big ski area too, and the chance to stay at the Cube – unlike anywhere you've ever stayed before **GETTING THERE** Tröpolach, the village base for the Nassfeld ski area, is right next to the Italian border in the southern Austria region of Carinthia. Ryanair flies to Klagenfurt from Stansted, but alternatives include Trieste (105km) and Ljubljana (145km) **TRANSFERS** The tourist office arranges taxis or minibuses to meet Ryanair flights into Klagenfurt. The trip takes 75 minutes, and costs €40 each way. You pay the driver but should book in advance (+43 (0)676 83103600; www.kaernten-transfer.at). A private taxi will cost around €175 (try Taxi Gratzer: + 43 (0)428 23066; www.taxi-gratzer.at) **WHERE TO STAY** The Cube (+43 (0)428 58412020; www.cube-nassfeld.at) has rooms sleeping from two to eight. Staying in a double ensuite room costs from €94 per person per night, including lift pass, breakfast, dinner and the chance to try lots of alternative snowsports. If you like the sound of the area, but not the Cube, the super-stylish four-star Hotel Carinzia (+43 (0)428 572000; www.falkensteiner.com) has doubles from €260, half board; minimum three nights **WHERE TO SKI** Don't miss the Carnia run (piste 80), a 7.6km red that takes you from 1,822m back to the village. Good intermediates and above should head

to the Rudnigsattellift and Trogkofelbahn (lifts 21 and 22), from where there is a good choice of testing red and black runs, and a couple of unpisted itinerary routes **➔ WHERE TO EAT** On the mountain, try the Watschiger Alm (+43 (0)428 58170) for authentic Austrian food. For a taste of Italy, head just over the border to Albergo Al Gallo Forcello (+39 0428 90014; www.forcello.com) or Albergo Wulfenia Livio (+39 0428 90506; www.livio.at). The Cube has its own restaurant, but it's a bit school dinners. A good alternative is the Bar Alpin (www.alpin-carinzia.at), a pizzeria beside the Olympic Express lift. This close to Italy, the pizzas are excellent. Alternatively, book in to the Lux restaurant at the Hotel Carinzia (it's sometimes reserved for residents, call to check) **➔ WHERE TO PARTY** Après ski is liveliest at the Barenhütte, a traditional wooden barn between the Cube and the end of the Carnia piste. There's music, lots of beer, and excellent ribs to keep revellers' strength up. In the Cube Club, in the concrete-heavy basement of the hotel, the party often keeps going till 5 a.m. or later **➔ HELP!** If you're on a tight budget, you'd be mad to introduce a middle man, and the Cube doesn't work through UK tour operators **➔ TOURIST OFFICE** +43 (0)428 58241; www.nassfeld.at

Five More... On a Budget

KRANJSKA GORA, SLOVENIA

➔ **STATS: Town altitude:** 810m; **Highest lift:** 1,630m; **Lifts:** 21; **Pistes:** 30km; **Closest airport:** Ljubljana – 66km

➔ **WHY?** The hotels are cheaper than in the western Alps, but that's just the start. It's with the incidentals – drinks, lunches, ski hire and so on – that you really save money. Kranjska Gora's slopes won't keep expert skiers occupied for long but, for intermediates, they are fine for the weekend, and it's an attractive town

➔ **GETTING THERE** Fly to Ljubljana with Easyjet, or Klagenfurt in Austria, about the same distance, with Ryanair. Taxis are great value – it will cost about €70 from Ljubljana, and take about 1 hour (+386 (0)31 378978; email: info@vandrovc.si). There are also coaches (see www.alpetour.si for timetables)

➔ **WHERE TO STAY** Try the four-star Hotel Lek (+386 (0)45 881520; www.hotel-lek.si; doubles from €144, half board). If it's full, the tourist office can help book an alternative

➔ **WHERE TO PARTY** There's a selection of cosy bars for après ski and some nightlife later. Most popular is the strangely named Papa Joe Razor bar, while the Vopa Pub has live music at weekends and is open till 3 a.m.

➔ **TOURIST OFFICE** +386 (0)45 809440; www.kranjska-gora.si

BRIDES-LES-BAINS, FRANCE

➔ **STATS: Town altitude:** 600m; **Highest lift:** 3,230m; **Lifts:** 183; **Pistes:** 600km; **Closest airport:** Chambéry – 90km

➔ **WHY?** The bargain basement of Les Trois Vallées, the old spa town of Brides is linked by a long gondola to Méribel (it takes 25 minutes). You feel a bit like the poor relation as you take the gondola down from buzzy Méribel to quiet Brides at the end of the day, but you're still getting the world's number-one linked ski area – at a fraction of the price

➔ **GETTING THERE** Hiring a car at Chambéry usually works out cheapest. For details of scheduled buses see www.altibus.com. Alternatively, Ski Weekends (0870 4423400; www.skiweekends.com) runs ski weekends to Brides-les-Bains by coach from the UK. You get 3 days on the slopes, and it costs £169, half board

➔ **WHERE TO STAY** The two-star Hôtel les Alpes (+33 (0)4 79 55 21 08; www.alpeshotel.fr; doubles from €105, half board) is 30m from the gondola. You can book all the accommodation in town through the tourist-office website, and it also organizes short-break packages, from €257 for 4 nights, including half board and a lift pass

➔ **WHERE TO PARTY** It's far quieter than elsewhere in the Three Valleys, but there are a few pubs like Le Jack and La Petite Auberge, and Le Blue Night, a club open till 4 a.m., in the casino

➔ **TOURIST OFFICE** +33 (0)4 79 55 20 64; www.brideski.com

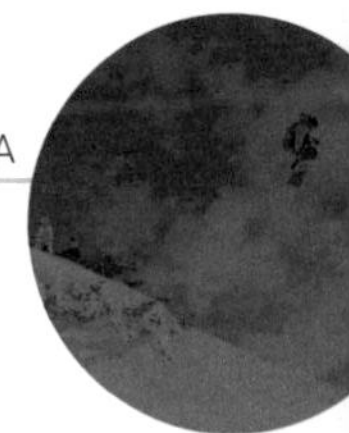

LE CHÂBLE, SWITZERLAND

STATS: Town altitude: 821m;
Highest lift: 3,330m; **Lifts:** 89; **Pistes:** 410km;
Closest airport: Sion – 64km

WHY? What Brides is to Méribel, Le Châble is to Verbier – the cheap option down on the valley floor. But, in many ways, Le Châble has the edge. The gondola up to Verbier takes less than 10 minutes, and there are regular buses too, and it also gives quick access to Bruson, on the opposite side of the valley from Verbier, home of the area's quietest pistes

GETTING THERE Sion is 45 minutes' drive away, but lack of flights means you are better off flying to Geneva, 160km away, then catching the train. From the airport station, it takes 2 hours 12 minutes to reach Le Châble. The return ticket will cost CHF102/£47

WHERE TO STAY Max and Millies (+41 (0)27 776 40 07; www.bedandbreakfastverbier.com; doubles from CHF190/£88, including 'Australian' breakfast) is a friendly, relaxed and nicely decorated place close to the lift and station

WHERE TO PARTY Le Châble has a few nice bars – La Ruinette, below Max and Millies, and the cosy Rosbif, but it's sleepy compared to Verbier. The final gondola stops just before 7 p.m., the bus just before 8 p.m. but, if you do decide to stay up in Verbier for a night out, you can usually hitchhike the five-minute drive back down

TOURIST OFFICE +41 (0)27 775 38 88; www.verbier.ch

BARÈGES, FRANCE

STATS: Town altitude: 1,250m;
Highest lift: 2,350m; **Lifts:** 43; **Pistes:** 100km;
Closest airport: Pau – 80km

WHY? The Pyrenees are overlooked by many Brits but offer attractive villages, good skiing, and prices well below those of the Alps. The spa village of Barèges is linked to nearby La Mongie, and together they make up the largest ski area of the Pyrenees, known as the Domaine Tourmalet. The skiing is mainly suited to intermediates, but there is some good off piste too

GETTING THERE Ryanair fly direct to Pau. Hiring a car will probably work out cheapest for the hour-and-a-half drive. A taxi will cost around €150 (+33 (0)5 62 46 14 61; www.alliance-taxis-lourdes.com)

WHERE TO STAY There is a choice of friendly two-star hotels, including La Montagne Fleurie (+33 (0)5 62 92 68 50; www.hotel-bareges.com; doubles from €48), the Alphée (+33 (0)5 62 92 68 39; doubles from €44) and Central (+33 (0)5 62 92 68 05; www.central-tourmalet.com; doubles from €48)

WHERE TO PARTY Taking the spa waters is the main evening activity, but there are some convivial drinking spots too. Try the Sabathie, next door to the butcher's, and the Isba. The restaurant La Rozell in Rue Ramond comes highly recommended

TOURIST OFFICE +33 (0)5 62 92 16 00; www.bareges.com and see also www.tourmalet.fr

PILA, ITALY

STATS: Town altitude: 1,800m;
Highest lift: 2,700m; **Lifts:** 14; **Pistes:** 70km;
Closest airport: Turin – 150km

WHY? Cheap Ryanair flights to Turin, cheap hotels and cheap food and drink when you get there. Pila is not going to win any beauty contests, but the north-facing pistes are superb for intermediates, there's just the right amount of them for a long weekend, and it's often very quiet

GETTING THERE From Turin, the quickest and easiest option is to hire a car for the 1 hour 40 minute drive to Pila. Alternatively, take the airport shuttle train to Dora station (15 minutes) and change on to the train to Aosta (direct, 2 hours 15 minutes), from where a gondola runs all the way to the ski resort (18 minutes)

WHERE TO STAY The three-star, piste-side Etoile de Neige (+39 0165 521541; doubles from €104, half board) has good food, or try the friendly Lion Noir (+39 0165 521704; www.lionnoirhotel.it; doubles from €114, half board)

WHERE TO PARTY Quiet during the week, it livens up at weekends, and you'll find some drinking buddies in Gallagher's Irish Pub and La Niche disco

TOURIST OFFICE +39 0165 521148; www.pila.it

10

Gourmet

ALTA BADIA, ITALY

THE FARMING communities of the Südtirol can muster twelve Michelin stars – not bad when the whole of Los Angeles merits twenty-one.

'SO, YOU LIKE TO START WITH SOME BUBBLES?' Can there be a more delicious phrase, particularly when spoken in an Italian accent, after a long journey and a hard week, by a man proffering a chilled bottle of Prosecco?

We are in San Cassiano, a tiny village of 900 residents in a snowy corner of the Südtirol, a province that was part of Austria for five centuries but given to Italy after the First World War. Few Britons have ever heard of San Cassiano, and it feels undiscovered and isolated. Locals speak Ladin, a language understood only in this and a couple more valleys. In appearance, it's just like any other modest alpine village – there's a quiet high street, a big church in the centre and a ski lift heading up to the runs far above. Except this sleepy place has a secret: it is the foodie epicentre of the Alps' most gourmet region.

San Cassiano boasts no fewer than three Michelin stars, while the neighbouring village of Corvara, just down the road, can add another to the tally. In all, the farming communities of the mountainous Südtirol can muster twelve Michelin stars – not bad when Los Angeles can manage only twenty-one.

The man proffering the Prosecco is Norbert Niederkofler, one of Italy's most famous chefs. Born in the nearby Valle Aurina, he started out as a downhill ski racer but gave it up at eighteen and started training in the kitchen. Today, his restaurant, the St Hubertus, within the Rosa Alpina hotel, has two Michelin stars, and he is constantly flying from London to New York

Norbert Niederkofler surveys his creations

Lobster for lunch and homemade truffles for supper

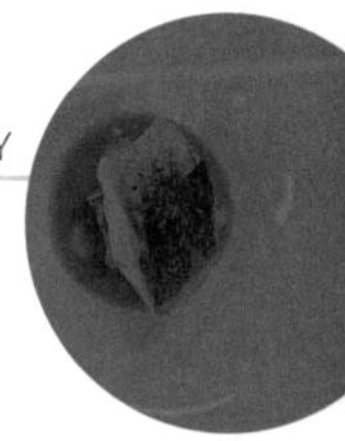

to Singapore to handle restaurant openings and do guest spots at top hotels and restaurants. We later learn that Tom Cruise and family were here the week before and Norbert cooked for them in a private chalet up the mountain.

He explains that, though it feels cut off, this area, just south of the Brenner Pass into Austria, is actually on an ancient trading route, and the culinary traditions, like the language, people and history, are a unique mix of influences from the north and south.

'The key is that the Mediterranean influence lightens the heavy Austrian dishes,' Norbert explains, 'so we'll use olive oil instead of butter or lard, for example.'

He says his philosophy is to offer simple, basic food, using three or four balanced ingredients, almost all of which are from the valley or the surrounding area. Soon after, Robin and I are being led into the cosy, traditional restaurant to try it out first hand.

The fact that the menu is the size of a broadsheet newspaper sets the tone. Soon the team of waiters is scurrying around us, bringing course after course. There are only eleven tables in the restaurant but no fewer than six waiters and twelve kitchen staff. After some Ruinart champagne and homemade bread (with a choice of French salted butter or olive oil from Umbria), we start in earnest.

First there's a little sardine, orange and fennel salad, served with a 2006 Keller Riesling, followed by scampi on a slice of calf's head, with black truffles from Umbria, then a plate containing four bowls

Previous spread: Sea bass and artichokes at the St Hubertus Below: Don't expect to ski much after a Club Moritzino lunch

The dramatic spires of the Sella Massif

of foie gras, each prepared a different way – one with the foie sautéed and served on crème brûlée, another with it poached in mulled wine and served on tangerine ragoût. By now I'm pretty full, but we've yet to reach the main course, and the menu stretches away down the page.

Next comes sautéed sea bass with oysters and artichokes, then Cajinci, the local type of ravioli, filled with Graukäse, a flaky, intensely flavoured cheese, then suckling pig, saddle of deer with rosehip gnocchi, fresh apple mousse surrounded in batter and, finally, a gingerbread soufflé with spiced oranges and cassis sorbet.

Then there's the wine. With each course, our sommelier, Christian, cracks open a new bottle, and there's an incredible variety. South Tirol is known for white wines – Gewürztraminer and Sauvignon Blanc, Riesling, Sylvaner, Veltliner and Kerner – but the Pinot Noir is delicious, and the absolute speciality is the sweet dessert wines, which aren't saved until dessert. About three courses in (once again my notes grow a little hazy) we have an ice wine made by Tramin using Gewürztraminer grapes. It's sweet but not sickly, an intense burst of flavour.

By the end, I'm playing a desperate game of catch-up and my plate is surrounded by five fine glasses which I haven't yet managed to finish. Norbert comes out to join us to see what we think.

'How many courses was it? I don't know – I never count because I don't have to do the washing up,' he says. Later analysis of menus and notes reveals there were ten wines and no fewer than nine courses, not including the breads at the start or the selection of chocolates and miniature cakes served on a slate at the end. It's taken four hours, cost €134 per head (before the wine) and has been without doubt the grandest meal I've ever eaten. So what is Norbert's favourite dish?

'Oh well, I don't think you can beat my mother's dumplings and cabbage salad.'

He is heading off to get to bed, as he needs to be up early for a TV appearance, and we lever ourselves from our chairs in order to waddle around the village to aid digestion. But, before we leave, it becomes clear that the gastro-marathon is only just beginning.

'The really great thing about all these restaurants in the area getting Michelin stars is that it has raised the standards of every other restaurant here too,' enthuses Norbert. 'So even the huts and restaurants on the mountain cook their particular style of food brilliantly.'

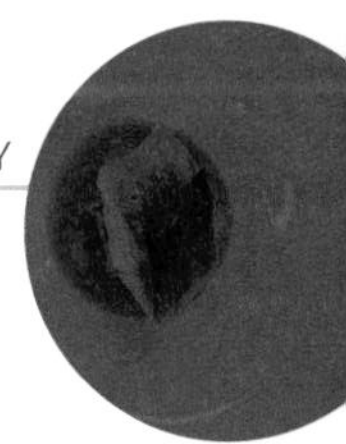

He gives us a list of suggestions, and our work for the next day is cut out.

They say that nothing clears a hangover better than mountain air, and the view as we ride up the lift above San Cassiano is a sight for a sore head. We're in the heart of the Dolomites, and the mist swirls around the jagged teeth which poke up all around us. The Italians claim this ski region – the Dolomiti Superski – to be the biggest network in the world, with 460 lifts and 1,220km of piste, all on the same lift pass, although you need to go by bus between many of the twelve ski areas.

Dominating the skyline from wherever you look is the bulk of the Sella Massif, a vast cathedral of dolomitic limestone with numerous spires, rising up to 3,150m. Its vertical walls are all but impenetrable, but lifts and pistes run right around the gentler slopes at its base, enabling skiers to make a 26km-long tour around it. Doing this full circuit, the Sella Ronda, takes a full day, though, and we have more epicurean matters to attend to.

The skiing here isn't steep or challenging, and there's limited off piste. Instead, it feels like a more genteel activity, mainly concerned with travelling

Tom skiing above Corvara

SKIING HERE is a genteel activity, with repeated stops at restaurants and bars to take in the view.

Jimmi showing off some homemade schnapps

Forget peach schnapps, here they use grass

about from village to village, stopping at restaurant and bar to take in the view. We head past the villages of Corvara and Colfosco, up to the Passo Gardena, from where the pistes head down to the better-known villages of Selva and Val Gardena.

Up on the pass at 2,222m is Jimmy's Hut, a wooden chalet with a terrace looking directly up at the Sella Massif. It's known for traditional food, such as polenta with melted local cheese, tagliatelle with wild mushrooms and mountain ham. But Jimmi Schrott, the owner, who comes to greet us in a chef's white hat, seems more concerned with getting us to taste his homemade schnapps. To my mounting concern, he begins to fill the bar with unlabelled bottles, and starts proffering glasses.

Now, homemade schnapps is traditional across the Alps, made with whichever flowers or fruits grow nearby. You've probably tried cherry-, apricot- and raspberry-flavoured versions, and perhaps the floral genepy, beloved in France. Here, though, things are rather more earthy. We start with some Enzian schnapps, made from the root of a bush, still visible in the clear bottle. It's tooth-enamel-stripping stuff, strangely meaty, and there's a guffaw from the bar as I down it and grimace. 'Good for the pulse!' says Jimmi, smacking his fist into his chest.

Next comes a bottle containing twigs (gingery and actually surprisingly pleasant), then one with pine cones. Suddenly, Jimmi remembers something and runs off to the kitchen, returning with a large, rusty-lidded jam jar, filled with grass. 'It's hay schnapps!' he beams. Here, it seems, nothing goes to waste ...

The surrounding valleys are full of similar huts, each with a different culinary tone. Norbert recommends the Scotoni hut beneath the Lagazuoi peak for its steaks, the Bioch, between San Cassiano and Corvara, for its traditional dishes such as 'pearl soup', made with barley, and the nearby La Brancha for sausages.

If you want more Michelin cuisine on the piste, aim for the one-starred Hotel La Perla, right next to the slopes in Corvara. It has a casual restaurant at lunchtime, and in the evenings, there's the cosy, romantic La Stua de Michil ('Michael's Living Room', after the boss Michil Costa), hidden behind a low wooden door in the middle of the building. It opens to reveal a womb-like, wood-panelled room like a rustic chalet from a century ago, with table settings of red roses and green leaves. A gilt picture frame can be turned on to become a screen showing a live video feed from the kitchen.

Even after last night, I'm tempted by the lunchtime specials – pheasant pie with foie-gras parfait and raspberry jelly, or cauliflower-cream soup with scallop and salmon caviar – but decide to save myself for supper.

Before that, though, we have to move from the traditional luxury of the five-star Rosa Alpina to the Las Vegas Lodge, a mountain refuge with eleven

The stunning view from the mountain-top Las Vegas Lodge

Las Vegas

Club Moritzino's chefs' brigade

rooms, sitting alone at the top of a mountain at 2,017m, where we are to consume our next feast. Ulli Crattolave, the owner, meets us at the bottom of the piste in San Cassiano then takes us up to the hotel, Robin sitting behind him on his skidoo, me towed along on a sledge with the luggage behind. It's a great ride, though, the snow beginning to fall in thick flakes, which are lit up by the skidoo's lights as we power up the empty piste.

When we get there, it's clear this is like no other mountain refuge. Built in 2005, there were two architects, one from Corvara, the other from California. The result is a stunning, modernist version of a mountain hut. There's lots of wood, but it's smooth and light and everything feels airy and spacious. There's a roaring fire set behind a square piece of glass, and low-lit lounging areas straight from a hip Shoreditch bar.

The food's not half bad either. We have salad, then deliciously salty homemade ravioli filled with radicchio and mountain ham, followed by lamb chops with red wine and sautéed potatoes, then chocolate pears. It costs €20 and, whisper it, is rather more up my street than the foie-gras-fuelled blow-out of the night before. Though we crave an early night, the Italian families sitting by the fire don't meet many Brits and, before long, we are downing the fig vodka with them, just to keep up appearances.

Waking up on the top of the mountain and seeing the sun rise over the Dolomites through the wide windows of the Las Vegas Lodge would be worth the trip even if you only ate sandwiches the entire time, but today we have our final gastro extravaganza – lunch at the legendary Club Moritzino. It's another mountain restaurant, at 2,077m close to the top of the Piz La Ila gondola, which ascends from La Villa, a village down in the valley between San Cassiano and Corvara. It has two claims to fame – its seafood, which arrives fresh from Chioggia on the Adriatic six days a week at 6 a.m., and its celebrities.

1 | *After a long lunch, diners at Club Moritzino sing and play harmonica*

2-3 | *The Dolomiti Superski area offers unrivalled views and a huge area of pistes*

4-6 | *The Las Vegas Lodge, at 2,017m – a modern take on the traditional mountain refuge*

SASSICAIA
1994
BOLGHERI SASSICAIA
SASSICAIA
1995
BOLGHERI SASSICAIA
SASSICAIA
1996
BOLGHERI SASSICAIA

1|2

|3

|4

|5
6

CLUB MoRITZINo
m.2100
RIF. PIZ LA ILA
MoRITZINO
ALTA BADIA
Defected
Accapellas

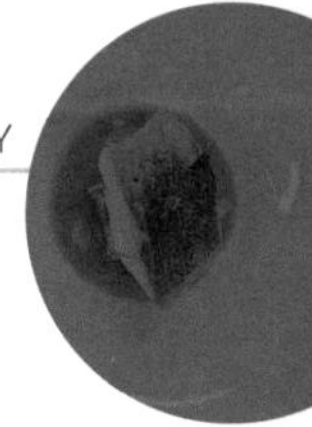

'I opened this place in 1970, just for fun,' says Moritz Craffonara, the sixty-four-year-old owner, as he relaxes back in his chair with a glass of Sauvignon Blanc. 'My first customer was Bridget Bardot's husband ...'

With that, he jumps up to show me his photos of the famous visitors – there are Formula One drivers, Tour de France cyclists, Prince Albert of Monaco dancing on a table, Ursula Andress, Alberto Tomba, not to mention the Aga Khan and George Clooney.

Back at the table, in a sunny conservatory outside the wooden chalet containing Club Moritzino's buzzy bar, it quickly becomes clear this isn't a place to come for a quick pitstop before getting back out on the pistes. We start with a carpaccio of amberjack with cucumber salad and caviar, move on to calamari stuffed with scampi and vegetables, then lobster spaghetti, with a slightly spicy tomato sauce (this isn't a few scrapings of white meat lost in pasta but half a whole lobster). Then there's a vodka-filled lemon sorbet, apple strudel and tiramisu, plus a long glass containing a creamy cocktail. Our waiter says the ingredients are a *'secreto,'* but it tastes very much of whisky to me.

By the time we get up to leave it's gone 5 p.m. The diners at the other tables have joined us and are singing traditional Venetian gondoliers' songs, playing the harmonica, and swaying slightly. At long last, we rise from lunch but, before we go, we poke our noses past the thick, noise-cancelling wooden walls, into the bar. There, Leo Lippolis, a DJ from Messina, is playing rocking house music, working up the crowd by scratching the records with his foot, his nose, then a ski.

We could head off straight away, ski down to the village and pack up ready for our flight, but it seems a shame not to join the happy, dancing crowd. We'll just stay for a quick glass of wine. And maybe they've got some nibbles ...

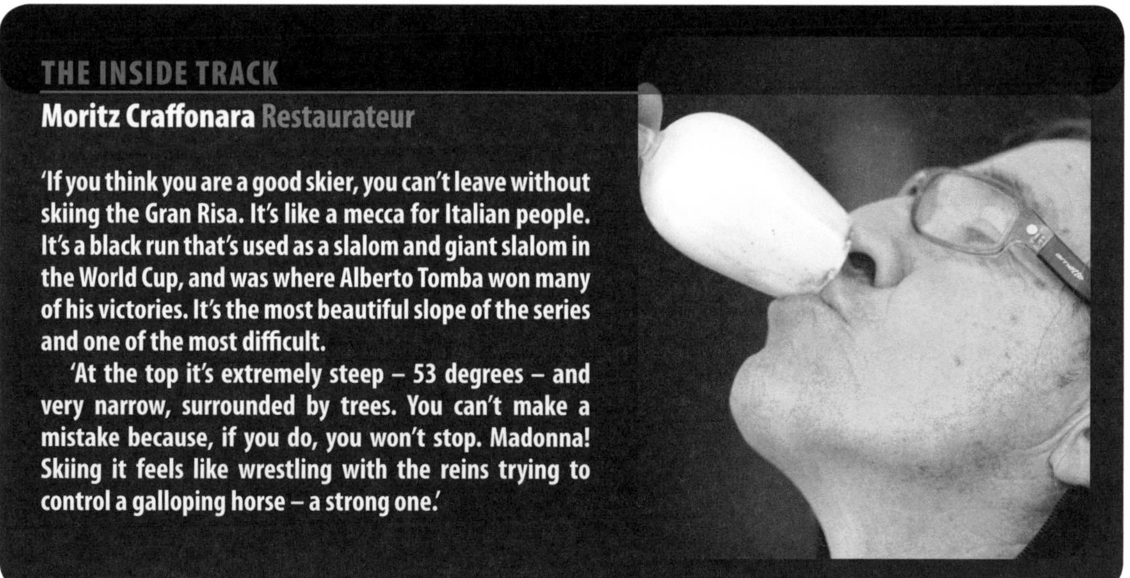

THE INSIDE TRACK

Moritz Craffonara Restaurateur

'If you think you are a good skier, you can't leave without skiing the Gran Risa. It's like a mecca for Italian people. It's a black run that's used as a slalom and giant slalom in the World Cup, and was where Alberto Tomba won many of his victories. It's the most beautiful slope of the series and one of the most difficult.

'At the top it's extremely steep – 53 degrees – and very narrow, surrounded by trees. You can't make a mistake because, if you do, you won't stop. Madonna! Skiing it feels like wrestling with the reins trying to control a galloping horse – a strong one.'

Beat this, Oakenfold: DJ Leo Lippolis shows his trademark ski-scratch

STATS **Town altitude:** 1,537m **Highest lift:** 2,530m; **Lifts:** 51
Pistes: 130km **Lift pass:** €34 per day **Closest airport:** Bolzano – 77km

The Knowledge
Alta Badia, Italy

➔ WHY? The farming villages that dot this remote valley conceal a surprising secret – they are bedecked with Michelin stars, and the trickle-down effect means even the humble mountain huts serve fantastic food **➔ GETTING THERE** Alta Badia is not a resort but the name of a valley containing the villages of San Cassiano, Corvara and Colfosco. Bolzano airport is very convenient but is currently served only by weekly charters (bookable through Inghams, 0208 780 4444; www.inghams.co.uk). Best for short breaks is Innsbruck, 133km and 1 hour 45 minutes' drive away, but Verona (229km) and Venice Treviso (186km) are also possibilities **➔ TRANSFERS** A taxi from Innsbruck will cost €240 each way for a standard-sized car (call +39 471 849472; www.garniflora.it). This means hiring a car will usually be cheaper. Terravision (+39 331 7814916; www.lowcostcoach.com) runs coaches which meet Ryanair flights to Treviso; they cost €29 return and take 3 hours to reach Cortina. From there, the tourist office of Corvara (email: corvara@ altabadia.org) lays on taxis to Alta Badia, for the set price of €20 return These take 30 minutes **➔ WHERE TO STAY** The utterly traditional Hotel Rosa Alpina in the village of San Cassiano is justifiably famous for its high standards (+39 0471 849500; www.rosalpina.it; doubles from €355, including breakfast). Totally different is the Las Vegas Lodge (+39 0471 840138; www lasvegasonline.it; from €84 per person per night, half board), a modernist take on the mountain refuge, up on the hill at 2,050m **➔ WHERE TO SKI** Don't leave without doing the Sella Ronda, a full-day, 26km circuit around the beautiful Sella Massif that will take you over four major passes and through the villages of Selva and Arabba. Much of the skiing here is about cruising and looking at the view, but there's one stunning off-piste itinerary – the Val Mezdi. It starts from the top of the Sass Pordoi cable car, at 2,950m, on the far side of the Sella Massif from Alta Badia. After a bit of skating and climbing, you pass the Boe hut, then ski down a vertical-sided gorge right through the middle of the jagged Sella peaks, popping out back at Colfosco

➔ LIFT PASS The Alta Badia pass (€34 per day) covers enough lifts to keep you going for a couple of days, but if you want to complete the Sella Ronda circuit, you need the Dolomiti Superski pass (€39 per day), which gives direct access to 500km of pistes and, if you're prepared to take bus connections, a total of 450 lifts and 1,220km of pistes. Given the minimal price difference, it's worth going for the latter unless you're positive you're staying in the local area **➔ WHERE TO EAT** On the mountain, book a table at Club Moritzino (+39 0471 847403; www.moritzino.it), above the village of La Villa, for a seafood extravaganza. Or go to Jimmy's Hut (+39 333 4332262), on the Passo Gardena, for hearty food, schnapps and great views. For Michelin stars, besides the St Hubertus, the two-starred restaurant within the Rosa Alpina, there's La Siriola (+39 0471 840092; www.siriolagroup.it) within the Hotel Ciasa Salares, also in San Cassiano, and La Stua de Michil (+39 0471 831000; www.hotel-laperla.it) within the Hotel La Perla beside the piste in the village of Corvara **➔ WHERE TO PARTY** After nine courses, you're unlikely to want to do too much dancing, which is good, because nightlife options are limited. The best party takes place weekly on Wednesday nights at the Las Vegas Lodge, with guests ferried up by piste basher **➔ HELP!** Momentum Ski (0207 371 9111; www.momentum.uk.com) offer three-night packages at the Rosa Alpina from £774, including flights and transfers **➔ TOURIST OFFICE** Alta Badia: +39 0471 836176; www.altabadia.org. Südtirol: +39 0471 999999; www.sudtirol.info

Five More...
For Gourmands

KALTENBACH, AUSTRIA

STATS: Town altitude: 560m; **Highest lift:** 2,500m; **Lifts:** 35; **Pistes:** 155km; **Closest airport:** Innsbruck – 50km

WHY? Kaltenbach sits close to the start of the Ziller valley, along from party capital Mayrhofen, but few people have ever heard of it. It's a quiet, traditional village, but gourmets should ignore the village and head straight up in the lift to the Kristallhütte, a beautiful mountaintop hotel at 2,147m, with 8 rooms and sensational food

GETTING THERE A taxi pick-up from Innsbruck will cost around €100 for up to 3, €140 for up to 7 (+43 (0)528 562260; www.taxikroell.com), or hire a car

WHERE TO STAY The Kristallhütte (+43 (0)676 88632400; www.kristallhuette.at) has doubles from €230, half board, which includes a 4-course dinner. There are regular champagne-tasting sessions too. It's a wooden chalet-style building, but with lots of modern art, and every room has a balcony with stunning mountain views

WHERE TO EAT At the Kristallhütte there is little choice on the set menu – you might have an amuse-bouche of velvety pumpkin soup, a prawn risotto followed by a slab of roast venison. Puddings are dramatic creations. The next day, if you're still hungry, visit the Michelin-starred Restaurant Alexander in the Hotel Lamark, in the village of Hochfügen at the foot of the slopes. Chef Alexander Fankhauser is a former Austrian chef of the year

TOURIST OFFICE +43 (0)528 32800; www.ski-optimal.at, and www.zillertal-mitte.at

MEGÈVE, FRANCE

STATS: Town altitude: 1,113m; **Highest lift:** 2,353m; **Lifts:** 107; **Pistes:** 445km; **Closest airport:** Geneva – 70km

WHY? In the 1960s Megève was the place for the Parisian beau monde to take the mountain air – Brigitte Bardot and Sacha Distel were regulars. Today, Courchevel has eclipsed it on the glitz front, but Megève retains its reputation as a place of fine food and wine

GETTING THERE A taxi from the airport will take about an hour and cost €200 for up to 3 (+33 (0)4 50 93 03 25; www.taxis.a-megeve.com). There are 3 public buses a day, taking 85 minutes and costing €70 return (details: www.borini.com)

WHERE TO STAY The Hôtel le Manège (+33 (0)4 50 21 41 09; www.hotel-le-manege.com; doubles from €320) is a smart four-star 100m from the pistes. British specialist Stanford Skiing just operates in Megève and offers 3-night weekend breaks from £390, including transfers but not flights, staying half board at its chalet Rond Point

WHERE TO EAT There are over 80 restaurants in the resort, but don't miss a Michelin-starred blow-out in one of the two leading establishments: La Ferme de Mon Père, set in an old barn, with glass sections in the floor through which you look to the cellars below, and the Flocons de Sel, where you should try the 6-course tasting menu

TOURIST OFFICE +33 (0)4 50 21 27 28; www.megeve.com

COURMAYEUR, ITALY

STATS: Town altitude: 1,200m; **Highest lift:** 2,755m; **Lifts:** 19; **Pistes:** 100km; **Closest airport:** Geneva – 105km

WHY? It's said that Courmayeur is unique in having more mountain restaurants than it does lifts, and food and drink are taken very seriously here. It's a charming old village, with great views of Mont Blanc and excellent piste skiing for a weekend, if not a full week

GETTING THERE A taxi will cost over €300, so a hire car from Geneva is the best option (always book a car from the Swiss, not the French side, for easy access to the motorway). You pass Chamonix and come straight through the Mont Blanc tunnel, which has a toll of €40 return

WHERE TO STAY The Pavillon (+39 0165 846120; www.pavillon.it; doubles from €230, half board) is a comfortable four-star with sauna and pool, close to the cable car. The three-star Hotel Bouton d'Or (+39 0165 846729; www.hotelboutondor.com; doubles from €125) gets glowing reports for its friendly owners

WHERE TO EAT Long mountain lunches are the order of the day. Try the Rifugio Maison Vieille, at the top of the Maison Vieille chair lift, the Rifugio Pavillon, on the Mont Blanc side, and La Grolla and Zerotta on Val Veny. In the evening, head to La Maison de Filippo in Entrèves, just outside the village, for fabulous local specialities in a traditional chalet, and a set menu of over 30 courses

TOURIST OFFICE +39 0165 842060; www.aiat-monte-bianco.com

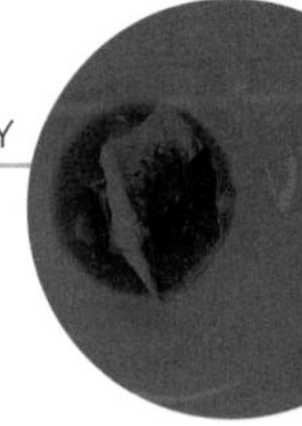

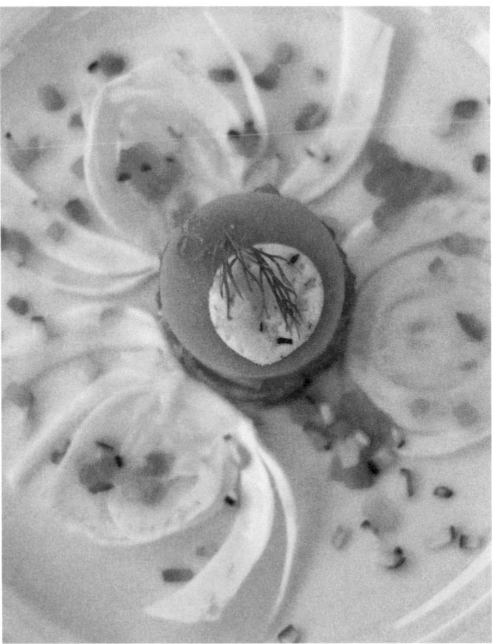

BAQUEIRA-BERET, SPAIN

➲ **STATS: Town altitude:** 1,500m; **Highest lift:** 2,510m; **Lifts:** 33; **Pistes:** 104km; **Closest airport:** Toulouse – 166km

➲ **WHY?** The best resort in the Spanish Pyrenees, Baqueira-Beret is, famously, the favourite destination of the Spanish royal family, and there are restaurants fit for a king. The usual Spanish dining rules apply – lunch stretches from 2 p.m. to the end of the afternoon, dinner is at 10 p.m. Don't ignore the skiing altogether though; there's some excellent off piste, which is totally overlooked by Europe's powder hounds
➲ **GETTING THERE** A hire car is the most sensible option. A taxi from Toulouse will cost €175 each way; book through the hotel
➲ **WHERE TO STAY** La Pleta (+34 (0)973 6455500; www.lapleta.com; doubles from €266, including breakfast) has five stars and the resort's best restaurant
➲ **WHERE TO EAT** The Del Gel al Foc restaurant in La Pleta has an excellent-value tasting menu – at €38, including wine, it features delights such as a starter of bloody Mary with Galician cockles, followed by lamb with honey and lavender. Also try the suckling pig at La Borda Lobato and head to the Casa Irene nearby for fresh fish. There are lots of good tapas bars in the village too
➲ **TOURIST OFFICE** +34 (0)973 639010; www.baqueira.es

KLOSTERS, SWITZERLAND

➲ **STATS: Town altitude:** 1,190m; **Highest lift:** 2,844m; **Lifts:** 51; **Pistes:** 305km; **Closest airport:** St Gallen – 119km

➲ **WHY?** Famous for being Prince Charles's favourite spot, Klosters actually feels surprisingly down to earth – it's certainly not full of Rollers and fur coats like St Moritz. The food, though, is seriously lavish, especially in the mountain restaurants
➲ **GETTING THERE** Fly to Zurich, 147km away, then take the train – it takes 2 hours 30 minutes from the airport, changing at Zurich main station and Landquart. Taxi will take about the same time and cost around CHF550/£255 (+41 (0)81 416 16 16; www.stiffler-ag.ch)
➲ **WHERE TO STAY** The traditional Walserhof (+41 (0)81 410 29 29; www.walserhof.ch; doubles from CHF300/£140, including breakfast) is where Prince Charles stayed and has a Michelin-starred restaurant, presided over by Swiss celebrity chef Armin Amrein
➲ **WHERE TO EAT** Bruhin's at the Weissfluhgipfel, at the very top of the linked Klosters-Davos ski area, is the place for a blow-out lunch. Just below, the Parsenn Weissfluhjoch doesn't look anything that special but serves sensational food. In the woods as you descend the Parsenn mountain to Klosters are the rustic Schwendi huts, great for lunch or afternoon drinks – try the Schwendi Ski und Berghaus, and the Alte Conterser Schwendi
➲ **TOURIST OFFICE** +41 (0)81 410 20 20; www.klosters.ch

Skidepot

11

Groups

ST ANTON, AUSTRIA

What sets St Anton apart is that it has something for everybody.

'ICH BIN SO SCHÖN, Ich bin so toll, Ich bin der Anton aus Ti-r-ol-a!' We're on the terrace outside the Mooserwirt and five hundred happy skiers are stamping their boots and singing along in unison while downing huge glasses of *weissbier* and tiny chasers of schnapps. It's an impressive place: though it closes at 8 p.m. every night, the Mooserwirt is reputed to sell more beer than anywhere else in Austria. From that, you might expect it to be a colossal nightclub in Vienna or Salzburg, but it's not even in a town. Actually, it sits on the mountain, beside a piste just above the village of St Anton. I down another shot, link arms with the group surrounding me and raise yet another toast to the best ski resort in the world.

This isn't just the drink talking. In my job I'm lucky enough to visit numerous ski resorts every winter. But, at the end of the season, when I go away with a group of friends for a proper holiday, I always come back to the same place – right here.

In truth, of course, what is the best resort in the world depends on what you're looking for. Extremists could make a case for La Grave, Chamonix and Jackson Hole, party animals for Ischgl, Mayrhofen or Verbier, intermediates for Whistler, Vail and the Trois Vallées. But what sets St Anton apart is that it has something for everybody and so is the perfect place for a big group of friends.

There's a charming, traditional village centre and a pedestrianized high street that's usually covered in snow. There's a huge linked ski area with fast, modern lifts and 280km of pistes. Mile-hungry intermediates can do long all-day expeditions to the linked resorts of Zürs and Lech. It's just an hour's drive from Innsbruck or an easy two from Friedrichshafen and, with the

Built in 1912, this chalet is now St Anton's museum Previous pages: Afternoon tea at the Mooserwirt

station right in the centre of town, train transfers from Innsbruck and Zurich are a cinch too.

There's après ski to rival any in the world and, if you're still standing after supper, there are bars and clubs that keep rocking till 6 a.m. St Anton has mountain restaurants as good as any, from cosy huts with rough-hewn tables to smart dining rooms with starched tablecloths. Last year, one woman in my group was pregnant and didn't ski, and there was even enough to keep her busy, with the wonderful Wellness centre and its indoor/outdoor pool, the shops, the cafés to linger in and easy day trips to Innsbruck. And, last but not least, there is the legendary off piste.

Our first day is cold and cloudy, so we ski up and over the mountain, then descend in a near white out for lunch in St Christoph, a bleak cluster of houses perched 1,800m up on the Arlberg pass. It was founded by monks in 1387 so they could make nightly patrols to rescue lost travellers from the colossal snowdrifts that collect here then bring the unfortunates back to their hospice for food and shelter. Since 1978, the travellers have largely vanished, instead taking the Arlberg road tunnel which burrows through the mountain deep below. In their place come well-heeled skiers, drawn to the food and shelter in the Hospiz Alm, not a monastery but a renowned, and rather lavish, restaurant and hotel.

Walking from a blizzard into the hot fug of the Hospiz Alm is slightly dizzying. Waiters in *lederhosen*, smart felt jackets and wooden bow-ties are swirling around the tables, delivering huge plates of ribs and bowls of *Kaiserschmarren* (sliced-up pancakes) with

The Hospiz Alm in St Christoph

Waiters wear felt waistcoats and wooden bow-ties

The quick way to the restrooms

Group bonding in the Krazy Kanguruh

plums and cream. Our waiter takes us downstairs to see the wine cellar – past the wall showing photos of visiting royals and celebs (from Charles and Di to Vladimir Putin, Romano Prodi and Boris Becker), past the slide that removes the need for walking downstairs to the toilets in ski boots – and pushes open the creaking door with apparent pride. Inside, the walls are stacked high with vast bottles, each holding from three to eighteen litres. In fact, we're told, this is the largest big-bottle cellar in Europe, with individual bottles on sale for up to €48,000. We toy with a 12-litre bottle of Moët – that's a Balthazar, fact fans – but slink back to the table and order an Orangina instead.

Extracting yourself from the Hospiz Alm is nearly as difficult as getting out of one of St Christoph's epic snowdrifts but, eventually, we manage it and ski back into the main St Anton ski area, lapping tree runs as the snow falls ever heavier. Before long, we come to the biggest decision of any day in St Anton – whether to stop at the Mooserwirt, on the right of blue piste 1, or the Krazy Kanguruh, on the left. Today, we turn left towards the KK, ground zero for Alpine après ski, the seminal ski bar against which all others are compared.

Originally owned by Australian Desmond McGuinness, hence the Antipodean name, the KK only really began to take off when a young Swedish commercial-economics student, Gunnar Munthe, dropped out of his studies, ran away to St Anton and took the place over. His first day was 26 February 1974. He spent the next decade single-handedly inventing the concept of après ski (at least in the turbo-charged Tirolean sense), and he's still here today.

As we walk in, Bon Jovi's 'Livin' on a Prayer' is blasting out of the speakers, and hundreds of skiers are crowding the tables and benches, singing at the tops of their voices. Gunnar's on the microphone ('Come on, this isn't a gay bar – let's see the women on the tables, guys get down!'), but then comes over to hand us a drink. 'Another day at the office,' he says, a touch ruefully.

As well as its own house rules reserving tabletops for women, the KK has its own drinks. Warm up with a Squashed Frog (grenadine, Midoro and Baileys), then tackle a KK Killer (vodka, tequila, Bacardi, gin, Batida de Coca and, if there's room, orange juice). Then there are the shot girls who stand on the tables and squirt slugs of sour-apple schnapps and Jägermeister directly into the grinning punters' mouths. Round it all off with a Heisse Witwe (a 'hot widow'), a warm cherry liqueur with cream and cinnamon.

Oh yes: did I mention you still have to ski down? From the KK and the Moose, you have about another 200m of descent, on a dark and often icy piste. The first time I went to the KK, my friend Paul and I only stopped in for a quick *glühwein*. We left three hours later, unable to tell which way round to put our skis on.

This time we are slightly more restrained but are still in fits of giggles when we take our skis off at the bottom and start staggering along the high street back to the chalet. And that brings me to the only real snag to St Anton – finding somewhere to stay. Few places want big groups just for weekends for fear their rooms will sit empty for the rest of the week. Your choice is to split the group into different hotels (at the end of the day, you're unlikely to be spending much time in your room anyway); leave booking till the week before, when empty hotels will accept short bookings in favour of none at all; or go to a British-run company such as Flexiski or Kaluma Travel, which specializes in short breaks.

We're staying with Kaluma in Chalet Montfort, a short wobble down the high street from the main Galzig lift, where the piste from the KK and Mooserwirt ends. It's a stylish, modern place, opened in 2008; more boutique hotel than traditional chalet. It sleeps up to twenty-four and four nights cost from around £750, including food, drink, scheduled flights and private transfers, and a rep to reserve tables at the KK, ensure free entrance to clubs and lead the drinking games.

THE FIRST TIME I went to the KK, my friend and I only stopped in for a quick glühwein. We left three hours later unable to tell which way round to put our skis on.

After an afternoon's St Anton-style après ski, our pre-dinner drinks, taken lounging around on the square sofas in front of the hip rectangular fireplace, are a hazy affair. Dinner is a blur of toasts and tall tales. It's simultaneously smart and silly, in that wonderful skiing way, and culminates with the presentation of some rather fancy frozen chocolates, filled with cream, which are then passed around the table, from mouth to mouth, like a sort of no-holds-barred version of the old orange-under-the-chin game.

Afterwards we stop in at Bar Cuba, an underground bar on the main street, where a big group of well-spoken female lawyers are having a 'Chavs' night out' dressed in shell-suits and bum bags. I could muse here about the centuries-old tradition of rich people pretending to be poor in order to have fun, but that would use up space better spent telling you about Scotty's, on the ground floor of the Rosanna hotel. This is the place for a restorative pizza after descending from the KK or, later, a pint of their speciality green beer (a curiously opaque lime-green concoction, the contents of which I've never quite deduced).

After that it's on to Piccadilly's, a big club with dance floor and live music bar, the Funky Chicken around the corner for margaritas, then the underground Kandahar club, the final stop on the classic St Anton night out.

The church in Stuben

As I have breakfast the next morning, the girls in our group are still sloping in from the night before. St Anton is a great place for single girls – the number of young men who come to test themselves against the fabled off-piste routes is so great that the ratio of men to women is apparently seven to one.

While the girls head upstairs for a morning nap, I head off to spend the day with Piste to Powder, a group guiding service that's another of St Anton's key attractions. Hiring a guide privately would typically cost £250 a day – fine if there are five of you of similar ability to share the cost, ruinous if you're the only one who's up for it. Piste to Powder, set up by Graham Austick, who's originally from Newcastle, gets round this by running a number of guided groups every day, from first-time off-pisters to the gnarliest of freeskiers, to which you can sign up as an individual for £62 a day.

I'm with a guide called Thomas and two other Brits, and we head off to tackle some of St Anton's classic descents. First is the back side of the Valluga, the highest peak of the range, at 2,811m. Anyone can ride up to the summit in order to look at the view, but only those accompanied by a guide are allowed to take their skis, such is the seriousness with which the resort managers view the descent. The cable car is scary enough in itself – a tiny cabin the size of a

St Anton's off-piste is legendary

Milka
1|2
be there or be SQUARE
SQUARE BAR SQUARE
|3
|4
|5
|6
CHATEAU L'EGLISE-CLINET
1995
POMEROL
CHATEAU
GRAND MAYNE
grand cru classé
1986
SAINT-EMILION GRAND CRU

telephone box taking a maximum of four people at a time, it slowly inches its way up towards the peak as the icy slopes fall sickeningly away beneath it.

The run down, off the back of the mountain towards the village of Zürs, isn't actually terrifically steep, but it is dangerous. After a few turns, you must traverse sharply left before continuing down. In clear visibility, this is no problem at all but fail to make the turn and you'll ski straight off a cliff. The guide-only rule was instigated after several skiers did exactly that. After the initial nervous sections, though, the descent becomes a straightforward delight. For the next hour, we find ourselves alone, descending the silent Paziel valley, beyond sight of any lifts or sign of human life.

We stop for lunch in Stuben, the most low-key and unpretentious of the villages in the St Anton ski area. Ski down past the church, over a farmer's field, and you arrive at the glorious sunny terrace of the Berghaus Stuben, a traditional restaurant that's a world away from the €48,000 excesses of the Hospiz Alm and the party frenzy of the KK.

Above Stuben are two of the oldest, slowest chair lifts in the area, but they are also the favourites of those in the know, for these lifts, Albona 1 and 2, give access to a huge, north-facing mountainside, with wide powder fields, narrow couloirs and tree runs which normally have the area's deepest powder. With good snow, you could spend a week on these two lifts without getting bored but, today, we take off our skis and hike for thirty minutes to the top of the Maroikopfe, an adjacent peak crowned with a metal cross.

We pause, drink some water, then strike out away from Stuben's pistes over high alpine pastures and then through the forest towards Langen, a couple of houses and a railway station on the way to Switzerland. The descent takes well over an hour and, as we wait with aching calves for the train from Zurich that will drop us back in St Anton, we look back on a day of real adventure. Instead of just frenetically lapping lifts, we've been travelling through the mountains on skis, from village to village over ridges and through forests – from St Anton to Zürs, to Stuben and, now, Langen.

The train eventually pulls up and we get on, standing with our skis in the corridor, looking into the compartments at the suited businessmen on their way to Innsbruck. Almost immediately we're in a tunnel, shooting under Stuben's slopes, back towards another big night of après ski in the best resort in the world.

WE TOY with a twelve-litre bottle of Moët – that's a Balthazar, fact fans – but order Orangina instead.

1 *The big-bottle wine cellar at the Hospiz Alm – some go for €48,000*

2 *Lunchtime beers in one of the piste-side tents*

3 *An afternoon sharpener in the Square Bar*

4 *Preprandial snifters at Chalet Montfort*

5 *St Anton's high street at night*

6 *Dinner around Chalet Montfort's huge table*

MOOSERW

THE INSIDE TRACK

Gunnar Munthe Owner of the Krazy Kanguruh

'I'm sixty-two now – this is my thirty-fourth season in St Anton – so when I've survived the zoo that is the après-ski session in the KK, I don't even want to think about going down to town in the evening to stand in another club and drink. Instead, I'll go for a nice quiet meal. Actually finding a quiet place to eat or drink in St Anton is almost impossible, but my favourite is Benvenuto, tucked away from the high street in the Wellness Centre. The food is fantastic, a sort of Italian–Asian fusion, the service great, and there's an open kitchen so you can watch the cooking. My favourite is the grilled tuna, with a citrus and soy sauce – a phenomenal meal.'

Benvenuto: +43 (0)544 630203; www.benvenuto.at

The Knowledge
St Anton, Austria

STATS **Town altitude:** 1,304m **Highest lift:** 2,811m; **Lifts:** 85 **Pistes:** 280km
Lift pass: €39 per day **Closest airport:** Innsbruck – 100km

WHY? The resort that has it all – great skiing, legendary nightlife, a pretty, traditional town centre, great food – and all within easy reach of the airport **GETTING THERE** Innsbruck is closest, and driving from there only takes an hour. Friedrichshafen (served by Ryanair from Stansted) is 125km away and Zurich 200km. St Anton has a railway station in the centre of the village and is on the key line between Switzerland and Austria. To get there by train go to Zurich (direct by TGV from Paris in 4 hours 20 minutes). From Zurich there are direct trains to St Anton, which take 2 hours 30 minutes **TRANSFERS** From Innsbruck airport, you take a local bus or taxi to the town's station, from where there are direct trains to St Anton, taking 1 hour 10 minutes and costing around €40 return (timetables at www.oebb.at). Taxis work out very reasonably if you are in a group – a car for one to three people costs €175 each, but a people carrier for up to eight costs only €195 each way (contact Taxi Harry: +43 (0)544 62315; www.harry.co.at). A shuttle bus runs from Zurich (3 hours 15 minutes) and Friedrichshafen (2 hours) airports and costs €45 each way (contact +43 (0)558 2226; www.arlbergexpress.com) **WHERE TO STAY** Chalet Montfort caters exclusively for groups (see Kaluma, below). The Hotel Anton (+43 (0)544 62408; www.hotelanton.com; doubles from €190, including breakfast) is a cool modernist place above the Café Anton, right in front of the Galzig lift. The Lux Alpinae (+43 (0)544 630108; www.luxalpinae.at; doubles from €262, half board) is another miminal temple of wood and glass (minimum stay four nights). For something more traditional, try the Schwarzer Adler (+43 (0)544 622440; www.schwarzeradler.com; doubles from €200, half board), which is right on the high street. The tourist-office website also has an excellent list of smaller hotels and bed and breakfasts **WHERE TO SKI** Beginners and intermediates will love the sunny, wide pistes on Rendl, a separate ski area on the other side of town from the main lifts. Alternatively, head for the Muggengrat and Madloch lifts above Zürs, for some beautiful long reds and blues. Experts will relish the endless off-piste possibilities above Stuben. There are also lots of unpisted ski routes, marked in dotted red lines on the map. Schindler Kar (SR15) and Mattun (SR16) are favourites. For guiding, contact Piste to Powder (+43 (0)664 1746282; www.pistetopowder.com). One interesting trip few people do is to take a taxi round to Kappl, a village close to Ischgl in the Paznaun valley, then ride the lifts and ski (with a guide) all the way back to St Anton down the deserted Malfontal

WHERE TO EAT If you're going to the Hospiz Alm in St Christoph, you should book a table (+43 (0)544 63625; www.hospiz.com). A more relaxed and equally delicious spot is the Berghaus Stuben (+43 (0)558 2714; www.berghaus-stuben.at), which has a great terrace. On cold days, sit by the fire and indulge in Tirolean specialities at the Rodelalm (+43 (0)699 10858855), beside the toboggan run and blue piste 24. The Anton Café, at the bottom of the Galzig lift, does excellent food all day. At night, most people eat in hotels or chalets, but there are some good options, including the Verwall Stube at the top of the Galzig lift (+43 (0)544 62352501). Scotty's (+43 (0)544 62400), inside Mark Warner's Hotel Rosanna, does great pizza

WHERE TO PARTY Afternoon après ski is taken so seriously many people never make it out again in the evening. The big boys are the Krazy Kanguruh (+43 (0)544 62633; www.krazykanguruh.com) and the Mooserwirt (+43 (0)544 63588; www.mooserwirt.at). For something more chilled, check out the guitarist at Underground on the Piste (+43 (0)544 62000), just below the museum (it also does an excellent fondue). At night, the favourites are the Kandahar (open till 6 a.m.), the Funky Chicken and the Post Keller, all a few wobbly steps apart on the high street **HELP!** Kaluma Travel (0870 4428044; www.kalumatravel.co.uk) offers four nights from £750, half board, including flights and transfers, but this will depend on group size **TOURIST OFFICE** +43 (0)544 622690; www.stantonamarlberg.com

Five More... For Groups

VAL D'ISÈRE, FRANCE

STATS: **Town altitude:** 1,850m; **Highest lift:** 3,456m; **Lifts:** 89; **Pistes:** 300km; **Closest airport:** Chambéry – 80km

WHY? The skiing in the Espace Killy (made up of Val d'Isère and Tignes) is very hard to beat – with lots of challenging pistes and off-piste areas and large numbers of high-altitude runs where excellent snow is all but guaranteed. Look hard enough and Val d'Isère even has a pretty centre and an old church too, and the nightlife is arguably the best in France. Only absolute beginners might not be well suited to it

GETTING THERE Best to hire a car at Chambéry for the 2-hour drive. A taxi for up to 4 will cost around €235 (+33 (0)6 14 18 26 11; www.aarthur.fr). Or take the train to Bourg St Maurice (direct TGV from Paris in 4 hours 45 minutes), from where there are regular buses

WHERE TO STAY Les Crêtes-Blanches (+33 (0)4 79 06 05 45; www.cretes-blanches.com; doubles from €118, including breakfast) is a good option for weekenders. The tourist office can help with last-minute bookings

WHERE TO PARTY Après-ski gets going in Bananas, a cosy hut on the left at the bottom of the pistes. Later on, the Morris Pub often has live bands, but most nights end up in Dick's Tea Bar (this was the original one), open till 4 a.m.

TOURIST OFFICE +33 (0)4 79 06 06 60; www.valdisere.com

SAALBACH, AUSTRIA

STATS: **Town altitude:** 1,003m; **Highest lift:** 2,100m; **Lifts:** 54; **Pistes:** 200km; **Closest airport:** Salzburg – 90km

WHY? This is another Austrian classic. The large, old village is clustered around a church and is mainly traffic-free. There are great mountain restaurants, extensive (if a little low) ski area, and renowned, rowdy après ski. The slopes are mainly south-facing, so get lots of sun – good for tans, bad for the snow conditions

GETTING THERE A shuttle bus runs 5 times a day from Salzburg airport, costing €65 return per person. Book at www.holiday-shuttle.at or call +43 (0)699 81558969. If you're in a group, though, it might be cheaper to book a private minibus, which would cost €150 each way for up to 4, €190 for 8 (+43 (0)654 16261; www.taxi-saalbach.at)

WHERE TO STAY The Hotel Haider (+43 (0)654 16228; www.hotel-haider.at; doubles from €146, half board, with drinks at dinner) is right next to the main lifts and has a sauna and whirlpool. The four-star Kunst-Hotel Kristiania (+43 (0)654 16253; www.kunsthotel.at; doubles from €196, half board) is a high-quality, traditional Tirolean-style place

WHERE TO PARTY The après ski is so enthusiastically pursued here that it seems to start shortly after lunch. The Bauer's Skialm, an old cowshed at the bottom of the nursery slopes, gets packed inside and out and is lots of fun, or try the Bäckstättstall. Stop in for drinks at Zum Turm, a former jail beside the church. For clubbing, it's off to the Arena and the King's Disco

TOURIST OFFICE +43 (0)654 1680068; www.saalbach.com

LES DEUX ALPES, FRANCE

STATS: **Town altitude:** 1,650m; **Highest lift:** 3,550m; **Lifts:** 51; **Pistes:** 220km; **Closest airport:** Grenoble – 115km

WHY? Fans call Les Deux Alpes the 'Las Vegas of the Alps' because of the vibrant nightlife (not après ski, but late-night partying), but there's no getting away from the fact that it's an ugly, purpose-built place, strung out along the roadside for more than a kilometre. But the plus points outweigh such qualms – there is excellent high, snow-sure skiing on a glacier, a huge terrain park for boarders, it's cheaper than most big French resorts,

experts can travel over the top of the mountain and down into La Grave (with a guide), and then there's that nightlife …

➲ **GETTING THERE** There are public buses (see www.transisere.fr for timetables), but a private minibus may work out around the same price or cheaper – a minibus for up to 8 will cost €285 (+33 (0)4 76 06 48 66; www.actibus.eu)

➲ **WHERE TO STAY** There are lots of apartments in the resort which sit empty for much of the time but which the tourist office can help you rent. You'll probably have to take it for the week, but this will still work out extremely good value. Alternatively, try the Chalet Mounier, probably the most attractive hotel in town (+33 (0)4 76 80 56 90; www.chalet-mounier.com; doubles from €198, half board) or the cheap and cheerful two-star Carlina (+33 (0)4 79 08 00 30; www.hotel-le-carlina.com; doubles from €103, including breakfast)

➲ **WHERE TO PARTY** Smithy's is an institution, a wooden barn on two floors but, with 30 bars in town, you have plenty of choice. Open till 4 a.m., L'Opéra is more like a city nightclub than a ski-resort disco – don't expect Austrian-style Alpenpop here. The Avalanche is another fave

➲ **TOURIST OFFICE** +33 (0)4 76 79 22 00; www.les2alpes.com

SÖLL, AUSTRIA

➲ **STATS: Town altitude:** 703m; **Highest lift:** 1,830m; **Lifts:** 94; **Pistes:** 250km; **Closest airport:** Innsbruck – 73 km

➲ **WHY?** Söll is a small, pretty village at the heart of one of Austria's largest interlinked ski areas – the Skiwelt. The slopes aren't especially high, but are great for cruising intermediates. The resort is also known for full-on après ski. The only drawback is that you have to take a ski bus from the village to the lifts

➲ **GETTING THERE** A private minibus will take about an hour from Innsbruck and cost €232 for up to 8 people (+43 (0)533 36161; www.taxi-stefan.at). It takes only a few minutes more from Salzburg airport, and will cost €24 more

➲ **WHERE TO STAY** The Hotel Feldwebel (+43 (0)533 35224; www.feldwebel.at; doubles from €110, half board) is a central three-star, which has had good reports for its food and is beside the pedestrianized area

➲ **WHERE TO PARTY** Major après ski goes on at the Salvenstadl and Hexenalm, starting around 3.30 p.m. At night, the Whisky-Mühle is the famous focal point and not for the faint hearted. The Rossini is recommended for a (slightly) quieter night

➲ **TOURIST OFFICE** +43 (0)505 09210; www.wilderkaiser.info and see also www.skiwelt.at

MORZINE, FRANCE

➲ **STATS: Town altitude:** 1,000m; **Highest lift:** 2,466m; **Lifts:** 209: **Pistes:** 650km; **Closest airport:** Geneva – 75km

➲ **WHY?** An attractive old town with good restaurants and nightlife, Morzine is the best spot in the giant Portes du Soleil ski area for groups. Intermediates will love cruising the extensive, tree-lined runs. The whole party will appreciate the quick and easy transfer from Geneva. Only experts might bemoan the fact that the low altitude of most slopes will mean they may miss out on the best snow conditions

➲ **GETTING THERE** If you're in a group, a private minibus will work out cheaper than taking the public bus. A minibus from Geneva airport will cost around €180 for up to 8 people (+33 (0)6 09 33 99 44; www.acces-taxi.com) and take an hour

➲ **WHERE TO STAY** The two-star Chalet Hôtel Fleur des Neiges (+33 (0)4 50 79 01 23; www.chalethotelfleurdesneiges.com; doubles from €130, half board) is an attractive wooden chalet with good 'country cooking'. Or try the three-star Neige Roc (+33 (0)4 50 79 03 21; www.neige-roc.com; doubles from €280, half board) which has an indoor pool and is close to the lifts to Avoriaz

➲ **WHERE TO PARTY** The Dixie Bar is good for après ski, as is the Cavern. Later, get the group along to L'Opéra or Le Paradis for some dancing – they are sure to like the latter's mirrored walls and red tiger-stripe upholstery!

➲ **TOURIST OFFICE** +33 (0)4 50 74 72 72; www.morzine-avoriaz.com

12

At Home

CAIRNGORM, SCOTLAND

UNDERGROUND
Euston
Keep clear

IT'S FRIDAY NIGHT, and my colleagues are powering down their computers and asking if I'm coming to the pub. 'Well, all right, if you twist my arm. But just for an hour or two – then I'm going skiing.'

At 9 p.m. I'm moving with the slightly merry throng of suited commuters streaming into Euston station. Most jump on trains bound for the home counties, but I'm heading to a quieter platform over on the far side of the station – it should by rights be platform nine and three quarters – where a rather special train is waiting, its engine humming softly.

Intercontinental flights and double-decker planes I take for granted, but this humble train, the Caledonian Sleeper, never fails to excite me. Mainly it's the fact that I'll board the train here in grimy, manic London, surrounded by 10 million people, and get off – without a single change – in the middle of the Highland wilderness. Partly it's that it feels so anachronistic – being greeted by your carriage steward, shown to your compartment, stipulating whether you prefer tea or coffee in the morning then heading down to the dining car; partly that it's so easy – no check-in, no security, no baggage reclaim.

You feel like you're in Scotland the moment you step on board. The cabins have tartan blankets, Highland mineral water and packets of shortbread. The jolly staff all chat away in broad Celtic accents. As we start moving at 9.15 p.m., Robin and I take our seats in the dining car and order some haggis, neaps and tatties (a snip at £4), washed down with Deuchars IPA and Tennants. There are even haggis-flavoured crisps.

At the other tables around us, and on the sofas at the far end of the car, people are drinking other Scottish beers or getting stuck into the wide selection of malt whiskies. By the time we reach Watford I'm half expecting a ceilidh to kick off.

But no matter how much whisky you drink, sleeping on the sleeper is an acquired art. W. H. Auden's famous 'Night Mail' travelled much of the same route as us, but his famous rhythms are way off. What he should have written is: 'This is the Night Mail crossing the, creak, border, bringing the cheque and, thump, thump, the postal order, letters for the rich, letters for the BANG'. Standard-class cabins have a window, basin and two bunks. First-class is the same, but each passenger has their own cabin and one bunk is folded away. The Orient Express it ain't, but the sheets are clean, the pillows comfortable and I eventually drift off.

It's a wonderful shock to open the blind in the morning to find we are passing through Dalwhinnie station and the ground is completely covered in snow. Just before 8 a.m., we arrive in Aviemore, our destination. It's bitterly cold and deserted and, as we stop to look at the haggis display in the butcher's window – 'Scotland's black-pudding champion', says the sign – Euston seems a world away.

The ski resort, known as Cairngorm Mountain, is a fifteen-minute drive away (the taxi rank is outside the station; there are regular buses; or you can hitch). We're lucky – it has snowed earlier in the week and, as our cab climbs up to the car park by the lifts, we pass drifts several feet deep. The sun is just coming out, the white, whale-backed mountains look stunning and yet the car park is almost deserted. Why isn't everyone here?

'The thing about Scottish skiing is that it's a lottery,' says Bob Kinnaird, the resort's chief executive, who greets us and gives us a tour. 'People come one weekend, and it can be utter crap and they say, "How can you compare this to the Alps?", but then another weekend they come and it's amazing and they say, "Why isn't everyone doing it?"'

Bob has the best office of any British chief executive – skis in one corner, ice axe hanging on a coat hook and a view looking directly up at the mountains. He's much-admired by his staff, and refreshingly plain speaking about the harsh realities facing Scottish skiing.

Friday night, 8.30 p.m., London – the white weekend starts here

BY THE TIME WE reach Watford, I'm half expecting a ceilidh to kick off.

The sleeper approaches Aviemore

The wind-lashed Cairngorm Mountain railway

The statistics are pretty grim. In the peak years of the 80s, skiers would together notch up 300,000 days on Cairngorm's pistes each winter, and the car park would be filled with coaches from Manchester, Liverpool and even London. These days, the number of 'skier days' hovers around 50,000.

Many people put this down to poor snows and climate change, but a far more important blow has been the advent of the low-cost airlines. A big proportion of skiing in Scotland was short breaks to supplement the main annual trip to Europe but, today, it's almost as easy for most Britons to reach the Alps as it is to come here.

'If you're sitting in London thinking, "Shall I jump on a plane and go down to the Alps or up to Scotland?", there's no choice – nine times out of ten you're going to head south,' says Bob.

Then there's the cost. Scottish skiing's one key advantage used to be the price but, today, the difference is minimal. A one-day pass in Cairngorm,

which has twelve lifts and 30km of pistes, costs £28. A one-day pass for the Portes du Soleil, with 220 lifts and 650km of pistes, costs, er, £28.

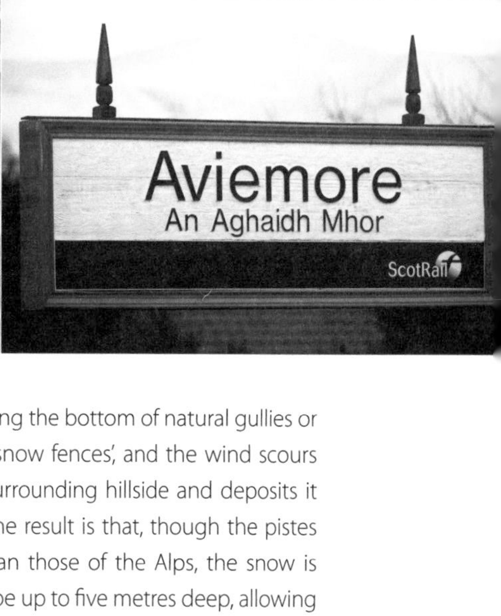

As if to underline the problems we've been discussing, by the time we've finished our interview a bitter wind has blown up and half the lifts have had to close. Still, the snow on the few runs we do ski is excellent and there are few other people around. It quickly becomes apparent that, as well as being a nuisance, the wind actually plays a vital role here. The pistes either run along the bottom of natural gullies or between wooden 'snow fences', and the wind scours the snow off the surrounding hillside and deposits it on to these runs. The result is that, though the pistes are far narrower than those of the Alps, the snow is protected and can be up to five metres deep, allowing the ski season to run from December to the end of April and, in 2008, even into May.

For lunch, we head to the Ptarmigan restaurant, which at 1,097m is Britain's highest. To be honest, though the view is fabulous, inside it's more like a school cafeteria than a charming mountain hut, and people are queuing at the counter for macaroni cheese, jumbo sausages and chips.

Afterwards, I head out with Bob, and Heather Morning of the Cairngorm Ranger Service, to ski the East Wall, a black run at the furthest extreme of the ski area. As we traverse across towards the start of the run, the wind picks up still further, gusting up to nigh on 90kmph and whipping the snow up so we can no longer see our skis. It starts to hail, then rain.

When we finally reach the shelter of the Cas Bar, a cosy pub/café next to the car park and bottom lift, Bob's apologetic about the terrible conditions, but I'm grinning from ear to ear. Cairngorm may not have any really testing pistes, but the weather had created a truly challenging and memorable run.

I've gradually come to understand the appeal of this place. On any normal skiing criteria – number of lifts, quality of snow, cost – Scotland simply can't compare with the Alps. But then it's not actually like the Alps. It's different, more like the Arctic, and the barren mountains feel wilder and more remote than the Alps' pretty valleys dotted with farms. It's somewhere untamed and dangerous.

At 2 a.m. that night Heather is called out on a rescue – two people have become disorientated and wander around lost for hours before they are found. They were lucky – the previous season saw five deaths, including those of a young couple who perished in terrible weather conditions just a few minutes' walk from the car park.

Aviemore on a Saturday night is pretty wild, too. In Café Mambo, we're sitting having a drink when a girl comes over to our table and promptly collapses. It's not yet 9 p.m. Soon there are no fewer than three hen parties in the one bar, eyeing each other disapprovingly.

The town is strung along a single main road, dotted at regular intervals with pubs, bars and restaurants. Most of the latter seem at pains to offer foreign food – there's La Taverna and Pancho's Pizzeria for Italian food, Spice of India, and Roo's Leap, which promises 'the Down Under dining experience' but whose menu offers Mexican, Jamaican and Japanese.

One lone establishment seems to have decided it will single-handedly fly the flag for Scotland. In the Cairngorm Hotel, both carpet and wallpaper are tartan, bagpipe music is playing, and the walls are covered in stags' heads, antlers and swords. Here the dishes have names like 'Chicken Ben Macdui' and 'John McNab's Midnight Feast'. It's highly touristy, but all good fun, and the bar next door is lively and welcoming.

THE BARREN mountains feel wilder and more remote than the pretty valleys of the Alps.

1 *Milly, a Cairngorm rescue dog*

2 *Ninja Turtles and Wonder Woman hit Café Mambo*

3 *More traditional Scottish entertainment at the Rowan Tree Hotel*

4 *Window display in Aviemore high street*

5 *A herd of reindeer range free on Cairngorm*

6 *More unusual wildlife outside the Vault*

1|2
SINGLE MALT
Distilled at
THE BALVENIE
SCOTLAND
DOUBLEWOOD
3
Haggis
Baby Haggis £2.55
Medium Haggis £3.99
£2.95/lb 6.50/kg
4
5
6

IT FEELS like we could be on expedition in Antarctica, but in a few hours I'll be back on the train to London.

The hard way up…

We later learn that the best place in town for food and a (slightly) quieter drink is the Old Bridge Inn, reached by crossing the bridge over the tracks at the railway station, then turning right and walking for a couple of minutes down Dalfaber Road. Next door is the popular Aviemore Bunkhouse, where dormitory beds cost £15 a night and private rooms for two start at £40.

We're staying a couple of miles down the road at the delightful Rowan Tree Hotel. It has log fires, a snug bar, newly decorated and spotless rooms and a truly gourmet restaurant, which serves things like scallops with saffron ravioli and roast venison with beetroot fondant.

Back in Café Mambo, the party is in full swing until 11.30 p.m., when everyone promptly downs their drinks and walks out. We follow the crowd and find out why. The Vault, Aviemore's only nightclub, is open till 3 a.m., but everyone must be inside by 11.45 p.m. It's not quite the Coco Club, but it is packed with people desperate to party like there's no tomorrow.

Turns out there is a tomorrow, and it arrives rather too soon. At 9 a.m. the next day, I'm slogging uphill on touring skis, heading for the summit of Cairngorm. For the uninitiated, ski touring is all about leaving the busy pistes and lift queues behind and heading out into the wilderness, using skins to enable you to ski up hills instead of down.

The skins, synthetic versions of the seal skins of yesteryear, are stuck to the bottom of the skis, and have fibres in just one direction, so you can slide forward but not back. The tricky thing is getting them to stick to the skis in the first place. It's like wrapping Christmas presents – the Sellotape always wants to stick to your hands, that precious but thinly veneered antique tabletop or itself rather than to the wrapping paper. Now imagine doing that with a 1.5m-long

And the quick way down – local guide Ian Sherrington on the south side of Caingorm

bit of Sellotape on a windy mountainside, with your hands getting more numb by the second.

My guide, George Reid, is sixteen years older than me but sets a stiff pace. As we near the top of Cairngorm, only twenty minutes uphill from the Ptarmigan restaurant, the clouds lift and a startling view emerges from the gloom. If we look back, we see the slopes, the people, the restaurant, the car park and, beyond, the landscape-blotting concrete mass of Aviemore's Macdonald Highland hotel. Look forward, and we see nothing but frozen lochs, soaring rockfaces and snowy peaks, and an arctic plateau that stretches away into the distance. In fact, it's at least 25km to Braemar, the nearest human habitation.

We set off on a day-long foray into the wilderness. We ski down a steep gully called Coire Raibert, skirt the shores of half-frozen Loch Avon, hurry past the path of a large recent avalanche, then start uphill again, heading towards Ben Macdui, Britain's second highest mountain. As we cross Loch Etchachan (the name means juniper, which grows on the ground around the area), the sun comes out. The loch is completely frozen and covered in snow, and we strike out directly across its pancake-flat surface, the mountains rising up all around us.

There are marks in the snow left by hares but no sign of human existence save for the tracks of our skis, stretching out behind us across the frozen lake. It feels as if we could be on expedition crossing Antarctica and yet, in just a few hours, I'll be back on the train to London.

Shortly before 1 p.m. we reach the top of Ben Macdui. Rather than an obvious, pointy peak, the top is wide open and gently rounded, and covered in sastrugi, wave-like snow formations made by the constant wind. Standing on the very summit is like being on a raft in the middle of a frozen sea.

THE WIND whips up the snow so we can no longer see our skis.

Tom descends towards Loch Avon

We eat our sandwiches sheltering from the wind, and George tells me about the 'grey man' of Ben Macdui, a sort of Yeti character occasionally glimpsed by otherwise hardy, sensible mountaineers. But before he reaches the end of the story, the sun and the expansive view have suddenly disappeared.

We are in the middle of a featureless plateau. The temperature is well below freezing. I've spent a fair amount of time in the mountains, but it very quickly dawns on me that, if I were alone here, I would be in grave danger. Thankfully, George is unfazed, takes a bearing and skis off, compass in hand, with me poling along close behind for all my life is worth.

At 9 p.m. we're at Aviemore station as the Caledonian Sleeper chugs into the platform. Christina, our host from the journey up, is hanging out of the window and welcomes us back on board. We take our places in the dining car and watch as the Highlands slide past our window in the silvery moonlight.

THE INSIDE TRACK

Heather Morning Mountain Ranger

'If you're looking for somewhere a little bit different to stay, try the Lazy Duck in Nethy Bridge, thirteen kilometres north of Aviemore. It's a cracking little place, a converted boathouse surrounded by woods, with a stunning view of the mountains, and ducks, chickens and squirrels roaming around outside. It sleeps up to eight people, but it only costs £10 each, so you could easily book out the whole place for a romantic break for two. There's a lovely wood-burning stove, and the beds are upstairs in the loft. Don't forget to visit Mr Mustard, the butcher in the village, whose meat is so good people come from miles around.'

The Lazy Duck: 01479 821642; www.lazyduck.co.uk

Riding the rails in the Vans terrain park

STATS **Town altitude (Aviemore):** 220m; Ski area base station altitude: 655m
Highest lift: 1,097m; **Lifts:** 12 **Pistes:** 30km **Lift pass:** £28 per day
Closest airport: Inverness – 67km

The Knowledge
Cairngorm, Scotland

WHY? Not just a pale imitation of the Alps but a unique wilderness experience. Travel up on the Caledonian Sleeper and you can have two days' skiing and pay for only one night in a hotel **GETTING THERE** The Caledonian Sleeper travels direct to Aviemore from London Euston, also stopping at Watford, Crewe and Preston. The trains run every night except for Saturday, leaving Euston at 9.15 p.m. and arriving in Aviemore at 7.40 a.m. For details, call 08457 550033 or see www.firstgroup.com/scotrail. 'Bargain berth' tickets are available from £19 each way but in very small numbers. You're more likely to pay around £112 for a standard-class return
TRANSFERS From Aviemore, it's about 12km to the Cairngorm mountain ski lifts. The taxi rank is right outside the station and the drive takes about 15 minutes **WHERE TO STAY** The Rowan Tree Hotel (01479 810207; www.rowantreehotel.com; doubles from £75, including breakfast) is 3km outside Aviemore and is cosy, scrupulously clean and does excellent food. In the village of Boat of Garten, just north of Aviemore, the Boat (01479 831258; www.boathotel.co.uk; doubles from £70, including breakfast) also gets good reviews. The Aviemore Bunkhouse (01479 811181; www.aviemore-bunkhouse.com; doubles £40) is beside the Old Bridge Inn behind the station. The Cairngorm Hotel (01479 810233; www.cairngorm.com; doubles from £88, including breakfast) is right opposite the station
WHERE TO SKI You'll easily be able to explore the whole ski area in a day. The most challenging runs are the East and West Wall gullies over to the far left of the ski area. Experts also like to climb up to the summit of Cairngorm, then traverse across to the 'Headwall', where they jump off the cornice on to an extremely steep slope before rejoining the Traverse piste. Ski touring is the only way to properly appreciate the remoteness of the Cairngorm plateau. Ben Macdui is the most popular day trip, and there are several different route options to get there. Steeper ski tours are possible on the stunning peaks to the west of Ben Macdui – Cairn Toul and Braeriach. The weather conditions make touring here extremely dangerous – be prepared
EQUIPMENT Hiring ski-touring equipment in Britain isn't easy – nowhere in London does so. In Aviemore, head to Cairngorm Mountain Sports (01479 810903; www.braemarmountainsports.com), which opens at 8.30 a.m. and charges £35 for two days' hire of touring skis, boots, skins, poles and crampons **WHERE TO EAT** Locals love the Cairngorm Mountain Café (01479 812473; www.mountaincafe-aviemore.co.uk), above Cairngorm Mountain

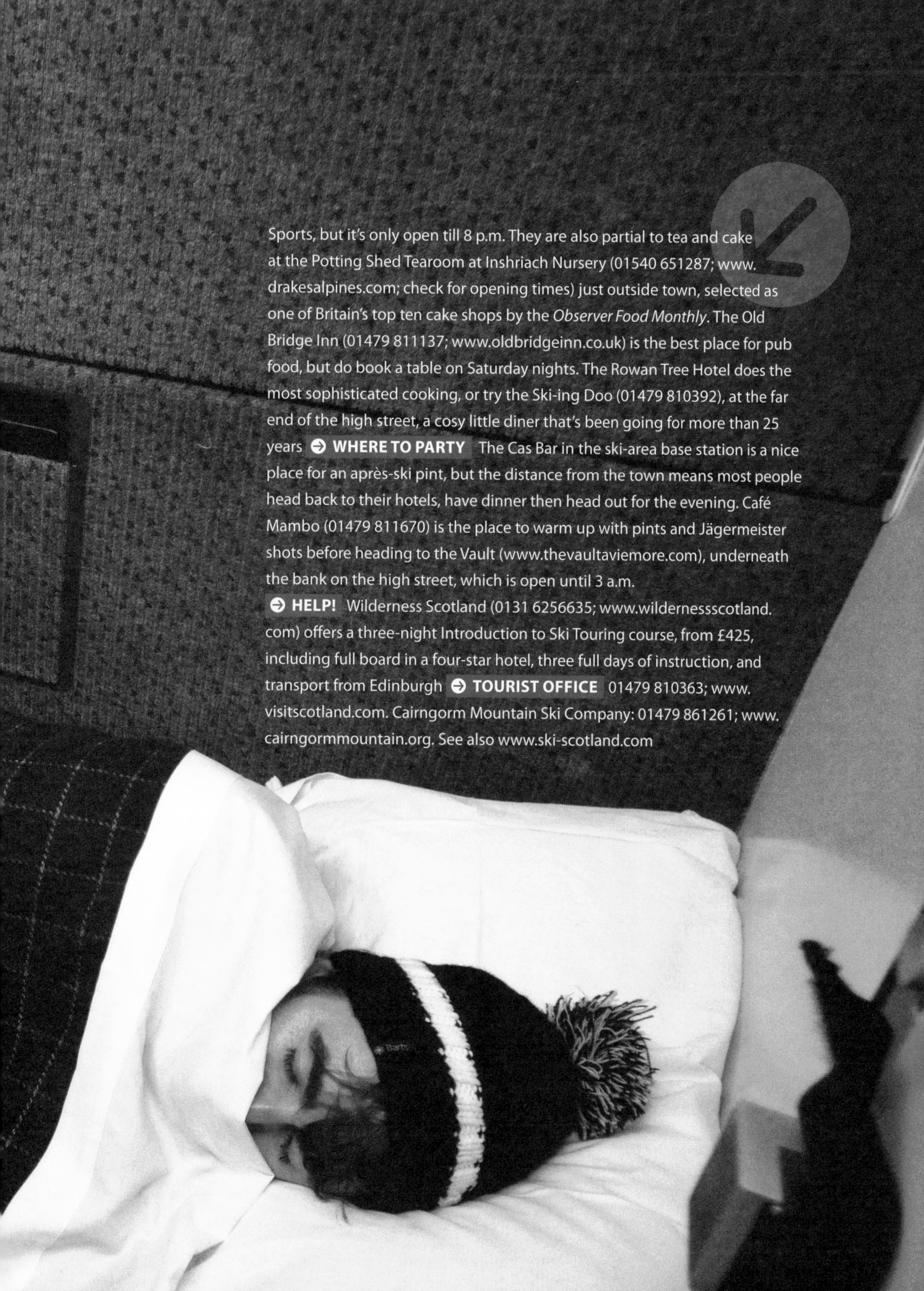

Sports, but it's only open till 8 p.m. They are also partial to tea and cake at the Potting Shed Tearoom at Inshriach Nursery (01540 651287; www.drakesalpines.com; check for opening times) just outside town, selected as one of Britain's top ten cake shops by the *Observer Food Monthly*. The Old Bridge Inn (01479 811137; www.oldbridgeinn.co.uk) is the best place for pub food, but do book a table on Saturday nights. The Rowan Tree Hotel does the most sophisticated cooking, or try the Ski-ing Doo (01479 810392), at the far end of the high street, a cosy little diner that's been going for more than 25 years **➔ WHERE TO PARTY** The Cas Bar in the ski-area base station is a nice place for an après-ski pint, but the distance from the town means most people head back to their hotels, have dinner then head out for the evening. Café Mambo (01479 811670) is the place to warm up with pints and Jägermeister shots before heading to the Vault (www.thevaultaviemore.com), underneath the bank on the high street, which is open until 3 a.m.

➔ HELP! Wilderness Scotland (0131 6256635; www.wildernessscotland.com) offers a three-night Introduction to Ski Touring course, from £425, including full board in a four-star hotel, three full days of instruction, and transport from Edinburgh **➔ TOURIST OFFICE** 01479 810363; www.visitscotland.com. Cairngorm Mountain Ski Company: 01479 861261; www.cairngormmountain.org. See also www.ski-scotland.com

Five More... At Home

NEVIS RANGE, SCOTLAND

STATS: Car park altitude: 91m; **Highest lift:** 1,221m; **Lifts:** 12; **Pistes:** 20km; **Closest airport:** Inverness – 85km

WHY? Scotland's highest skiing, accessed by its only gondola, with stunning views. Then there are the Back Corries – an off-piste area offering Britain's most challenging lift-accessed skiing. High winds build up large cornices on the side of Aonach Mor, providing the perfect launching pad for extreme skiers, and there are gullies with descents of up to 500m at up to 35 degrees. Lots of ski touring possibilities up Ben Nevis too

GETTING THERE The ski area is 11km north of Fort William, 2 hours and 30 minutes' drive from Glasgow and 90 minutes from Inverness. There are also direct Caledonian Sleeper services from London, Watford, Crewe and Preston

WHERE TO STAY The Ben Nevis Inn (01397 701227; www.ben-nevis-inn.co.uk; dormitory beds from £14 per night) at the start of Glen Nevis just outside town, is a fun place in dramatic surroundings that is very popular with climbers and hosts regular live music. The Grange (01397 705516; www.grangefortwilliam.com; doubles from £95, including breakfast) is a superior bed and breakfast which hosted the stars of *Rob Roy* during filming. In town, the Alexandra (01397 702241; www.strathmorehotels.com; doubles from £99) is comfortable, if a little bland, but it couldn't be more central

WHERE TO PARTY There are lots of good pubs on Fort William's pedestrianized high street, several with live music at weekends. The best is the Grog and Gruel – it has a selection of real ales on tap including delicious local heather ales (good chips too) and is open till 1 a.m. at weekends

TOURIST OFFICE 01397 705825; www.nevisrange.co.uk; see also www.ski-scotland.com

GLENSHEE, SCOTLAND

STATS: Car park altitude: 650m; **Highest lift:** 1,068m; **Lifts:** 21; **Pistes:** 40km; **Closest airport:** Aberdeen – 110km

WHY? The largest of Scotland's five resorts

GETTING THERE Edinburgh has more flights than Aberdeen and is 134km away – driving from either airport takes about 90 minutes. The nearest stations are Perth or Pitlochry, both at least 60km away

WHERE TO STAY The Gulabin Lodge Bunkhouse (01250 885255; www.cairngormshostel.co.uk; from £17 per person, including breakfast) has basic accommodation close to the ski area. The Inver Hotel, 8km outside Braemar (01339 742345; www.inverhotel.com; doubles from £80, including breakfast) is a historic coaching inn overlooking the Balmoral estate. Otherwise, stay in Braemar, 15km to the north of the ski resort. Try the Braemar Lodge (01339 741627; from £70, including breakfast)

WHERE TO PARTY There's only one option in Braemar – the bar of the Fife Arms Hotel. It has occasional live music and discos, but best to take a pack of cards to play while enjoying your whisky

TOURIST OFFICE 01339 741320; www.ski-glenshee.co.uk; Braemar tourist information: 01339 741600

HILLEND, SCOTLAND

STATS: Car park altitude: 240m; **Highest lift:** 350m; **Lifts:** 3; **Pistes:** 800m; **Closest airport:** Edinburgh – 16km

WHY? OK, so it's a dry ski slope, and only really worth visiting if you happen to be going to Edinburgh anyway. But, if you are, you'd be crazy to miss it – Hillend,

or the Midlothian Snowsports Centre, to give it its proper name, is one of the largest artificial slopes in Europe. The longest run, accessed by chairlift, is 400m long, and is seriously steep at the very top. The views over the city are good too and, this being Scotland, there's often rain, which greatly improves the skiing surface

➔ **GETTING THERE** It's a 10-minute drive or taxi from the centre of Edinburgh

➔ **WHERE TO STAY** Edinburgh has endless options, including the original Malmaison (08453 654247; www.malmaison-edinburgh.com; doubles from £99)

➔ **WHERE TO PARTY** There's Café 360 at the ski slope, but it doesn't serve alcohol. Edinburgh is hardly short of nightlife, though: in the centre, the City Café on Blair Street is an institution. The clubbing scene is as hedonistic as anything in London – Cabaret Voltaire is the club of the moment

➔ **TOURIST OFFICE** Ski slope: 0131 445 4433; www.midlothian.gov.uk (the slope is run by the local council). City: 0131 473 3600; www.edinburgh.org

YAD MOSS, ENGLAND

➔ **STATS: Bottom lift station:** 600m; **Highest lift:** 725m; **Lifts:** 1; **Pistes:** 600m; **Closest airport:** Newcastle – 53km

➔ **WHY?** Believe it or not, you can go skiing on real snow, on real mountains, in England. Just not very often. There are at least 7 ski clubs in the north of England, some who set up temporary rope tows, others with more impressive facilities. Worth trying are the slopes on the Raise, an 883m peak next to the famous Helvellyn above the Lake District village of Glenridding (see www.ldscsnowski.co.uk) and Swinhope Moor, near Daddry Shield in the north Pennines (details: www.skiweardale.co.uk). Top of the tree is Yad Moss in the Lake District, which has a 560m long Poma lift, a Kässbohrer piste basher, and a new stone day lodge, thanks to lottery funding. For all resorts, it's a case of ringing the club's answerphone to check if there's enough snow for the lifts to operate

➔ **GETTING THERE** The Yad Moss lift is 10km south of Alston, Cumbria, on the B6277. Alston is 30km north-east of the M6 at Penrith

➔ **WHERE TO STAY** To be honest, this is more of a day-trip destination but, worth a visit in the Penrith area, is the Mardale Inn (01931 713244; www.mardaleinn.co.uk; doubles from £70, including breakfast) in the village of Bampton

➔ **WHERE TO PARTY** The George and Dragon is a nice village pub just north of the ski area in Garrigill

➔ **CLUB DETAILS** The Carlisle Ski Club: 01228 561634; www.skicarlisle.skiers.co.uk

For more on England's ski resorts, see www.snowlion.freeuk.com

MANCHESTER, ENGLAND

➔ **STATS: Town altitude:** 25m; **Highest lift:** 65m; **Lifts:** 3; **Pistes:** 290m; **Closest airport:** Manchester – 12km

➔ **WHY?** At the time of going to press, Manchester boasts the biggest indoor ski slope in Britain – the Chill Factore – although it now looks as if Ipswich's colossal Snoasis project, which will have a 415m-long slope, is to get the go-ahead. The Chill Factore's main slope is 180m long and 100m wide at the bottom, with a 40m vertical drop, and there are two 55m nursery runs. There's also a high-speed luge track 'inspired by the Cresta run in St Moritz'

➔ **GETTING THERE** The Chill Factore is part of the Trafford Centre complex, beside junction 10 of the M60, 7km from the centre of Manchester

➔ **WHERE TO STAY** Not only is the Great John Street Hotel (0161 8313211; www.greatjohnstreet.co.uk; doubles from £110) one of the city's hippest boutique properties, from its swish roof terrace, complete with hot tub, you can gaze down into Granada studios and the hallowed cobbles of Coronation Street!

➔ **WHERE TO PARTY** There are several après-ski venues within the complex. The Mont Blanc Restaurant and Chilli's Bar have views over the piste. There's the Eiger bistro, and the alpine-themed Castle in the Air pub (owned by JD Wetherspoons, so don't expect anything too alpine)

➔ **CENTRE CONTACT DETAILS** 0161 749 2222; www.chillfactore.com

13

Spa and Ski

AROSA, SWITZERLAND

WE PASS wooden shepherds' huts, waterfalls and wild deer in the woods.

CHUGGING UP THE mountainside in a tiny blue train, the scene could scarcely be more typically Swiss. We pass wooden shepherds' huts, waterfalls, wild deer in the woods, go through tunnels bored into the rockface and teeter over impossible bridges. The further we climb, the more snow there is, bending the silver-birch branches double under its weight, sitting a foot high on fenceposts and spraying off the tracks as the train carves through it.

We are heading for Arosa, in Switzerland's Graubünden region. Getting here is simple – fly to Zurich and go down the escalator to the airport station. From there, it's an hour and a half to Chur, where you walk out of the station and find the little train to Arosa sitting on the street outside. It runs every hour, at first weaving its way through the traffic like a tram then starting to climb in earnest, up the narrow valley, through forests and a few tiny hamlets – ring the bell if you want to stop – until, after an hour, it reaches 1,800m, where Arosa lies at the end of the line.

At the station, a chauffeur from our hotel is waiting to greet us, resplendent in his black uniform and

On the hour-long climb to Arosa, the little train crosses forty-one bridges

The Tschuggen's chauffeur meets the train

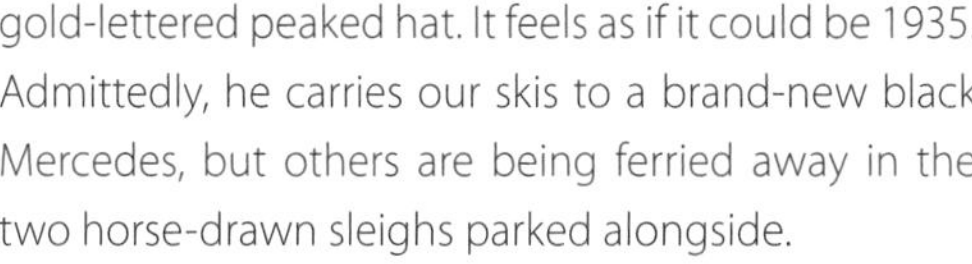

gold-lettered peaked hat. It feels as if it could be 1935. Admittedly, he carries our skis to a brand-new black Mercedes, but others are being ferried away in the two horse-drawn sleighs parked alongside.

We've come not just for the skiing but for perhaps the ultimate in indulgent weekend breaks – a combination of action on the slopes and relaxation in a top-notch spa. And, for anything spa-related, it has to be Switzerland. It basically invented the concept, back in Victorian times – its sanatoriums were the original blend of luxury hotel and hospital, and the great and the good would come to the Swiss Alps to take the air.

The Tschuggen Grand, the hotel our chauffeur is driving us through the snowy streets towards, has been in the wellness business for almost eighty years. It started out in 1929 as a sanatorium for asthmatics, was burnt down then rebuilt in the 60s and run as a 'grand hotel'.

In 2002 the owners decided that their clientele's average age – well over sixty – was so high, it was in danger of dying out, so they held a competition to

STAR ARCHITECT Mario Botta came up with a better plan – to build the spa inside the mountain.

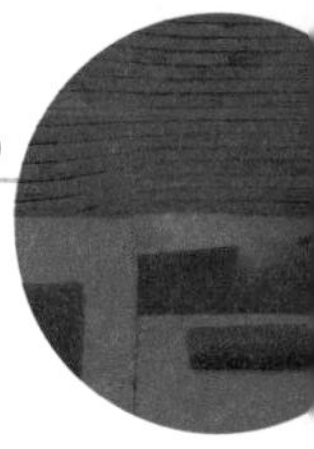

Alberto Colombo, the maître d'

An exuberant Rampazzi interior

design a spa with the wow factor that would attract younger guests. Five architects were shortlisted. Four wanted to build a huge new building beside the hotel, but the other, Mario Botta, had a better plan: to build the spa inside the mountain. Twenty-three thousand cubic metres of rock were excavated and helicopters ferried in nine 'light trees' – the sculpted skylights that are meant to echo the surrounding forest. In all, the hotel spent CHF35 million (about £17 million) building what it calls 'Europe's first super-spa', which finally opened on 1 December 2006.

Botta is Switzerland's most famous architect, with credits including the Museum of Modern Art in San Francisco and the restructuring of La Scala in Milan. He's known for cool minimalism, and the use of exposed stone, so it's something of a shock to find the interior of the hotel decorated in utterly flamboyant, if not screamingly camp, style. The lifts are covered in gold leaf; in the corridor, a model of a gold stag roams past two bright-blue easy chairs; and on the stairs is a stag-shaped floor-to-ceiling mirror. Instead of flower arrangements there are metre-long cactus leaves covered in silver leaf, or a pyramid of perfect green apples. The waiters are all Italian, wear black suits and have their hair slicked back. Alberto, the maître d', looks like an Armani model.

'We offer guests two worlds,' explains André, the manager, as he shows us around. 'The hotel is grand, formal and comfortable, the spa is totally different.'

In fact, the hotel, also refurbished in 2006, is the work of Carlo Rampazzi, a designer known for his love of bold colour. The bedrooms are an absolute riot: mine has an orange leather armchair, a padded headboard with an almost tartan design, a strange sculptural ceramic desk-light, a blue carpet and an orange ceiling.

Some people would probably hate it, but you have to admire Rampazzi's nerve, and it's a welcome relief from generic minimalism and the taupe-and-beige colour schemes that have become the standard luxury-hotel look the world over.

After waffles with whipped cream and jam in the plush drawing room, it's time to don our fluffy robes and check out the spa or *Bergoase* (mountain oasis), to give it its proper name. As I reach the end of the glass bridge that connects the hotel to the spa, a door automatically swishes open, revealing a scene from a Bond villain's lair.

Two women in white suits with gold braiding and epaulettes sit wearing serious expressions at a desk in front of me and, through the glass walls behind them, I catch a glimpse of a cavernous hall inside the mountain. The spa actually covers 5,000m^2 but, in true Bond style, there's a similar-sized area hidden underneath just for the staff, who come and go using their own access tunnel.

Crossing the bridge, you leave behind Rampazzi's explosion of colour and enter Botta's vision of

The spa's indoor-outdoor pool

calm. The *Bergoase*, spread over four floors, is made almost exclusively from Duke White granite from Domodossola, on the Swiss–Italian border, with floors made from light Canadian maple. In the lounge area, red leather chairs add the only splash of colour.

It's semi-open plan, with high ceilings, and there's a feeling of real space. From the vast pool area on the top floor, you can look diagonally down through glass walls all the way to the gym four storeys below, beside which natural mountain spring water bubbles up in a drinking fountain fashioned from a huge chunk of rock. It also helps the sense of calm and space that there never seem to be more than a couple of other people using the spa (it's free for guests, but non-residents have to pay CHF65). There are fifty white leather loungers beside the pool, each with a perfectly rolled red towel on top, but I only ever see two in use.

Of course, there's everything you could possibly want in a spa. The large gym is full of space-age machines. There are a dozen treatment rooms and two private spa suites, where you can sit drinking champagne with your partner in a circular jacuzzi directly under one of the light trees. There are several steamrooms and saunas, including a circular 'mountain sauna' that seats up to fifty, a chill-out room with fireplace, plus hair salon and solarium. This being Switzerland, there's also an on-site doctor offering a 'medical wellness' programme, so look no further for your Botox, collagen or non-surgical facelifts. The doctor even offers a programme of 'anti-ageing medicine', although I'm not entirely sure how that works.

Things get really interesting in the top-floor pool area. My favourite is the 'Arosa mountain grotto', where you pass through a rain curtain into a dark stone-walled booth where lights, sound effects, smells and countless different shower effects evoke the passage of the seasons. Spring has light, warm rain and a smell of apple blossom; in summer there's a smell of flowers, but also lightning and the rumble of thunder; winter has cold rain and a fresh lemon scent. Being blasted unexpectedly by jets of cold water then hot is half hideous, half pleasurable, but you do come out feeling invigorated.

Masochists can move on to the Kneipp Path, which recreates the experience of walking along a mountain stream. Underfoot are different textures of stone, and the stream suddenly switches from ankle- to waist- to knee-deep, and from warm, to hot, to icy cold.

The main pool covers 340m^2, with undulating granite walls and a sloped glass and maple ceiling, plus underwater lighting that makes it as turquoise as the Caribbean. I swim past various whirlpools and through the door to the outside pool. There, I sit in a chair, under a warm waterfall, as the snow falls heavily all around. It's blissful, until Robin comes along and insists I demonstrate, repeatedly, the local practice of jumping from the warm pool and rolling in the snow.

The hotel's private monorail

Now, as Dr No or Goldfinger would be well aware, no hi-tech lair of villainy is complete without a futuristic transport system – and the Tschuggen has just that: a private, driverless monorail that whisks guests from the hotel directly into the heart of the ski system. Before this opened in 2008, guests had to be driven down to the lifts in the centre of the village but, with this 'coaster' and a small piste that returns to its base, the hotel is now genuinely ski-in, ski-out, a rarity in a traditional Swiss village.

In contrast to the space-age spa, Arosa itself could not be more charming and traditional. Cars are banned between midnight and 6 a.m. to ensure the villagers' sleep isn't disturbed and the roads are left covered in snow to preserve the Alpine appearance.

We find ourselves skiing beside the village church and past endless chocolate-box-perfect chalets. It isn't a big ski area – there are thirteen lifts and 60km of piste – but there's great variety, with lots of gently sloping blues and a couple of steep blacks. Because it's in a big open bowl, there's also lots of scope for learning to ski in the deep snow between the pistes. The snow record here is good, and the slopes are relatively high – mostly between 2,000m and 2,600m.

Tom skis beside the Inner-Arosa church

IN CONTRAST TO the space-age spa, Arosa could not be more charming and traditional.

Lunch is in the Hörnli Hütte, a stone hut at 2,511m with beds for mountaineers. Built by the Swiss Alpine Club in 1903, it's the kind of place where everyone coming into the restaurant greets everyone else with a cheery *'Gruetzi Mittenand'* ('Hello, everybody,' in the local dialect of Swiss German). As we get stuck into a *rösti*, a plate-filling meal of grated and fried potato, with cheese and bacon, followed by a *Schümlipflümli*, a coffee with plum schnapps and cream, our guide, Ella Alpiger, explains how advanced skiers can do a series of day-long tours from Arosa to the neighbouring villages. The classic is to set off from this hut, ski down to the tiny resort of Tschiertschen, ride the lifts to the top, then descend off piste to the village of Lenzerheide. From there you take the bus to Davos and ski to Langwies, a hamlet one stop down the train line from Arosa.

That afternoon, it clouds over, so we ski the trees, lapping the lower section of the Weisshorn cable car. Ella skis the powder like a demon – and we later prise from her that she used to be in the Swiss downhill team, until she broke her back in training a week before the Turin Olympics, and was dropped.

A couple of hours later, I'm standing in a darkened treatment room in the spa, listening to soft oriental music, wondering if that big, greasy *rösti* was such a good idea. The spa's treatment list is as long as your arm, from facials and manicures through seaweed wraps and milk and honey baths to reflexology, lymphatic drainage massages, acupuncture, Shiatsu and all sorts of Ayurvedic cures. I'm getting a Thai Yoga massage, a 105-minute-long mix of reflexology, Shiatsu and passive hatha yoga, meaning that the masseur physically pushes and pulls you into the positions, while you just sit and relax. My masseur, Steven Singh, trained in Bangkok (although, disappointingly, he's actually from Bedford) and explains how the treatment tones the spleen, liver and kidneys. Before we start he says I shouldn't worry if I feel any 'release of energy'.

Being an uptight Brit, I spend the first half-hour wondering whether 'release of energy' means 'fart', and worrying about the *Schümlipflümli*. But when

THE INSIDE TRACK

Susanne Hörtnagl Lifeguard

'If you've had enough of the spa and the healthy living, head down to the Casino, close to the station in the main part of town. It's a big building with two or three bars. One of them is full of fifty-year-olds, but one of the others, Nuts, is much more lively and fun – that's where all the staff go on their day off. There are DJs there at the weekend and it's open till 4 or 5 a.m. Start with an aperitif in the Eden Bar on the main street, eat at the Grottino Pizzeria, then head off to Nuts. You can always put in more time in the gym tomorrow.'

Nuts: +41 (0)81 377 39 40; www.disconuts.ch

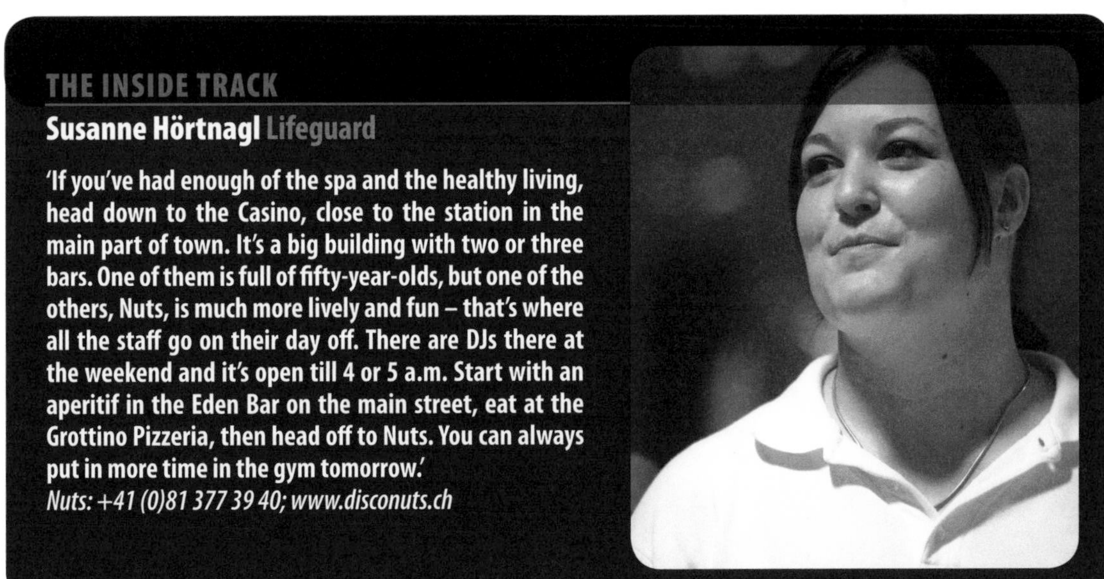

1|2
|3
|4
|5
6

Skiing back to the hotel. Its 1960s exterior belies the luxury inside

I leave, though I'm slightly spaced out, my heavy, post-skiing muscles feel magically restored.

Of course, spa-ing isn't cheap. My treatment costs CHF250, a little over £100. Staying at the hotel costs from £90 per person per night to well over £1,000 for one of the suites, including access to the spa. It also includes the most lavish breakfast you'll ever eat – coffee served in silver pots, eight types of muesli and hams, twenty types of bread, champagne on ice.

Now, how to round off such a healthy day? By going for a massive cheese fondue, of course, in the hotel's Bündnerstube, its traditional Swiss restaurant. Here the fondue is made even richer by the addition of truffles from Lombardy. Add some white wine, a few beers and a few games of bowling in the adjacent alley and my energy flow is quickly all over the shop again.

We ski the next morning, then come down for a shower and to be dropped back at the station by the chauffeur. Maybe it was all the icy spa water or the yoga, or maybe it was the half-metre of fresh powder but, as the train slowly trundles down the mountain, I've never felt better.

1 *Crossing the glass bridge from the cosy hotel to the space-age spa*

2 *Smart receptionists await*

3 *Bubbling massage seats at the edge of the main pool*

4 *The 'mountain sauna' has an outdoor terrace so you can run out and roll in the snow*

5 *Swimming past the outdoor waterfall*

6 *Workout done, how about a hot chocolate in the hotel lounge?*

STATS Town altitude: 1,739m Highest lift: 2,653m; Lifts: 13
Pistes: 60km Lift pass: CHF56/£26 per day Closest airport: Zurich - 130km

The Knowledge
Arosa, Switzerland

WHY? A classic Swiss resort, which now boasts the Alps' most stunning spa **GETTING THERE** Zurich airport is served by numerous flights from the UK, but a cheaper alternative may be to fly with Ryanair to Friedrichshafen, 160km away in Germany. You can also go to Zurich by train (4 hours 20 minutes on direct TGV from Paris Est) **TRANSFERS** The quickest way is to drive from Zurich, which takes a little over 2 hours (hire a car or call for a taxi pick-up, which costs around CHF500/£230 each way for up to 3 people, CHF600 for up to 7; Taxi Koller: +41 (0)81 377 35 35). However, most people find taking the train a more relaxing option (not least because the road up to Arosa has 360 bends), and the total journey will take just under 3 hours. From the airport station, take the train to Zurich Main Station (15 minutes), then Chur (90 minutes). From Chur, the tiny Arosa train takes an hour to trundle up to the resort. From Friedrichshafen, a shuttle bus meets arriving planes and takes 2 hours 30 minutes to reach Arosa and costs €89 return (+49 (0)7541 39 86 15; www.graubuenden-express.com)

WHERE TO STAY The Tschuggen Grand (+41 (0)81 378 99 99; www.tschuggen.ch; doubles from CHF390/£180, including breakfast and entry to spa) . The other option is to stay somewhere cheaper and pay CHF65/£30 to access the spa. The Eden Arosa (+41 (0)81 378 71 00; www.edenarosa.ch; doubles from CHF310/£144, including lift pass) is the funkiest place in town. The Alpensonne is a good, cheaper option (+41 (0)81 377 15 47; www.hotelalpensonne.ch; doubles from CHF165/£77, half board)

WHERE TO SKI An excellent area for intermediates: the runs are mainly in a wide, open bowl. Two great blue runs are at either side of the ski area – to the far left is Piste 1 and to the far right, in the quieter Prätschli area, is Piste 9, which takes you down a high ridge, through trees, and ends up by the lake in the village. More advanced skiers will enjoy the steep black Piste 11 from the top of the Weisshorn and, if there's powder but poor visibility, the tree runs beside the bottom section of the Weisshorn cable car. If you hire a guide there are also some excellent day trips to neighbouring resorts

➔ WHERE TO EAT On a ridge at the top of the ski area, the Hörnli Hütte (+41 (0)81 377 15 04; www.skiclubarosa.ch/Hoernli_Huette) is good for lunch, and you can also stay overnight. The Carmennahütte, on red Piste 5, is the spot to relax in the sun with an afternoon beer. Off the mountain, most people eat in their hotels, but the Grottino Pizzeria (+41 (0)81 377 17 17; www.grottino.ch) and the smart Le Bistro (+41 (0)81 378 68 68), inside the Hotel Cristallo, are recommended **➔ WHERE TO PARTY** The bar and the Kitchen Club at the Hotel Eden are the liveliest spots in town – the club goes on till 5 a.m. at weekends. There's also Nuts disco inside the Casino (see inside track) **➔ HELP!** Made to Measure Ski (01243 533333; www.mtmhols.co.uk) offers a 4-night break at the Tschuggen Grand, including flights and transfers from £879 per person

➔ TOURIST OFFICE +41 (0)81 378 70 20; www.arosa.ch

Five More... Spa and Ski

BAD GASTEIN, AUSTRIA

➜ STATS: **Town altitude:** 1,000m; **Highest lift:** 2,686m; **Lifts:** 44; **Pistes:** 201km; **Closest airport:** Salzburg – 96km

➜ WHY? The Gastein valley boasts 17 springs, through which 23 million litres of water bubbles every day, and has been prized as a spa destination since Roman times. The water is piped into both private hotels and public spas, like the vast Alpentherme (www.alpentherme.com), which has 6 different 'thermal worlds', and the beautifully designed Felsentherme (www.felsentherme.com). There are also the Heilstollen, or 'healing caves' – deep tunnels into the mountains where the air is supposed to have beneficial effects for a wide range of conditions. There's extensive skiing too

➜ GETTING THERE Lots of options: it's just over an hour's drive from Salzburg in a hire car, or there are regular buses, 6 times a day, costing €44 return and taking 90 minutes (times and tickets at www.rainer-reisen.at; +43 (0)643 23000). Or take the shuttle bus or taxi from the airport to Salzburg station, from where there are direct trains taking 1 hour and 36 minutes (see timetables at www.oebb.at)

➜ WHERE TO STAY Built in 1938, the Villa Solitude has 9 stylish, wood-panelled suites (+43 (0)643 45101; www.villasolitude.com; doubles from €200, half board). Or try the three-star Hotel Mozart (+43 (0)643 426860; www.hotelmozart.at; doubles from €80, including breakfast), so-called because Mozart's mother used to come to town to take the waters (although this hotel wasn't built till the 1920s)

➜ WHERE TO PARTY Spa-ing and partying might seem a contradiction but, this being Austria, you can always find some après ski. Try the Hexenhäusl in Mozartplatz, the Weinfassl, and the Silver Bullet in the Salzburgerhof hotel, which has live bands from 5 p.m. The Gatz nightclub is in the same hotel

➜ TOURIST OFFICE +43 (0)643 233930; www.gastein.com

VALS, SWITZERLAND

➜ STATS: **Town altitude:** 1,250m; **Highest lift:** 2,941m; **Lifts:** 5; **Pistes:** 25km; **Closest airport:** Zurich – 170km

➜ WHY? The Therme Vals is a place of pilgrimage for design fans – celebrated architect Peter Zumthor has created a brutal landmark from 60,000 slabs of Valser quartzite. Initial reviews called it 'a lesson in courage and aesthetics'. Water containing calcium, sulphate, hydrogen carbonate and iron emerges from the mountain at 30°C and feeds the spa's 6 pools. The pretty, wooden chalets of the village of Vals contrast with the spa's breathtaking modernism. The ski area is tiny, but high, quiet and with an impressive vertical drop

➜ GETTING THERE Take the train from Zurich airport to Ilanz station (2 hours 15 minutes, change at Zurich main station and Chur), from where local buses run up to Vals (30 minutes). Or just hire a car in Zurich for the 2-hour drive

➜ WHERE TO STAY The Therme Vals (+41 (0)81 926 80 80; www.therme-vals.ch) also has a hotel, offering a range of different room types, with doubles from CHF214/£105, including breakfast, and hotel guests can use the spa until midnight 3 times a week. Alternatively, stay elsewhere in the village and buy an entrance ticket to the spa (CHF40/£20)

➜ WHERE TO PARTY Don't expect anything wild, but there's après ski at the Fleebar at the bottom lift station, and a disco in the village called G's

➜ TOURIST OFFICE +41 (0)81 920 70 70; www.vals.ch. See www.vals3000.ch for details of the ski area

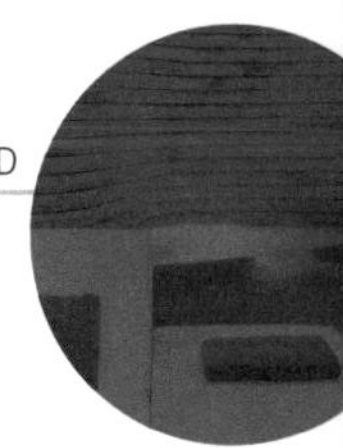

VIGILIUS, ITALY

STATS: Town altitude: 1,486m; **Highest lift:** 1,814m; **Lifts:** 4; **Pistes:** 5km; **Closest airport:** Bolzano – 24km

WHY? A stunning spa, accessible only by cable car, this is the favourite hotel of Reinhold Messner, the climbing world's number-one star. It's the work of Matteo Thun, another star architect but, unlike the Therme Vals' hard lines and cold surfaces, the Vigilius is all about warm wood, and it blends into the larch forest that surrounds it. The treatments range from the traditional alpine haybath to eastern delights like Watsu and Shiatsu. There's some limited skiing right outside the hotel, or you can also head to nearby Merano 2000 (www.merano2000.net), which has 40km of piste, or the 12 other nearby resorts which make up the Ortler Skiarena (www.ortlerskiarena.com). The hotel also offers snowshoeing, cross-country skiing, winter hiking and curling

GETTING THERE You can fly to Bolzano via Rome with Alitalia, and it's a 20-minute taxi ride to the village of Lana, from where the cable car goes up to the Vigilius. However, it's probably easier to fly direct to Verona (125km, 2 hours) or Innsbruck (75km, 90 minutes), and hire a car. The hotel will organize a taxi transfer for €200 one way from Verona and €180 from Innsbruck

WHERE TO STAY The Vigilius (+39 0473 556600, www.vigilius.it) has doubles from €320, including breakfast and use of the local ski lifts

WHERE TO PARTY You're stuck on a mountainside in a forest, and supposed to be here to detox. However, the good news is there are 2 restaurants (one offering South Tirolean specialities, the other Mediterranean) and an extensive wine cellar

TOURIST OFFICE +39 0473 561770; www.lana.info

LERMOOS, AUSTRIA

STATS: Town altitude: 1,005m; **Highest lift:** 2,100m; **Lifts:** 15; **Pistes:** 47km; **Closest airport:** Innsbruck – 75km

WHY? At the foot of the Zugspitze, the iconic mountain that separates Austria and Germany, is the village of Lermoos, home to the Mohr Life resort. It's a 200-year-old hotel which has been redeveloped with some bold modern architecture. The local Lermoos-Biberwier area has just about enough skiing for the weekend, but close by are the other resorts of the Zugspitz arena (www.zugspitzarena.com), together notching up 152km of piste

GETTING THERE Lermoos is under an hour's drive from Innsbruck airport. A taxi arranged by the hotel will cost €105 each way

WHERE TO STAY The Mohr Life resort (+43 (0)567 32362; www.mohr-life-resort.at) has double rooms starting at €178, half board

WHERE TO PARTY The Lahme Ente and Entenschirm, at the bottom of the Grubigstein lift, promise the liveliest après ski in the region

TOURIST OFFICE +43 (0)567 320000300; www.lermoos.at

PRAGELATO, ITALY

STATS: Town altitude: 1,534m; **Highest lift:** 2,825m; **Lifts:** 78; **Pistes:** 400km; **Closest airport:** Turin – 60km

WHY? A relaxing spot to get away from it all for a weekend of ski and spa, Pragelato is a new, self-contained luxury hotel complex owned by the Kempinski chain, linked by cable car to Sestriere and the Milky Way ski area. The Mineralia Wellness Centre has saunas, Turkish baths, a big indoor pool and an extensive treatment list

GETTING THERE The drive from Turin airport takes a little over an hour – choose between the more direct but curvy A55, or the longer, straighter A32. The hotel will arrange a taxi, but it costs €200 each way, so a hire car will be cheaper

WHERE TO STAY There's just the one option – the Pragelato Resort (+39 0122 740011; www.pragelatoresort.com; 'chalet suites' from €344, including breakfast)

WHERE TO PARTY Après ski is a 10km taxi ride over the mountain in Sestriere, but Pragelato has a good restaurant, and a pianist and singer entertain in Ritrovo, the cosy wood-panelled hotel bar. Nearby is the Antica Osteria, a renowned restaurant in a converted cowshed

TOURIST OFFICE Sestriere: +39 0122 755444; www.sestriere.it

14

Heliskiing
KRASNAYA POLYANA, RUSSIA

THE CLOSER it comes, the harder the throb of its rotors beats the pit of my stomach.

I DIDN'T TELL MY MUM where I was going. I know I shouldn't have lied, it's just 'heliskiing in Russia' would have conjured up all sorts of images in her naturally nervous mind, all of them very bad indeed. Things like ancient, war-damaged helicopters, unpatrolled mountains just waiting to avalanche, trigger-happy mafiosi in hooker-filled bars and pilots who keep out the cold with liberal doses of homemade vodka. She wouldn't have slept a wink until I was safely back home.

As the vast, soot-stained Russian chopper lumbers towards us on the first morning, I begin to feel a teensy bit nervous myself. The closer it comes, the harder the throb of its rotors beats the pit of my stomach. The downdraft sends snow and ice blasting into my face. Every instinct screams 'Run away' but, like the other skiers around me, I fall to the ground, cowering face down and eyes shut. The noise grows so loud it seems clear the pilot is going to land directly on top of us. And my mum doesn't even know I'm here!

Suddenly, the tempest eases. I look up to find the helicopter on the ground, its nose just over a metre from where I'm crouching. The rotors are still thwacking the air above, but it's so close we are now

An Mi-8 thunders over Krasnaya Polyana

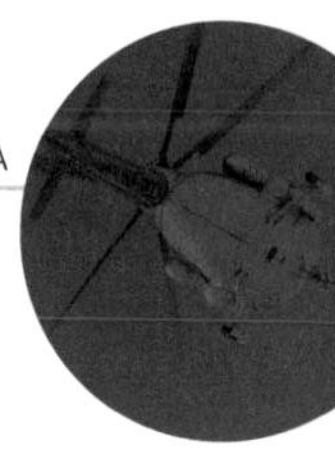

in the eye of its storm. Heart in throat and buttocks clenched, I stumble blindly on board.

I'm sorry if this sounds a little over-dramatic, but this was my first taste of heliskiing, and it was happening not in some jolly, familiar Swiss resort, where helicopters are buzzy little things with names like Squirrel and Gazelle, but deep in southern Russia, where the choppers are giant warbirds. Ours was a Mil Mi-8, designed as a dual-purpose attack and military-transport helicopter. It has room inside for up to thirty troops, and the machines have seen service everywhere from Afghanistan to Angola. And, at the risk of confirming my mother's worst fears, ours didn't exactly look new.

We are staying at Krasnaya Polyana, 540m up in the Caucasus mountains and two hours inland from the Black Sea resort of Sochi. On the surface, it's an unremarkable little place, a drab rural town where unmade roads divide a jumble of ragged wooden houses. Rubbish lies strewn around the verges, being picked at by scavenging pigs, and packs of dogs keep up a night-long howling rota. Rusting Ladas cough and splutter through the muddy potholes.

The rural town is in the grip of a skiing revolution

But Krasnaya is in the grip of a revolution, a skiing gold rush which is changing the town far more than the fall of the Soviet Union ever did. Amazingly, in July 2007 it was announced that this ramshackle town, which at the time had just four rickety old two-man chair lifts and a couple of narrow and patchy pistes, had been selected to host the 2014 Winter Olympics, beating off Salzburg in Austria, and Pyeongchang in Korea. The result is that anything between £6- and £12 billion of investment is pouring into the valley (which is even more mind-boggling when you think that the 2006 Turin Winter Olympics are estimated to have cost just £1.5 billion).

Already, things are changing. Look long enough, and the procession of muddy Ladas will be interrupted by a brand-new Mercedes or BMW. The pigs will look up as a pair of skiers in the latest Prada gear swagger past, top-of-the-range skis balanced on their shoulders. New hotels and apartment blocks are being built and, instead of the one tiny current ski area, which claims 25km of piste, there will be lifts in at least three new separate sectors. Most important will be the Roza Khutor area, 6km to the east of the main village, which by 2014 will have forty pistes and fifteen lifts, as well as downhill and slalom courses designed by Switzerland's Bernard Russi, and grandstands for five thousand spectators with standing room for another thirteen thousand. Gazprom, the energy giant, is developing its own ski area at nearby Psekhako Ridge, where a gondola and five more lifts have already been completed and the Olympic cross-country skiing and biathlon events will take place.

We're staying at the Radisson SAS Lazurnaya Peak, a four-star hotel that could have been teleported from Val d'Isère. The rooms are comfortable, there's a pianist in the cocktail bar, and there's a big outdoor swimming pool. Down the road is Atmosphere, a top-notch French restaurant housed in a traditional Alpine chalet. Inside, brush past a thick velvet curtain and you are in a world of black-tie-wearing waiters, fine wines and cigar humidors.

Krasnaya is 45km from the airport at Sochi, the city on the Black Sea which will host the opening Olympic ceremonies and the non-skiing events. In 2005, it took over two hours to cover that distance, much of it on unmade roads. Now, it's a forty-minute blast on new tarmac. The airport has a new terminal, and now there are numerous daily flights from Moscow. Local officials say direct flights from Europe will start soon.

Olympics or not, it will be a few more years before there are enough pistes to justify the journey from Britain but, when it comes to off piste, the resort is already world class.

'I spent years travelling around the world and the Soviet Union looking for the best skiing, from Siberia to Kazakhstan to Kamchatka,' says Marc Testut, a former mountain guide from Chamonix who now runs Yak and Yeti, the company which organizes the heliskiing here. 'Krasnaya came out on top.'

Above the town lie bowl after bowl of perfect, untouched powder. It's almost entirely unglaciated, so there are no concerns about suddenly vanishing in a crevasse, and the influence of the nearby Black Sea seems to make for an exceptionally stable snowpack. There's lots of it too – by mid-winter it's usually several metres deep. The only snag is that to get to all this perfect powder, you either need to take a very long hike, through woods where bears are common, or a helicopter.

Once inside the chopper, my fears subside. We lift off with unexpected smoothness and start skimming above the pine forests. Inside, it's vaguely like a tube train: two long benches down either side and the odd empty crisp packet floating about. There's lots of room too. Instead of thirty troops, there are just ten skiers and boarders, plus two guides and three crew.

Pro skiers compete at the Nissan Russian Adventure (www.nissan-sportsadventure.com)

ABOVE THE TOWN lie bowl after bowl of perfect, untouched powder.

KRASNAYA IS in the grip of a revolution, a skiing gold rush that is changing the town far more than the fall of the Soviet Union ever did.

The rickety old chairlift climbs through the forests

At the top of the ridge, around 2,800m, the pilot touches the wheels down on the snow and hovers – land properly and the helicopter would disappear into the deep snow. Denis, our French guide, jumps out, and his Russian assistant Georgey throws him the skis. Then, like a row of paras, we shuffle along to the front of the chopper, turn left to the open hatch, and jump – almost a metre down – to land in the soft snow. There's a roar of engine noise, a blast of spindrift and the old bird veers violently off back down the valley. Suddenly, we're alone.

I stand and look around. There's almost too much to take in. We can see for miles, with the peak of Mount Elbrus, Europe's highest mountain, poking up in the far distance. From our ridge we look down in every direction to vast snowy bowls falling away into wooded valleys. There's not a single sound, and not a single ski track.

Denis remains the picture of Gallic nonchalance. 'We go?' he shrugs, and darts off.

Most of the runs start with a short, steep section, sometimes requiring you to jump down a metre

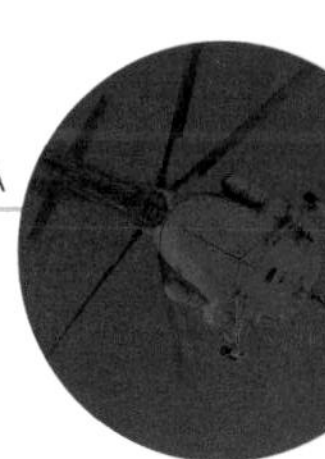

Snowboarders wait for the heli pick-up

or so off the lip of a cornice. Then they level off for maybe 600m of open powder fields before you break into widely spaced silver-birch forest, much of it over gentle, rounded hillocks and all of it holding huge quantities of light, dry powder.

As soon as the group has skied a valley once, we move on to the next. On the busiest days there are two choppers taking turns to ferry four groups of ten skiers but, even then, you will only meet another group at the picnic-lunch stops.

When we get to the bottom of our first run the nerves of the morning's pick-up are forgotten. I'm gasping for breath but elated. In one run I've skied as much deep powder as in a normal week. 'Un-freakin-believable,' shouts one of the snowboarders. 'That was sick!'

'Pas mal,' concedes Denis, sparking up a fag.

Does it work for a weekend? Even without direct flights from Europe, short breaks here are becoming increasingly popular. If you can take three days off work to add to your weekend, sacrifice a day at each

One of the crew surveys a landing zone

Approaching a drop-off point

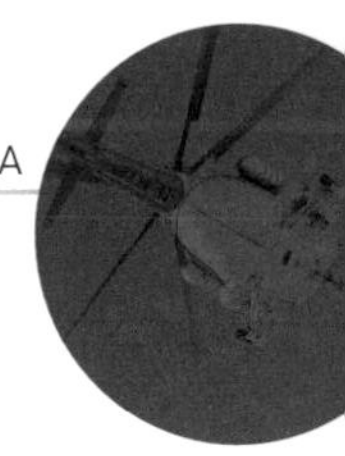

end to travelling, that leaves you with three days' heliskiing. Crucially, to get this kind of heliski terrain and this type of deep and light powder, your only alternative would be Canada or Alaska, both of which come with huge flight times and hideous jet lag.

Flying from London to Moscow takes four hours, and from Moscow to Sochi two. Of course, it's not cheap – a package including accommodation, all meals, skis and safety equipment will cost €2,500, and flights would take this to €3,000. But then, like drug addicts, people who know the thrill of floating through deep powder will, frankly, pay anything to get their next fix.

And what about the choppers? Testut refused to tell me exactly how old they are, insisting that the key thing is that they are immaculately well serviced. In any case, their twin engines make them safer than the small single-engined models normally used for heliskiing, and these have full night-flying and zero-visibility capabilities. They were built for battle, after all.

More reassuring is the operation's record: in more than ten years there's never been a hitch with the helicopters. Putin himself has entrusted his safety to them. (On condition of strictest anonymity, a local tells me Russia's leader is 'good on piste but still has a long, long way to go in the powder'.)

The rest of our trip continues in the same wonderful way. Six or seven drops a day, a picnic lunch in the snow, and more powder than at a supermodel's party. On our penultimate day we stumble across a group of American snowboarders filming a movie and give them a lift back in the helicopter. 'I do this all day every day all around the world,' said one, 'and it don't get no better than this.'

Next time, I'll have to take my mum.

THE INSIDE TRACK

James Moreland

Founder of Elemental Adventure Heliskiing

'Is all the development for the Olympics going to ruin Krasnaya? It won't happen overnight, but I think the equation is pretty simple: increase the number of people, decrease the quality of the experience. Hopefully, I am wrong, but I would say that, by 2014, Krasnaya Polyana will no longer be a great "destination heliski area" but will transform into somewhere that's good for a resort-based holiday with a couple of runs in the helicopter thrown in – a bit like in the Alps or Whistler. My message would be, if you are going to go, then do it sooner rather than later.'

The Knowledge
Krasnaya Polyana, Russia

STATS **Town altitude:** 540m **Highest lift:** 2,228m; **Lifts:** 4 **Pistes:** 25km **Lift pass:** £29 per day **Closest airport:** Sochi-Adler – 45km

WHY? Wild mountains, deep snow, strong vodka – Krasnaya has the best heliskiing in Europe and is just about accessible for a short break. Go before 2014 Olympic fever changes the place for ever **GETTING THERE** Krasnaya Polyana ('Red Meadow') is 60km from the Black Sea city of Sochi. To fly there, you currently have to change planes in Moscow – travel will take a full day each end of the trip. British Airways and British Midland fly direct to Moscow (4 hours), Aeroflot and at least 5 other Russian airlines fly from Moscow to Sochi (2 hours). See www.sochi-airport.com for details. Moscow's airports are quite a long way apart – make sure your UK and internal flights use the same airport **TRANSFERS** The recently completed road up to the resort means the drive now takes only 40 minutes. Your heliski operator will provide a minibus transfer; otherwise, taxis wait at the airport **WHERE TO STAY** New hotels are opening all the time. The smartest place in town is currently the Grand Hotel Polyana (+7 (0)8622 902902; www.grandhotelpolyana.ru; doubles from 8,700 roubles/£188 half board), but many visitors prefer the atmosphere in the older Radisson SAS Lazurnaya Peak (+7 (0)4954 11776; www.peakhotel.ru; doubles from 7,200 roubles/£155 half board). A cheaper option is the Deja Vu (+7 (0)8622 437777; email: deja-vuu@mail.ru; doubles from 3,900 roubles/£85) **WHERE TO SKI** More lifts are being built all the time, but even with the existing 4 chair lifts, there is some excellent skiing. From the top lift, traverse left or right for a huge range of off-piste runs. There are a couple of pistes, but these are certainly not worth travelling to Russia for. Obviously, with a helicopter, things become way more interesting. The longest established heliski operator is Yak and Yeti (Chamonix office: +33 (0)4 50 53 53 67; Krasnaya office: +7 (0)8622 336803; www.yak-yeti.com), which uses French guides assisted by locals. A typical run might descend 1,000m from a high alpine ridge then through silver-birch forests. Steep flutes and gullies will keep even the most advanced skiers and boarders excited **WHERE TO EAT** On the mountain, the restaurant at the bottom of the highest chairlift does great goulash soup. In town, Atmosphere (+7 (0)9183 060103; www.atmospher.ru) is the best option – a classy French restaurant. Those on a tighter budget recommend the café in the petrol station on the main road through town

➔ WHERE TO PARTY The Münchhausen bar, at the bottom of the ski lifts, looks like a traditional alpine après-ski bar but hosts some exceedingly wild parties. The nightclubs in the basements of the Grand and the Radisson hotels are open till 4 a.m. **➔ HELP!** Elemental Adventure (0207 836 3547; www.eaheliskiing.com) organizes heliski trips all over the world. Its 4-night trips to Krasnaya, including 3 days' heliskiing, powder skis, guides, Airbag avalanche backpacks and all meals, but not flights to Krasnaya, cost €2,500. Yak and Yeti (details as before) can also arrange packages – 4-night weekends start at €2,390
➔ TOURIST OFFICE Contact the Russian National Tourist Office in London: 0207 495 7570; www.visitrussia.org.uk

Five More... For Heliskiing

VALGRISENCHE, ITALY

STATS: Town altitude: 1,664m; **Highest lift:** 2,000m; **Lifts:** 3; **Pistes:** 8km; **Closest airport:** Turin – 75km

WHY? Valgrisenche is a small village on the south side of the Aosta valley, just over the mountain from Sainte Foy in France. There's a tiny children's and beginners' ski area, but it's also used as the base for Heliski Valgrisenche (+39 349 6649763; www.heliskivalgrisenche.it), a leading company run by an Italian guide, Danilo Garin, who spent many years working in heliski lodges in Canada. The company offers day, weekend and week packages. A 3-day weekend costs from €800 per person, based on a group of 4, including 6 helidrops and guiding and airbag rucksacks
GETTING THERE Hire a car for the easy 75-minute drive. A taxi will cost around €200 (+39 339 7113050; www.taxivalledaosta.com)
WHERE TO STAY The Hotel Perret, in Bonne, further up the valley from Valgrisenche at 1,810m, is close to the helipad (+39 0165 97107; www.hotelperret.com; doubles from €104, half board)
WHERE TO PARTY A drink in the hotel bar is about all you'll get
TOURIST OFFICE +39 0165 97225; www.skivallee.it

GRINDELWALD, SWITZERLAND

STATS: Town altitude: 943m; **Highest lift:** 2,971m; **Lifts:** 45; **Pistes:** 213km; **Closest airport:** Bern – 80km

WHY? Grindelwald is known as a place for sedate skiing and marvelling at the views of the Eiger, Mönch and Jungfrau mountains. But few appreciate that it's actually an excellent place to try heliskiing. Several guiding companies arrange heliski trips (the tourist office has details). Bohag, for example (+41 (0)33 828 90 00; www.bohag.ch) will pick you up from the helipad at the top of the Männlichen lift, and drop you at the Ebnefluh (3,800m) for your first run, then drop you at the Petersgat (3,200m) for your second – giving a total of 35km off-piste skiing, for a total of CHF350/£172, including guide, but based on a group of three minimum. Even those who don't want to heliski will relish a scenic flight over the Eiger and Jungfrau, from CHF90/£44
GETTING THERE From Bern, it's a 75-minute drive, and a taxi will cost CHF250/£116 for up to 3 (+41 (0)33 853 62 61; www.taxigrindelwald.ch)
WHERE TO STAY The Hotel Bodmi (+41 (0)33 853 12 20; www.bodmi.ch; doubles from CHF260/£128, including breakfast) has good food, is close to the slopes and doesn't get overrun with tour parties
WHERE TO PARTY There are some lovely mountain restaurants – the one by the railway at Brandegg feels like little's changed in a hundred years – but nightlife in the town is tame. The Challi-Bar in the Hotel Kreuz has DJs, the Gepsi-bar in the Hotel Eiger has live music (and 'grandma and grandpa nights', whatever they are). The late spot is the Mescalero disco
TOURIST OFFICE +41 (0)33 854 12 12; www.grindelwald.ch

ARTIES, SPAIN

STATS: Town altitude: 1,400m; **Highest lift:** 2,510m (in Baqueira-Beret); **Lifts:** 33; **Pistes:** 104km; **Closest airport:** Toulouse – 159km

WHY? The Parador hotel in the hamlet of Arties is 7km down the road from Baqueira-Beret in the Val d'Aran. It's used as the base for a heliski weekend offered by Pyroutdoor (+33 (0)6 80 14 76 70; www.pyroutdoor.com). For €2,180, you get 3 full days' heliskiing, 18 drops, guiding and accommodation at the Parador. Cheaper packages based on a mixture of skiing in the resort and heliskiing are also available, starting at around €700
GETTING THERE A hire car makes most sense – a taxi will cost €175 each way
WHERE TO STAY The Parador (+34 (0)973 640801; www.parador.es; doubles from €138) in Arties is a modern building but built in traditional mountain style, with heavy wood beams and big fireplaces
WHERE TO PARTY La Luna in Arties gets lively but, to celebrate your big final day heliskiing, head to Pacha in Baqueira, an outpost of the legendary Ibizan club
TOURIST OFFICE +34 (0)973 639010; www.baqueira.es

ABISKO, SWEDEN

STATS: Town altitude: 350m; **Highest lift:** 1,200m; **Lifts:** 1; **Pistes:** 0km; **Closest airport:** Kiruna – 80km

WHY? Abisko Mountain Lodge is 350km north of the Arctic Circle in Sweden, and heliskiing goes on until June here. Owned by outdoor fanatics Dick and Mina Johansson, it's an isolated centre for all types

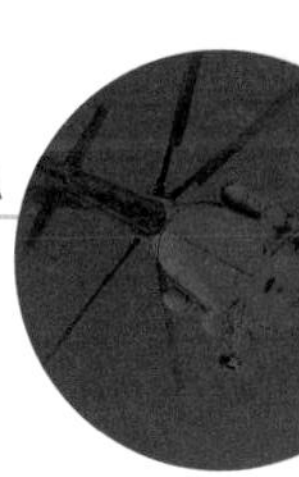

of mountain sports with one long chairlift leading to an off-piste run, plus it is only 30 minutes' drive to the resort of Riksgränsen. British heliski specialists Elemental Adventure (0207 836 3547; www.eaheliskiing.com) organize 4-day-long weekends here, with 2 days' heliskiing and 2 days in resort at Riksgränsen, from £1,550 including transfers from Kiruna airport. They can tailor-make shorter ones too

➜ **GETTING THERE** From Kiruna, regular buses run direct to the resort, taking around an hour (+46 (0)771 100110; www.ltnbd.se). A taxi will cost 1,550 SEK/£130 (+46 (0)980 12020; www.taxikiruna.se)

➜ **WHERE TO STAY** Abisko Mountain Lodge (+46 (0)980 40100; www.abiskomountainlodge.se) has double hotel rooms from 1,500SEK/£125, including breakfast, and also some self-catering cabins outside

➜ **WHERE TO PARTY** The lodge has its own bar. It's a long walk through the Arctic to anything else

➜ **TOURIST OFFICE** +46 (0)980 40200; www.abisko.nu

GRESSONEY-LA-TRINITÉ, ITALY

➜ **STATS: Town altitude:** 1,212m; **Highest lift:** 2,970m; **Lifts:** 37; **Pistes:** 180km; **Closest airport:** Turin – 96km

➜ **WHY?** The Monterosa area (made up of Champoluc, Gressoney and Alagna) is well known as a heliski hotspot. In Gressoney, you can sign up with the Guide Monterosa company (+39 0125 366019; www.guidemonterosa.com), which organizes weekend trips featuring 3 days' heliskiing, dropping you at points like the Colle del Lys (4,200m), Colle del Felik (4,100m), Colle di Verra (3,900m) and Tête de Valpelline (3,900m). The heliski package, including a 3-day ski pass and 2 nights' accommodation, with guiding costs €490, plus €100 per person for each drop

➜ **GETTING THERE** Hire a car for the 75-minute drive. A taxi will cost around €180 (+39 339 7113050; www.taxivalledaosta.com)

➜ **WHERE TO STAY** Accommodation is usually arranged as part of the heliski package and, otherwise, it can be hard to find a room without a minimum stay of a week here

➜ **WHERE TO PARTY** The Wunder Bar at the bottom of the slope in the Stafal part of the village (where the piste comes down from Champoluc) is the place for après ski. In the main, La Trinité, part of the village, the bar of the Hotel Dufour is the focus

➜ **TOURIST OFFICE** +39 0125 303111; www.monterosa-ski.com

Romance

ALMDORF, AUSTRIA

15

SWEETCORN HANGS drying in the midday sun, a man chops wood with an axe, a cat plays at our heels.

TO BE HONEST, it doesn't start well. No matter how good your intentions, the long-stay car park at Stansted airport at 5 a.m. is never going to be that romantic. As we board the bus to the terminal, my girlfriend Jill says she feels so tired she thinks she is going to be sick.

Still, slight hiccup over flight timings aside, I'm quietly confident I'm going to be able to pull off a weekend so lavishly romantic it will keep me in brownie points for a year. British men may be no match for the French or Italians when it comes to matters of the heart, but we do know the one key ingredient of romance. That's right – good organization.

Only with military-style planning can you create the impression of being relaxed and carefree on a date. Without it, you end up aimlessly trudging around looking in the windows of different restaurants saying, 'No, you choose,' or standing on windy street corners while a streetmap flaps in your face.

My plans were all in place. We'd fly to Klagenfurt (OK, Ryanair doesn't scream romance, but those plastic sachets of gin certainly get you in the mood) and pick up a hire car pre-arranged through Alamo. Then, just fifty minutes later we'd reach our accommodation – not a honeymoon suite in a swanky hotel, something far better than that: our own picture-perfect wooden chalet where we could hole up all weekend.

Finding a romantic wooden chalet for a weekend hadn't been easy. There's Chalet Mozart, a gorgeous chalet for two in Verbier, but it's booked up years in

The chalet's terrace, and the cute touches inside

Previous pages: Tom and Jill enjoy the wood-fired hot tub

advance and only available for full weeks. There are log cabins galore in the States but, in Europe, the chalets offered by holiday companies usually sleep at least ten. Sure you can just take an individual room, but the walls will be paper thin and dinners will be boozy affairs at shared tables, leaving little scope for staring into each other's eyes and whispering sweet nothings. Of course, the Alps are positively littered with pretty, privately owned chalets and you can rent many of them through agencies such as Interhome, but few are available just for weekends, and none offer any kind of catering, so your first romantic task for the weekend would be to hunt down a supermarket.

From the flat green valley floor we take a narrow lane, snaking up the steep mountainside towards the tiny ski area of Falkert. Halfway up, we come upon our destination, a tiny cluster of wooden chalets clinging to the hillside, roofs covered in snow, little plumes of woodsmoke puffing from the chimneys. This is Almdorf Seinerzeit, which translates as something like 'village in the meadow from the good old days'. As we crunch down the drive, it feels like we're entering an episode of *Heidi*. A man points out a parking space. He's wearing *lederhosen*.

Daniella, the beaming blonde manageress, leads us along a pebbly path to our chalet, oil lamps hanging from trees either side to light the way at night. We wind our way past a little pond and an outdoor wood-fired oven where joints of pork are being slowly roasted for supper. Sweetcorn hangs drying in the midday sun, a

Almdorf Seinerzeit – like stepping into an episode of Heidi

LIFT UP THE wooden step in the bathroom and you find a refrigerated compartment full of bottles of Veuve Clicquot.

man chops wood with an axe, stopping to smile and say '*Grüß Gott*' as we pass. A cat plays at our heels.

It's all so perfect, it doesn't seem real. And, actually, it's not. Almdorf isn't a real village at all but a re-creation of an idealized Alpine hamlet. There are twenty-two chalets in all, plus one for spa treatments and a village inn housing the restaurant. None is more than twelve years old.

But though it's all, essentially, fake, you'd never know, such is the incredible attention to detail. Our chalet was built in 2004 but is utterly traditional and cuter than a newborn kitten. Everything is made from wood – walls, floor, window frames, bed, shower. Even the tiles on the roof are wooden, and the gutters are made not of metal but of hollowed-out branches. The chalet has two bedrooms, one with a hand-carved wooden four-poster, the other with an even more dramatic bed made from huge polished pieces of timber and with a billowing white canopy.

There's a little kitchen, complete with wooden dressers stacked with crockery, and a living-room arranged around a fireplace. Luxurious modern touches are cunningly concealed – tug on an antique pulley and a flatscreen TV rises out of a wooden dresser. Lift up the wooden step in the bathroom and you find a refrigerated compartment full of bottles of Veuve Clicquot in different sizes. A small hatch in the wall swings open to reveal two champagne flutes – perfect for when you're lounging in the vast (wooden) bath.

It's homely and lovey-dovey rather than flashy or raunchy, though. Forget satin sheets: here you find fluffy red-and-white-checked duvets dotted with little hearts. The shelves are lined with books, an embroidered tea towel from 1915 hangs in the kitchen and little heart-shaped lavender bags sit next to the fresh roses on the windowsill. In some ways it's so sweet it borders on the sickly, but Jill loves it.

The chalet's four-poster

There's even a hayloft – a ladder (wooden) swings down from the roof, letting you clamber up to a snug mezzanine corner, with a mattress and bits of hay tucked around the rafters. Perfect for kids, or adults who just, er, fancy a roll in the hay.

Another of the chalets goes one better still. It has its own treehouse – a tiny wooden cabin high in the branches with a double bed inside and fabulous views out over the valley. You reach it by walking along a gangplank and crossing a drawbridge, which you can then raise behind you for the ultimate in romantic seclusion.

After lunch we drive five minutes up the road to the Falkert ski area. It's tiny – just five small lifts and a handful of runs – but even on a sunny Saturday, the total number of skiers using them is twelve. For this part of Austria, it's also quite high; the runs range from 1,700m to 2,300m. If you are a beginner, I can't think of anywhere better.

Back in the chalet, we've scarcely taken off our ski jackets when there's a knock on the door. 'So! Teatime!' beams Aldo, one of the waiters from the inn, as he presents a flask of steaming coffee and two slices of chocolate cake.

We sit eating on the terrace as the sun sets, while Reinhold, another of the Almdorf team, starts the wood fire that heats the outdoor hot-tub. This is reminiscent of a large wooden barrel sunk down into the terrace. After an hour or so the water's hot, so we flip open the lid and jump in. The view is stunning. Behind the wooden rail at the end of the terrace, the hillside drops away steeply all the way to the valley floor. It's almost dark, but the snow-covered mountains on the far side of the valley are still shining silver. The long-stay car park seems a very long way away.

Almdorf is so geared to romance you almost can't escape it. For dinner you have the choice of heading to the main restaurant in the village inn, eating in the

Supper in the village inn

Every chalet has a sun terrace

'world's smallest restaurant' (basically a tiny shed with a view, with one table for two and a little stove for the chef), or having the chefs bring the food to your chalet so you can spend the entire meal clasping hands and talking about the depth of your love. Being British, and hence genetically unsuited to that kind of thing, we opt for the restaurant.

Of course, what we do know is that the food of love is booze, so we get stuck into a lovely bottle of Austrian Grüner Veltliner. The menu is crammed full of Austrian specialities – after home-baked bread with fennel seeds we have deliciously salty cheese noodles, then baked pork with polenta and red-wine sauce and, finally, a buttermilk terrine with lemon sorbet. Andreas, the white-jacketed chef, comes out to present each course, and check we enjoyed the last.

There's a lovely, relaxed atmosphere in the restaurant, the food's fabulous, but something's not quite right. It's almost as if there are three people in this relationship. Oh yes, that's right: Robin is here too and, in between taking pictures, he is sitting down and eating with us.

Of course there's no nightlife, nothing to do after dinner at all in fact, and, after a stroll around the village, we're in bed by ten. I guess that's the point.

Next day we head to the area's main ski resort, Bad Kleinkirchheim, a fifteen-minute drive away. It's not Les Trois Vallées but it has a respectable 100km of pistes stretched out across two mountains. The highest point of the lift system, the top of the Kaiserburg, is a decidedly modest 2,055m, so you're unlikely to find the deepest snow here. But then you are not here for hardcore powder-hounding, you're here for romance and, for that, the area is perfect.

While there isn't the drama of the jagged, soaring peaks that surround Chamonix, the forest-covered mountains, with mists swirling about them, are more gently beautiful. You won't hear another English voice, so there's a sense of it just being the two of you on the mountain together. And, above all, it's incredibly quiet.

Little could break the dreamy spell of mountain vistas, healthy exercise and the *glühwein* glow more than a huge jostling queue, but we never see anyone else waiting for a lift at all. The runs are all but deserted.

And there are some great runs. Red number 11 swoops down through the forests for 4km, dropping 740m from the Maibrunn ridge back to the village, at 1,020m. Close by is the Franz Klammer World Cup Run – a 3.2km-long black used for men's downhill racing (Klammer, winner of Olympic skiing gold in 1976, is the area's most famous son). And, over on the Kaiserburg, there is some good easy off piste between the trees beside the Muldenlift T-bar.

But this place really isn't about gnarly skiing. They even put red sofas beside the pistes at various spots around the mountain, just in case you need a sit-down.

Other skiers are few and far between at Bad Kleinkirchheim

134

THE INSIDE TRACK

Franz Klammer Ski Racing Legend

'My favourite place to stop on the mountain is called Poldl's Weltcup Hut, above St Oswald. The owner, Leopold Gruber, is a close friend, and we used to race together in the World Cup. It's a traditional wooden chalet halfway up the mountain with a big terrace that gets the sun all afternoon. Leopold cooks outside on the terrace, so you can see what he's making. The Wiener schnitzel is fantastic, and you should drink a Poldilex, which means a small beer and a glass of pine-flavoured Zirbenschnaps. It's a great place for lunch, but it's very easy to get stuck there for the rest of the day.'

Zum Weltcup Poldl: +43 (0)664 1844353

We stop at Maibrunnalm, a restaurant on the ridge close to the start of the World Cup run, to sit in deck chairs, drink hot chocolate and soak up the sun.

At the end of the day, we ski down to find people lounging around in swimming costumes. The Römerbad, a huge Roman-themed spa, is right at the bottom of the main pistes, and swimmers splash about in its outdoor pool yards from where you step out of your bindings. You can include entrance to the spa with your lift pass and, since it only adds €20 to the cost of a weekend ticket, it's definitely worth it – but we are heading back to Almdorf, where we have an altogether more couply spa experience planned.

We tiptoe past the glowing oil lamps into the 'House of Senses' – another traditional chalet, but one that is full of massage and treatment rooms. Downstairs, Peter is waiting for us, stirring a big black cauldron that hangs from chains over a crackling fire. We're to have a traditional alpine hay bath – excellent for the circulation and immune system, apparently.

First, we get into two baths, side by side in front of the fire. They are made of wood, naturally, and have lids which fold down to keep in the heat of the water. Then Peter ladles in his concoction from the cauldron, a mixture of ninety-six herbs, including arnica. We sit there for twenty minutes, Jill looking as if she's going to faint, before getting out and moving over to two beds, where we are covered in hay for another forty minutes. Halfway through I remember I have hayfever and my eyes start to itch, but relationships are all about sacrifices, aren't they?

Next morning, there's a ring at the door. It's Karin, carrying a huge basket. She comes in, spreads out a tablecloth and puts down some fresh flowers, then starts to lay out a fabulous breakfast – hams, cheeses with grapes and walnuts, fresh breads, homemade jams, fresh orange juice and coffee, and boiled eggs, delivered on a little wooden tray.

It kind of sums it up – in Almdorf even breakfast is romantic. If a weekend here doesn't work wonders for your relationship, you may as well give up.

1 *Breakfast is laid out in the chalet, complete with rose*
2 *Having a traditional hay bath*
3 *The Römerbad's outdoor pool is at the foot of the pistes*
4 *Love is . . . a helping hand*
5 *Open fire and wall-to-wall wood in the chalet*
6 *Stopping off at the Millstätter See on the way home*

At Almdorf, even
breakfast is romantic
1|2
|3
|4
5
6

STATS (For Bad Kleinkirchheim) **Town altitude:** 1,090m **Highest lift:** 2,055m, **Lifts:** 26 **Pistes:** 100km **Lift pass:** €37 per day **Closest airport:** Klagenfurt – 60km

The Knowledge
Almdorf, Austria

WHY? The enchanting wooden chalets at Almdorf Seinerzeit are the perfect setting for romance, especially if your loved one is a fan of *Heidi*
GETTING THERE Ryanair fly to Klagenfurt, 50 minutes' drive away, but there are more frequent flights to Salzburg, 167km and a little over 2 hours away **TRANSFERS** Hiring a car will let you get the most from the pretty drive and enable you to move easily between Almdorf and the two nearby ski areas, but taxis are extremely reasonable too. From Klagenfurt, a car for up to 3 people costs €85 each way, a minibus for up to 8 costs €100 (contact Bacher Reisen: +43 (0)424 630720; www.bacher-reisen.at, or email transfer@bacher-reisen.at). From Salzburg taxis/minibuses cost €240/265
WHERE TO STAY Almdorf Seinerzeit (+43 (0)427 57201; www.almdorf.com) has chalets for 2 people from €290, including breakfast. Larger chalets with 2 double bedrooms cost from €750, including breakfast. For rustic, self-catering chalets throughout the Alps, try the booking agency Interhome (0208 780 6633; www.interhome.co.uk) **WHERE TO SKI** The Falkert ski area (+43 (0)427 572220; www.falkert.at), a couple of minutes up the road, is the perfect place for beginners, with a selection of gentle runs and no one around to watch if you fall over. For intermediates, the wide tree-lined slopes of Bad Kleinkirchheim are great for a couple of days. The best snow will usually be up on the Kaiserburg, where you can warm up on a couple of T-bars then take red piste 6 all the way back to the village, descending almost 1,000m. The other long swooping run is red piste 11, which notches up 4km. Advanced skiers can test themselves on the 3.2km Franz Klammer World Cup Run

WHERE TO EAT There are 22 restaurants up on the mountain, almost all of them charming traditional places offering local Carinthian specialities. Try the Maibrunnhütte (+43 (0)424 08262), at the top of the Maibrunnbahn chair lift, which has an excellent terrace for an afternoon beer or a Willi-Willi (pear schnapps). At Almdorf, you just have to choose whether to go into the cosy restaurant, eat in your chalet or book 'the world's smallest restaurant'. The chalets all have self-catering facilities too **WHERE TO PARTY** There are several bars for après ski around the bottom lift station – including the Almstube and Viktoria Pub. This is not the place for evening entertainment though. Just climb into your wood-fired outdoor hot-tub and watch the stars **HELP!** Unfortunately, no British tour operators feature Almdorf, so you have to book direct **TOURIST OFFICE** Bad Kleinkirchheim: +43 (0)424 08212; www.badkleinkirchheim.at

Five More... For Romance

GRIMENTZ, SWITZERLAND

➲ **STATS: Town altitude:** 1,570m; **Highest lift:** 2,900m; **Lifts:** 47; **Pistes:** 220km; **Closest airport:** Sion – 19km

➲ **WHY?** Grimentz, tucked away up the picturesque Val d'Anniviers, is the very epitome of the chocolate-box-pretty Swiss village. The fifteenth-century Burgher's House is still the village's focal point, and the narrow streets are lined with sun-darkened barns, chalets and the characteristic granaries known as 'raccards'. In summer, the balconies would be dripping with flowers but, in winter, you may be compensated by a taste of 125-year-old Vin des Glaciers from one of over a hundred cellars. The skiing above the village offers spectacular views of the Moiry Glacier and the Rhone Valley far below. There are 11 lifts and 50km of pistes in the local area, but the lift pass covers the others in the valley (stats above)

➲ **GETTING THERE** Assuming you can't get a flight into Sion, from Geneva airport (115km away) take the train to Sierre, then the Postbus (see www.sbb.ch for timetables), which will take about 3 hours in all. Or hire a car for the 2-hour drive (a car is useful for getting to the other resorts in the Val d'Anniviers). Finally, you could fly to Bern, hire a car and whizz through the new Lötschberg tunnel in 1 hour and 45 minutes

➲ **WHERE TO STAY** Hotel Alpina (+41 (0)27 476 16 16; www.alpinagrimentz.ch; doubles from CHF318/£156 half board) is newly built but traditional in style and elegantly furnished, with comfortable lounge, sauna and jacuzzi; a more modest option is the Moiry (+41 (0)27 475 11 44; www.hoteldemoiry.ch; doubles from CHF176/£86 half board), owned by the Salamin family for generations. Ask for a room in the Chalet Arolle annexe for a pretty outlook

➲ **WHERE TO PARTY** As you come off the slopes, drop in at the Snow Bar Chez Florioz. If you want more than the cosy hotel bars, the Disco Shadock will see you through until 3 a.m.

➲ **TOURIST OFFICE** +41 (0)27 475 14 93; www.grimentz.ch

KLEINE SCHEIDEGG, SWITZERLAND

➲ **STATS: Hotel altitude:** 2,061m; **Highest lift:** 2,971m; **Lifts:** 45; **Pistes:** 213km; **Closest airport:** Bern – 75 km

➲ **WHY?** Kleine Scheidegg, a high mountain plateau between the towns of Grindelwald and Wengen, has one of the most iconic views in Europe – it sits right under the 'Big Three' peaks, the Eiger, Mönch and Jungfrau. Here, you and your loved one will be drawn a little closer by the vicarious thrill of danger as you look through the telescopes at climbers struggling up the Eiger's north face. During the day, it's busy with skiers and tourists simply coming to gawp, but the trick is to stay the night in the hotel here, which could scarcely be more atmospheric. You'll get first tracks in the morning too

➲ **GETTING THERE** From Bern airport, hire a car and drive in an hour to Lauterbrunnen. Park in the multi-storey (CHF38/£19 for 3 days) and pick up the Wengernalpbahn cog railway, which takes 45 minutes to reach Kleine Scheidegg (last ascent is usually 4.30 p.m.; check at www.jungfraubahn.ch). Or from Zurich airport, catch the train via Interlaken and Wengen, about 3 hours and 30 minutes in total – but utterly spectacular (see www.sbb.ch)

➲ **WHERE TO STAY** The Hotel Bellevue des Alpes (+41 (0)33 855 12 12; www.scheidegg-hotels.ch, doubles from CHF310/£152 half board) was built in 1856, and has a delicious faded grandeur. It has been host to pioneers of skiing and climbing, including those, from Barrington to Lauper, who scaled the north face of the Eiger, as well as to ladies and gentlemen who wanted to enjoy fresh mountain air in their accustomed luxury. Bedrooms vary in size and furnishings but all have character. Through lace and velvet curtains you glimpse the most majestic peaks. If you want something simpler, the Hotel Jungfrau at Wengernalp (+41 (0)33 855 16 22; www.wengernalp.ch; doubles CHF400/£196 half board) is a smaller 19th-century hotel set alone on the mountainside at 1,900m

➲ **WHERE TO PARTY** Sit in the bar of the Bellevue, with storms raging around, while Mario the barman mixes cocktails that are, just like the hotel, from another era – Kir Royal, Gin Fizz, Whisky Sour. What could be more romantic?

➲ **TOURIST OFFICE** Wengen: +41 (0)33 855 14 14; www.wengen.com. Grindelwald: +41 (0)33 854 12 12; www.grindelwald.com

SERRE CHEVALIER, FRANCE

➲ **STATS: Town altitude:** 1,400m; **Highest lift:** 2,830m; **Lifts:** 66; **Pistes:** 250km; **Closest airport:** Turin – 105km

➲ **WHY?** Serre Chevalier is a big area of linked pistes, reached from a string of a dozen villages and the town of

Briançon. All very well, but far more romantic is to retreat to Le Pi Mai, a hideaway hotel alone on the mountain far above the bustle of the valley. Since there are only 6 bedrooms, you're not going to find your fellow guests crowding you, either

➜ **GETTING THERE** The easiest option is to hire a car for the 90-minute drive from Turin airport or 2-hour drive past La Grave from Grenoble. Buses are infrequent. A taxi from Turin will cost €260 (+33 (0)6 13 51 17 66; www.taxi-serre-chevalier.com)

➜ **WHERE TO STAY** Le Pi Mai (+33 (0)4 92 24 83 63; www.lepimai.com; doubles from €224, half board) is a delightful farmhouse-style hotel perched alone at 1,985m. You arrive by the Fréjus cable car from the village of Villeneuve (last ascent 4 p.m.) and take a 5-minute blue run, or 15-minute walk, down to the hotel. Don't worry about your luggage, as staff will help. Rooms are a blend of modern and traditional style, and the hotel even has its own supply of spring water

➜ **WHERE TO PARTY** The Loco Loco down in Villeneuve is one of Serre Chevalier's hotspots, but there's no way to get back up to the hotel, so you had better settle in to enjoy each other's company and the peace and quiet

➜ **TOURIST OFFICE** +33 (0)4 92 24 98 98; www.serre-chevalier.com

GSTAAD, SWITZERLAND

➜ **STATS: Town altitude:** 1,050m; **Highest lift:** 2,979m; **Lifts:** 62; **Pistes:** 250km; **Closest airport:** Geneva – 95km

➜ **WHY?** What could be more romantic than snuggling up together all cosy and warm in a real igloo? Well, now you can, thanks to the 'igloo village' built each winter at 1,500m above Gstaad. There's a big communal igloo for eating, and then individual bedroom ones around the outside, with smooth ice walls and candles burning in icy alcoves. You sleep in double sleeping bags but, if you get really cold, there's a little wooden sauna

➜ **GETTING THERE** The train is simple, and it's a romantic trip. From the station at Geneva airport, it takes 2 hours 36 minutes to Gstaad's station, with one change in Montreux. The train runs all the way alongside Lake Geneva

➜ **WHERE TO STAY** The Igludorf (+41 (0)41 612 27 28; www.iglu-dorf.com). Standard igloos sleep up to 6 and cost CHF119/£58 per person, but that's no good. You need the 'romantic igloo' at CHF279/£137 per person, for which you also get a fondue dinner and a welcome glass of Prosecco and plate of mountain ham. The company also builds similar igloo villages in Garmisch in Germany, and Engelberg, Davos and Zermatt. If you only fancy one night in the ice, stay the second down in town at the five-star Palace Hotel (+41 (0)33 748 50 00; www.palace.ch; doubles from CHF720/£353, half board), a grand fairytale castle. Or try the funky Zloft in the village of Saannenmöser, just outside Gstaad (+41 (0)33 744 69 69; www.zloft.ch; doubles from CHF175/£86)

➜ **WHERE TO PARTY** There's a bar in a larger communal igloo nearby. Down in Gstaad, head for Richi's Pub, then the GreenGo nightclub of the Palace Hotel

➜ **TOURIST OFFICE** +41 (0)33 748 81 81; www.gstaad.ch

SAMOËNS, FRANCE

➜ **STATS: Town altitude:** 720m; **Highest lift:** 2,561m; **Lifts:** 78; **Pistes:** 265km; **Closest airport:** Geneva – 70km

➜ **WHY?** Samoëns is the little valley village at the base of Flaine's wonderful Grand Massif ski area. It's charming in its own right, but nothing compared with a night on the mountain in the Gîte du Lac de Gers, at 1,533m. A wooden chalet, it overlooks a snow-covered lake in the Sixt Fer à Cheval Nature Reserve. You may be able to spot chamois as you drink a glass of local wine before a dinner of Savoyard specialities

➜ **GETTING THERE** The drive from the airport takes just over an hour. Hire a car, or book a taxi, which will cost around €150 each way for up to 3 (+33 (0)4 50349676; www.taxidechavassine.fr). There are 3 daily buses too, operated by SAT, costing €74 return and taking 1 hour and 40 minutes (details: www.altibus.com; +33 (0)4 79 68 32 96)

➜ **WHERE TO STAY** The Gîte du Lac de Gers (+33 (0)4 50 89 55 14; some details on the Samoëns tourist-board website; doubles from €110, including breakfast). You have to get there on skis – halfway down the Cascades piste, down from Flaine towards the hamlet of Sixt, you'll come across a phone. From this, you call the owner, Laurence, who'll send a skidoo down to drag you up to the gîte. In Samoëns, try the Neige et Roc (+33 (0)4 50 34 40 72; www.neigeetroc.com; doubles from €230, half board)

➜ **WHERE TO PARTY** In Samoëns, there's Covey's Irish Pub or Le Savoie. At the gîte, it's a case of a glass of Genepy and a stroll under the stars

➜ **TOURIST OFFICE** +33 (0)4 50 34 40 28; www.samoens.com

16

Piste Perfection

LES TROIS VALLÉES, FRANCE

THE STATISTICS alone are mind-boggling – there are 183 lifts and 600km of pistes.

Sometimes it doesn't quite feel like France

LES TROIS VALLÉES is Britain's favourite place to ski. A vast ski area linking the French resorts of Courchevel, Méribel and Val Thorens, it attracts around 300,000 of us each year. And, like so many others, this is where I came to learn to ski on annual family holidays during my teenage years.

But familiarity breeds contempt. In Méribel, which alone gets 150,000 Brits a year (and was founded by a British colonel), it often feels as if you go all day without hearing a French voice. In other resorts, the couloirs, those steep, narrow ribbons of snow with rock walls on each side, are given evocative names based on local folklore. Here, one of the most famous is called 'The Plumber's Crack'. Elsewhere, your après-ski drink might be served with a delicious slice of *tarte tatin* or some finely smoked mountain ham. Here, ovens on the bar gently reheat a choice of Pukka Pies.

Five or six years ago, I decided I'd had enough. I didn't want to spend my holidays with braying public schoolboys called Chopper and Toby throwing rubber chickens across the bar at each other, rugger-style, before downing toffee vodkas to a chorus of 'Down it! Down it!' From now on, I thought, it would be remote slopes and authentic little villages for me. And yet, I was tempted back here during the research for this book. And, within a few hours, I realized I'd made a mistake – this place is simply far too good to leave to Chopper and Tobes.

For piste skiing, no other ski area can come close. True, there are moments when the Britishness gets a bit much but, really, that's a small price to pay for such outstanding terrain.

The statistics alone are mind-boggling. This is the world's biggest linked ski area, with 183 lifts and 600km of pistes. Other areas claim to be bigger – the Dolomiti Superski boasts 1,220km, the Portes du Soleil 650km, but neither area's pistes are properly linked up like those of Les Trois Vallées. Here, provided there's enough snow, you can ski all 600km without ever setting foot in a bus or taxi.

Of course, if you're just here for the weekend, all this is a bit academic. But it's the quality as well as the quantity of the slopes that is so impressive. We arrive at lunchtime and cruise over to the pistes above Courchevel. Despite the fact that it's after 2 p.m., the pistes we're on – Stade, Granges and Chapelets – are still beautifully groomed, their surface free of moguls, ice patches, rocks and snowballs: perfectly smooth, in fact, except for thousands of little, inch-high ridges. This is 'corduroy', the pattern left behind by huge combs dragged behind the piste bashers as they prepare the slopes at night.

In bad weather, you might not even notice it but, in sunshine, the pattern comes alive, one side of each tiny ridge catching the light, the other in shadow. And, like a blank wall tempting a graffiti artist, as you stand at the top of the slope, the corduroy calls out for you to come flying down and carve through the symmetry with a big, rounded, high-speed turn.

Slightly confusingly, there are actually four valleys in Les Trois Vallées. Standing looking upwards in Brides-les-Bains, the spa town at the very bottom of the ski area, the Courchevel valley is at the far left, Méribel in the centre, Val Thorens on the right, and the 'fourth valley', the slopes above a village called Orelle, further right still. Each valley has several villages along its length – Courchevel, for example, actually has four main villages, with names designating their altitude in metres. At the bottom is Courchevel 1300, aka Le Praz, then there's Courchevel 1550, 1650 and 1850, the latter arguably being France's glitziest resort, much loved of late by Russian oligarchs and boasting hotels like the Cheval Blanc, owned by the boss of Louis Vuitton. Time-pressed millionaires can fly in to the village's own airport, a sort of tarmac ski-jump affair on the mountainside (well worth standing beside to marvel at the pilots' skill as they come in to land).

La Tania sits among wooded slopes
Previous pages: Perfect corduroy on the Granges piste above Courchevel

Tom skiing above Méribel

In all, Les Trois Vallées has no fewer than fourteen villages, so intermediates can strike out on huge expeditions, travelling from valley to valley, village to village, stopping for coffee on a mountaintop here, for lunch down in a little hamlet there.

With people staying in Courchevel crossing over to Val Thorens and vice versa, some key lifts in the central, Méribel, valley, can get busy in the afternoon, but the slopes at either edge of the area – those above Courchevel 1650 on the left and above Orelle on the right, are very often empty. But, frankly, such is the sheer number of pistes that you can usually find a peaceful slope wherever you are.

The other big benefit, and one few people realize, is that, in Les Trois Vallées, there's a sort of anti-weekend effect. Because almost everyone here has come for a full week and so are travelling on Saturday or Sunday, the weekends are by far the quietest times on the slopes

The Dent de Burgin, 2,739m, sits between Courchevel and Méribel

– the exact opposite of the conventional ski resort.

But there's a problem, a reason for this lack of weekenders. Two, in fact. First is transport – getting here from Geneva or Lyon takes a good three hours. Those coming for a week can take the Eurostar, which runs overnight services direct from St Pancras to Moûtiers, a fifteen-minute bus ride down the valley, but these only go out on Friday nights, returning on Saturday nights, so don't work for weekenders.

Second is accommodation. Such is the demand for week-long stays that hoteliers are loath to release a room just for the weekend and thus have it sitting empty during the week. If you did manage to book a room for the weekend, it would probably cost you about the same as keeping it all week anyway.

Thankfully, there is a way round these obstacles. Firstly, you fly to Chambéry, from where the transfer takes just ninety minutes. Until recently, Chambéry was served only by weekly charter flights but now low-cost carriers such as Astraeus, Flybe and Jet2 are opening it up.

THE CORDUROY CALLS out for you to come flying down and carve through the symmetry with a big, high-speed turn.

And, secondly, in answer to the accommodation problem, there is La Tania, a quiet, unpretentious, family-orientated village built for the 1992 Olympics amid forest slopes halfway between Courchevel 1300 and Méribel. Here, prices are lower, everything is more relaxed and yet lifts run straight up to the Col de la Loze, from where you can swoop down to either Courchevel or Méribel. It's like getting straight into the heart of Les Trois Vallées through the little-used back door.

And here, in La Tania, is the British-run Hotel Telemark, that rarest of things in the Alps, let alone Les Trois Vallées – a hotel set up specifically with weekenders in mind.

Now, the Telemark isn't going to worry the Cheval Blanc. The rooms are quite small, there's a slight smell of ski boot about the place and the bar is more about watching rugby with a pint than sipping Cristal with your loved one. It's still not exactly cheap – around €120 per night, per person, including a three-course dinner – but for weekends in Les Trois Vallées, that represents good value.

It's clean, jolly and friendly and, on our first night staying there, the new arrivals from Britain chat excitedly to those on neighbouring tables at dinner about the weekend to come. Afterwards some are heading by taxi (ten minutes and €10) for some proper nightlife in Méribel, where Dick's Tea Bar and Le Loft keep rocking till 4 a.m. – but La Tania itself also has a couple of decent bars. The après-ski favourite, right at the bottom of the pistes, is Le Ski Lodge, where it's happy hour from 4 p.m. to 6 p.m. and pints cost €4. For a slightly classier evening drink, we wander down from the hotel, over the piste, where the bashers are working away flattening and smoothing snow, headlamps blazing, to the Taiga, a traditional chalet with exposed stone walls and wooden beams and a selection of champagne sitting in ice buckets on the bar.

To make the most of a day in Les Trois Vallées, you need to do some planning. At breakfast tables across the region, skiers study their piste maps, working out the day's itinerary. We start off up to the Col de la Loze, a windy, exposed spot where, if the cold gets too much, you can shelter and drink hot chocolate inside the Chalet Roc Tania.

From here we shoot down into Courchevel's long, wide main valley, then take the big cable car up to Saulire, the high point of Courchevel's ski area. As the cable car rises up over Saulire's steep cliffs, you can scope out the couloirs dropping below. On the far right is the Grand Couloir, a steep black run that's often covered in huge moguls. The other couloirs are off piste – the best, for showing off at least, is Sous Téléférique, which runs directly below the line of the cable car. Make sure you time your run to give those on the lift a grandstand view.

From Saulire we drop down towards Méribel. In fact, there is an excellent off-piste route down – dropping off the other side of the ridge from where

1 *Ski jumping at Le Praz*

2 *The Hotel Telemark in La Tania*

3 *British papers, beers and voices at Pub Le Ski Lodge*

4 *You said it*

5 *Lost in the fog under the La Tania gondola*

HOTEL
TELEMARK
BAR
BISTRO
OUVERT JUSQU A 2h
PUB LE SKI LODGE
BAR
RESTAURANT
PRAT
du Jour

1|2

|3

|4
5

THE INSIDE TRACK

Doreann Mendelsberg Waitress

'If you want to find perfectly groomed corduroy in Courchevel, look for the signs at the bottom of some chair lifts, like Biollay, which tell you which slopes have been most recently prepared. My perfect pistes? I like the runs down to La Tania and Le Praz – I guess because they are low people tend to ignore them, but they are actually really great, and are perfect in bad weather because they are lined by trees on both sides, giving good visibility. I'd also have to mention Indians, in Courchevel 1650, because it's such fun – there's a tepee village, where actors dressed like Red Indians will dress you up in furs, facepaint and a head dress, do archery demonstrations and let you smoke a peace pipe – well, something with a bit of sage in it anyway!'

the cable car docks – but it gets a lot of sun and can be avalanche prone. Instead, we take Maudit, one of several long, curving reds, descending nearly 1,300m to the village.

On the far side are some of my favourite runs, the long blues and reds coming down under the Tougnète 2 chair lift and, further to the right, the quiet Choucas blue piste. If there's snow, this is a great place to venture beyond the edge of the piste and take your first steps towards powder skiing. Above, at the Tougnète pass, is Les Crêtes, a cute little restaurant that feels like a proper mountain hut and is famous for its sausages in wine.

In fact, although there are some hidden gems, eating lunch in Les Trois Vallées requires a certain amount of care, such are the number of big, soulless and extremely expensive self-service cafeterias. If you've €50 to spend, head to the Mont Bel-Air, a swanky place with a huge sunny terrace above Courchevel 1650. For something cheaper but still high quality, try Le Petit Savoyard, a locals' favourite in the centre of Courchevel 1650, or La Table de Mon Grand-Père, inside the Hotel les Peupliers in Courchevel 1300. For a birthday, wedding anniversary or proposal, there's only one choice. From Méribel, keep going over the Tougnète ridge and blast down the wide, open hillside towards St Marcel, a tiny hamlet in the Val Thorens valley which would be utterly ignored by visitors were it not home to a restaurant called La Bouitte. Confident skiers can veer off piste at the last minute and ski right to St Marcel; others should take the piste to St Martin de Belleville, a minute's drive away, from where the restaurant will pick you up. Housed in an eighteenth-century farmhouse, it doesn't look particularly fancy, but La Bouitte has a Michelin star and a menu full of foie gras, lobster and truffles. A two-course menu costs around €50 and, if you can't move after lunch, they have five lovely rooms to rent upstairs.

From St Martin de Belleville, you can easily head to Val Thorens, the highest resort in Europe. It sits at

The colossal Saulire cable car

COURCHEVEL
ATTENTION
BE CAREFUL

IT'S THE QUALITY of the slopes as well as the quantity that is so impressive.

Skiing out of the cloud on the Combe Saulire red run

Heavy snow hits La Tania

Tarte aux myrtilles *at the Chalet Roc Tania*

2,300m, the lifts go up to 3,230m and the snow will be markedly better than in La Tania (1,400m) or Méribel (1,450m). It's an unlovely place though – purpose built, full of concrete blocks and stranded far above the tree line.

Having forgone La Bouitte in favour of some chips from Méribel's piste-side snack bar, we have time to make it up to the Cime de Caron, the final ridge, from where we can look over into the empty slopes of the 'fourth valley'. Tempting as it is to plunge into it, we have to err on the side of caution and turn back.

In an area this big, you have to keep your eye on the time. The connecting lifts that take you from one valley to the next close shortly after 4 p.m. and don't wait for stragglers – and a taxi from Val Thorens back to La Tania will take nearly two hours and cost a couple of hundred euros.

Back in Méribel, there's just time to stop for an afternoon drink on the terrace of the Rond Point, a celebrated bar beside the green Rhodos piste. If it's sunny, bands play outside in the afternoon (this is where The Feeling started out before breaking into the Top Ten). From here, home is in sight: it's just two lifts back to the Col de la Loze and then a long, leisurely ski with burning thighs down through the trees to La Tania.

Over mussel ravioli and roast pork belly at the Telemark that night, we look back at our route and guestimate we might have covered 60km during the day. So just another 540km to go then.

STATS **Town altitude (La Tania):** 1,400m **Highest lift:** 3,230m; **Lifts:** 183 **Pistes:** 600km **Lift pass:** €44 per day **Closest airport:** Chambéry – 95km

WHY? At some point every skier must come to try out the world's biggest single ski area. La Tania provides a low-key back door that's perfect for weekenders **GETTING THERE** Every winter more scheduled as well as charter flights are using Chambéry, which is 90 minutes' drive away (see flightfinder on page 287). The alternatives are Geneva (135km) and Lyon (185km), both of which take more than 3 hours to drive. The train is an option too: during the winter, TGVs run direct from Paris Gare de Lyon to Moûtiers; they take about 4 hours. From Moûtiers, it's a short taxi or shuttle bus ride up to the resort. Unfortunately, the overnight ski trains direct from London don't work for weekends – they go out on Friday night but return on Saturday night **TRANSFERS** Many people use hire cars. Remember: if you are picking up a hire car at Geneva airport, you'll be given the option of booking from the French or the Swiss side of the airport. It's counter-intuitive given your destination is in France, but you should opt for the Swiss side, even though French cars can be cheaper. Swiss hire cars usually come with winter tyres and snow chains included in the price; French ones don't. Picking up from France is also more time-consuming. First, you have to go through French customs to get to the desk, then you have to take a big detour round the back of the runway. From the Swiss car-hire pick-up, you are straight on the motorway. Lots of companies offer private transfers. Three Valley Transfers (01782 644420; www.3vt.co.uk) charge £170 each way for a taxi for up to 3 people from Chambéry, and £190 from Geneva. With larger groups it works out cheaper – from Chambéry, a taxi for 8 costs £240. Alternatively, try Snow Trip (0845 2006794; www.snowtrip.co.uk) or Mountain Express (+33 (0)6 19 17 26 00; www.mountainexpress.co.uk) **WHERE TO STAY** The Hotel Telemark (+33 (0)4 79 08 93 49; www.hoteltelemark.com; doubles from €240, half board) in La Tania is one of the few places to welcome weekenders. Alternatively, the large Hotel Montana (+33 (0)4 79 08 80 08; doubles from €194, room only) is charmless, but is right in the centre

WHERE TO SKI The piste options are endless. The quietest pistes are at either extreme of the area – above Courchevel 1650 and in the 'fourth valley' beyond Val Thorens. Intermediates will relish the red runs down Mont Vallon, above Méribel. Don't ignore the local runs either – the long red Moretta Blanche and blue Folyères, which return through the trees to La Tania. There are also some extremely serious off-piste lines off the Col de la Loze both towards La Tania and over towards Méribel **WHERE TO EAT** La Bouitte (+33 (0)4 79 08 96 77; www.la-bouitte.com) in St Marcel is the place for a memorable meal or, if it's sunny, book a table on the terrace of Bel-Air above Courchevel 1650 (+33 (0)4 79 08 00 93). In La Tania, if you want to eat out, try La Taiga (+33 (0)4 79 08 80 33; www.easytaiga.com) or La Ferme de La Tania (+33 (0)4 79082325)
WHERE TO PARTY If you get stuck into après ski at the Rond Point in Méribel (+ 33 (0)4 79 00 37 51; www.rondpointmeribel.com) and miss the last lift, you can easily taxi back. In La Tania, the two evening options are the Pub Le Ski Lodge (+33 (0)4 79 08 81 49; www.publeskilodge.com) and the Taiga. Party seekers should take a taxi round to Méribel to Dick's Tea Bar (+33 (0)4 79086019; www.dicksteabar.com) and Le Loft (+33 (0)4 79003658; www.leloftmeribel.com)
HELP! Supertravel (0207 295 1650; www.supertravel.co.uk) offers 3-night breaks from £400 to the Chalet Cardamines, Méribel, half board but excluding flights or transfers. The Hotel Telemark does not work with any UK tour operators
TOURIST OFFICE +33 (0)4 79084040; www.latania.com

Five More... For Piste Perfection

SÖLDEN, AUSTRIA

STATS: **Town altitude:** 1,377m; **Highest lift:** 3,249m; **Lifts:** 34; **Pistes:** 150km; **Closest airport:** Innsbruck – 85km

WHY? High-altitude slopes and buzzing après ski make this a favourite with Austrian and German skiers, yet it is largely ignored by Brits. It's good for all abilities, and many of the slopes are on the Tiefenbach and Rettenbach glaciers, meaning good conditions are guaranteed. There are lots of cosy mountain huts, too, and don't leave without heading to the Tiefenbachkogl, at 3,250m, where a dramatic metal and glass viewing platform stretches out into thin air

GETTING THERE It's an hour's drive from Innsbruck, and a taxi for up to 4 will cost around €120/€24pp for 5 and above (Taxi Quaxis: +43 (0)525 43737; www.taxiquaxibusreisen.com)

WHERE TO STAY The four-star Hotel Stefan (+43 (0)525 42237; www.hotel-stefan.at; doubles from €190, half board) is right next to the Giggijoch lift station and does good 4-course dinners

WHERE TO PARTY There are 23 après-ski bars, and they get pretty full-on: try Giggi Tenne, Philipp, Joker and Kuckuck. There are 8 nightclubs too – Partyhaus is a big, modern 2-storey place, Fire and Ice goes through from 3 p.m. to 3 a.m. After the après-ski dancing on tables in ski boots is over, the Rodelhütte offers table dancing of an altogether less wholesome and less clothed variety

TOURIST OFFICE +43 (0)572 00200; www.soelden.com

TIGNES, FRANCE

STATS: 2,100m; **Highest lift:** 3,450m; **Lifts:** 96; **Pistes:** 300km; **Closest airport:** Chambéry – 130km

WHY? Altitude, the vast ski area, and direct access to the Grande Motte glacier, are Tignes' recipe for sensational skiing. The modern, purpose-built (some might say a little ugly) resort is linked to the slopes of Val d'Isère (to form the Espace Killy ski area), but those staying in cheaper, less pretentious Tignes can get to the best slopes first. The season is long, too, running until 1 May, but 7 lifts on the glacier are open in the mornings until September, giving a vertical drop of 750m and making this a mecca for professional ski teams to stay in shape over the summer

GETTING THERE Hiring a car is best, and the drive should take under 2 hours. A taxi will be expensive – around €230 each way (try +33 (0)6 32 19 29 62; www.thecoolbus.co.uk). Transavoie (+33 (0)4 79 68 32 90; www.transavoie.com) has regular buses from Chambéry to Tignes, taking 2 hours and 30 minutes and costing €70 return. Alternatively, go by train to Bourg St Maurice, 30km away, and pick up a taxi or local bus

WHERE TO STAY Unlike many properties, the Alpaka Lodge (+33 (0)4 79 06 45 30; www.alpaka.com; doubles from €180, half board) accepts weekenders. Plus, there's a lively bar serving more than 100 cocktails

WHERE TO PARTY The tiny Jam bar is an unpretentious skiers' favourite, or head for the Loop, both in the main, Le Lac, area. Grizzly's is a laid-back bar in the Val Claret part of the resort. For late-night action, it's Jack's in Le Lac, and the Blue Girl in Val Claret

TOURIST OFFICE +33 (0)4 79 40 04 40; www.tignes.net

ALPE D'HUEZ, FRANCE

STATS: **Town altitude:** 1,860m; **Highest lift:** 3,330m; **Lifts:** 87; **Pistes:** 249km; **Closest airport:** Grenoble – 75km

WHY? A rival for nearby Les Deux Alpes for the title of France's ugliest resort, but there is one huge compensation – the skiing. The town itself is higher than the pistes in many resorts, and the skiing goes all the way to the top of the Pic Blanc at 3,330m. The Sarenne run from the top of Pic Blanc is a classic, the longest black run in the Alps, descending for 16km and dropping 2,000m. There are some great off-piste variations too

GETTING THERE Hiring a car is simplest; the drive is around 90 minutes. There are public buses, but you have to change at Grenoble bus station and connections can make the journey a nightmare. A taxi will cost around €170 (Taxi Chalvin: +33 (0)4 76 80 38 38). There are private shuttle buses run by Bensbus: www.bensbus.co.uk

WHERE TO STAY Les Grandes Rousses (+33 (0)4 76 11 42 42; www.hmc-hotels.com; doubles from €240, half board) is a wooden chalet-style building – one of the few attractive ones in town – and has a swimming pool

WHERE TO PARTY The Underground is good for après ski with regular live music. Later on, popular bars include Crowded House, Zoo, Freeride and Smithy's. For clubbing, it's off to the Igloo and Les Caves

TOURIST OFFICE +33 (0)4 76 11 44 44; www.alpedhuez.com

LES ARCS, FRANCE

➲ **STATS: Town altitude:** 1,600–2,000m; **Highest lift:** 3,250m; **Lifts:** 141; **Pistes:** 425km; **Closest airport:** Chambéry – 125km

➲ **WHY?** In 2003, the already sizeable resort of Les Arcs (with 56 lifts/200km of piste) was joined to La Plagne by a huge double-decker cable car. Together they make up the Paradiski, a truly vast area of high-altitude, snow-sure pistes. Unfortunately, due to 'safety concerns', the cable car was shut for the whole 2007/8 season, but the resorts say the closure won't be repeated. In Les Arcs there are 4 separate villages, from 1,600–2,000m in altitude

➲ **GETTING THERE** Train is a good option – travel direct from Paris to Bourg St Maurice, from where a funicular railway runs up to Arc 1600 in just 7 minutes. Or hire a car for the hour-and-a-half drive from Chambéry. A taxi will cost €225 each way (+33 (0)6 14 18 26 11; www.aarthur.fr)

➲ **WHERE TO STAY** The best in the resort is the Hôtel Grand Paradiso (+33 (0)4 79 07 65 00; www.grand-hotel-lesarcs.com; doubles from €290, half board), in Arc 1800, which blends modern design with traditional materials. The tourist board has a central reservation service so can help if you want somewhere cheaper

➲ **WHERE TO PARTY** Arc 1800 has the widest choice of, and liveliest, nightlife. The Jungle Café and Benjy's are popular bars, the Red Hot Saloon has a big dance floor and live bands, and is often followed by the Apokalypse, open till 4 a.m., and the Igloo

➲ **TOURIST OFFICE** +33 (0)4 79 07 12 57; www.lesarcs.com. See also www.paradiski.com

AVORIAZ, FRANCE

➲ **STATS: Town altitude:** 1,800m; **Highest lift:** 2,466m; **Lifts:** 208; **Pistes:** 650km; **Closest airport:** Geneva – 75 km

➲ **WHY?** The highest resort in the Portes du Soleil region, it also gives the easiest access to the area's best pistes – which are an intermediate's dream. It's a purpose-built place and its modernist architecture has put some off but, like Flaine, is now starting to be seriously appreciated once more. Don't miss the bragging rights that come with braving the infamous black run, the Wall

➲ **GETTING THERE** It's on a cliff above Morzine (an hour's drive), but the transfer takes a while longer – you can drive up the twisty mountain road and park your car (the centre of Avoriaz is car-free), which takes 20 minutes, or else take a taxi or bus to Morzine, then catch the Prodains cable car to Avoriaz. A taxi from the airport will cost around €125 to Morzine, for up to 4 people, or €145 to Avoriaz (+33 (0)6 09 33 99 44; www.acces-taxi.com). There are 3 public buses a day from the airport to Prodains, taking 2 hours 10 minutes and costing €63 (timetables at www.altibus.com)

➲ **WHERE TO STAY** The Hôtel les Dromots (+33 (0)4 94 97 91 91; www.christophe-leroy.com; doubles from €290, half board) is a unique place to stay, an original 1970s building which has been recently renovated and is full of retro-futurist touches such as sloping walls with huge round windows in them

➲ **WHERE TO PARTY** The Place has live music and is a good place to get ready for a night out in Le Yak nightclub. Le Shooters is a favourite bar too

➲ **TOURIST OFFICE** +33 (0)4 50 74 02 11; www.avoriaz.com

Party

SNOWBOMBING, AUSTRIA

17

AT ABOUT 6.45 A.M., I realize that I'm not going to make it skiing today. We're dancing at a rave in an underground car park, DJ and stacks of pounding speakers at one end, a makeshift bar on trestle tables at the other. The tightly packed crowd wears sunglasses, skinny jeans and asymmetric hairstyles. We could be in Hoxton or Hackney but, in fact, when we finally emerge up the stairs into the frail morning light, it's into the high street of a charming, traditional Tirolean village.

It's been a very long night, and a very long winter. This morning is 6 April, the final day of the ski season in Mayrhofen. And while I've seen some pretty wild scenes over the past few months – from the Krazy Kanguruh, to Club Moritzino, the Vault, the Cube and the Coco Club – nothing has prepared me for this. Snowbombing is quite simply the Olympics of après ski, the climax of the season's party calendar, the ultimate end-of-term blow-out.

To be honest, it's not really après ski at all. This is a full-on music festival that just happens to be taking place in the mountains. This year (2008) more than twenty live bands and seventy-five DJs have been shipped out from the UK to provide entertainment. Headlining bands include Foals, Dirty Pretty Things, Madness and The Whip. The DJ line-up boasts Calvin Harris, Erol Alkan, DJ Yoda, Radio 1's Annie Mac and the Scratch Perverts and ranges from the old guard, like Joy Division co-founder Peter Hook, to young pretenders like the Filthy Dukes. Watching them are three thousand revellers, known as Snowbombers.

Maybe it's because it's 7 a.m. and starting to snow but, as I walk home, the whole idea seems like a stroke of genius. In the late 1990s, Gareth Cooper, a tour operator from Manchester, had started to become bored with the cheesy euro-pop played in ski-resort nightclubs. 'We thought, well, if the mountain won't come to the music, the music will come to the mountains,' he says. So he set about organizing the first Snowbombing, and the spring of 2000 saw two hundred people, a few DJs and their record bags head for a week in the tiny French resort of Risoul. It was chaotic and disorganized but great fun and, since then, the event has grown and grown.

After moving around for a few years, Cooper brought Snowbombing to Mayrhofen in 2005 and realized he had found the perfect location. For a start, this is a town that embraces après ski with a passion all winter long, so the locals were unlikely to be easily shocked. And, crucially for such a late event, should there be little snow, it's just a twenty-minute, free bus ride up the valley to Hintertux, a glacier ski area with the country's highest ski lift and guaranteed skiing all summer long – not that skiing is really that high on the agenda for many Snowbombers.

Holding the festival in the last week of the season is a great idea too, as it means the hotels, which would otherwise be all but empty, are delighted to welcome even the rowdiest British clubbers with open arms. Prices are low, the days are sunny and the evenings long and warm. For the Snowbombers, it works as a natural bridge between the end of the ski season and the start of the summer festival season.

As I wander back to the hotel, the previous day's action on the slopes is a distant but happy memory. Mayrhofen sits among green fields at 630m on the floor of the Ziller valley. Admittedly, this is a little low for a serious ski resort, but mountains rise up almost vertically on either side. To the south, Austria's largest cable car, with room for 160 people, rises up to the Ahorn, a quiet area of mainly beginners' slopes. To the north, a gondola takes you from the village centre to the far larger Penken area.

We had spent the morning exploring the latter's 92km of slopes and twenty-four lifts. Though it isn't a high area, with the top lift at 2,500m and most of the skiing under 2,000m, it had been snowing all the previous week and the conditions were excellent.

Heavy snow can't dampen an impromptu rave at 2,000m

SNOWBOMBING is quite simply the Olympics of après ski, the climax of the season's party calendar, the ultimate end-of-term blow-out.

Austria's steepest piste (allegedly)

There are lots of good intermediate runs here and pretty views across the Ziller valley, plus the Harakiri, a black run marked with special warning signs, which the resort claims is the steepest piste in the country, with a gradient of 78 per cent. 'It takes nerves of steel and advanced skiing skills to conquer this monster of a mountain,' it says on the piste map.

(Actually, I think there's a bit of hyperbole going on with the gradient because, yesterday, the monster was being conquered by numerous small children who went zooming straight down in a tuck, giggling manically.)

From the middle of the Penken ski area, a new cable car that holds up to 150 people whisks you up to the Horberg ridge, giving access to the long, curving red piste 16 and some equally long, beautiful off-piste routes. Though it is April, there was a metre of powder yesterday morning and I lapped the cable car, coming down steep, open snowfields, then between widely spaced bushes clinging to little gullies reminiscent of the heliskiing terrain above Krasnaya Polyana, Russia. I stuck to the north-facing slopes, where the snow was light and deep, but on the south-facing side opposite, suicidal snowboarders slid down between the scores of very recent avalanches, even as the spring sun grew ever warmer.

Facing the off-piste slopes is the huge funpark, with half-pipe, rails and massive kickers, all of them bigger than those anywhere else we've visited for this book. Top snowboarders from across Europe were doing colossal leaps, competing in the final of Snowbombing's Highway to Hell competition, while beats pumped out from the packed terrace of the Grillhofalm bar at the bottom of the park. Actually, I think the crowd was more interested in lying in the sun and checking out the DJ, each other and the bar than the spins, flips and leaps of the skiers and boarders above them.

Tricks in the park, with the Grillhofalm below

THERE ARE ONLY five hours in every twenty-four when there isn't some music event going on.

Dancing in the sun at the top of the Ahorn cable car

Arriving at the dance floor, on skis

Though the snow was deep, the sun was hot and, by 2 p.m., the powder was getting heavy and sticky. It was high time for the après ski to begin in earnest, so we settled in at the Mountain Stage, sitting on the snow by the top of the Penken lift, where the Sketches and I Call Shotgun were rocking out in the sun.

Snowbombing is very good at throwing up music venues in the most unlikely places. The night before we'd followed a trail of signs saying 'Madness this way'. In this resort, this week, madness was pretty much in every direction, but the signs guided us to a path through a forest, past a brass band playing Queen covers and to a clearing surrounded by a few wooden chalets. And there, the ska veterans of North London, in trademark sharp suits and hats, performed what must have been one of the most bizarre gigs of their career. A thousand partygoers, jumping around to 'Our House' and 'Baggy Trousers', in a dark and freezing Austrian forest.

Back down in town, the partying had kicked up a

gear by 4 p.m., when the Snowbombing Street Party took over Mayrhofen's main street. Snowbombers seem to love nothing more than fancy dress – all weekend the pistes and dance floors are dotted with superhero costumes – but this was the chance to really go to town. And so the street, where temporary bars and outdoor stages had been set out, thronged with Snow Whites and dwarves, every kind of lion, bear, badger and chipmunk, an excellent Adam Ant and a disturbingly well-executed Osama bin Laden.

Pacing yourself is an art form here. It would be even if you were here just for one night, but Snowbombing runs for a whole week, with entertainment on six days running from 12 noon to 7 a.m. Yes, there are only five hours in each twenty-four when there isn't some music event going on. Lots of Snowbombers do come for the whole week, buying a package of accommodation and festival wristband to gain access to the events, which starts at around £350. Unless you are still at university and

VANS

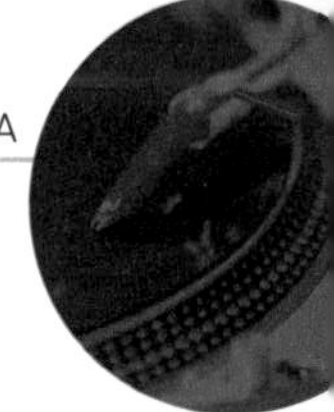

PRO SNOWBOARDERS from across Europe are doing colossal leaps.

so properly match fit, a long weekend will give you plenty of time to have your fill of partying. Fly to either Innsbruck (closer, at about sixty minutes' drive, but with fewer flights and more susceptible to fog delays) or Munich (about two hours' drive), from where the festival organizers arrange transfer buses.

Accommodation is better than at any festival you've ever been to. The party HQ is the Strass Hotel, a four-star place right beside the Penken lift, with a big spa, a bar for live music and several restaurants. Unless you really want to party twenty-four hours a day, I'd choose the Sporthotel Manni, where we're staying, just down the road from the Strass. Another four-star, it has spacious rooms, really charming staff, a roof-top swimming pool and lavish buffet breakfasts to feel guilty about missing each morning.

By 8 p.m. the fancy-dress street carnival was winding down and we were ready to tackle the next phase of the party marathon. We caught the Ahorn cable car, open late specially for the event, up to the other ski area on the south side of the town. At the top cable-car station, we picked up flaming torches then followed a line of lanterns over a few folds and hollows of snow until, suddenly, we came over the brow to see what must be the most memorable party venue in the world: a complex of huge igloos known as the Arctic Disco.

Out in the front were speakers and a long bar, and bonfires around which people were dancing. Inside, we pushed past some animal skins, headed down a long tunnel and emerged into one of four big, domed rooms made entirely of ice. The biggest – and here it starts getting really bizarre – had a DJ booth carved into the wall, in which Krafty Kuts was scratching away, to the crowd's delight. Around the back are several romantic smaller igloos where you can stay the night (expedition sleeping bags are provided) and get up to watch the sunrise over the mountains.

We danced inside the igloo until it grew so hot the walls were melting, then we danced some more outside under the starry sky. Eventually, we skidded and slipped back across the piste to catch the lift down to the town, and a hundred people started doing the conga around the cable car – hilarious and terrifying in equal measure.

The pros battle it out in the Highway to Hell competition

1|2
|3
|4
5
6

THE INSIDE TRACK

Olly Dixon DJ, Filthy Dukes

'If you need to take some time out from skiing, or partying too, go to the train station and hire a bike. It's cheap – €8 for half a day. Head south out of the village and cycle along following the river until you get to a deep gorge. Get off, leave the bikes (no one's going to steal them round here) and climb down the stairs to the bottom of the gorge, where there's a rocky beach beside the river. It's an amazing oasis of beauty, and the water is a stunning blue-grey, mineral-infused colour.'

Back on the valley floor, Snowbombing had taken over the town, with venues in every corner. We started in the Europahaus, the town's biggest venue, watching the Filthy Dukes, then moved to the Arena for DJ Yoda, back to the Europahaus for Erol Alkan, to the Schlüssel for Streetlife DJs and, finally, to the Garage for Tristan da Cunha. In all the venues the sound systems and light shows are almost as slick and professional as you'd find in a big London club, and yet the really nice thing, even the crucial thing, about the entire event, is that it still feels utterly uncommercial – more like a group of friends having fun than a business venture. The musicians finish their sets then come down to the dance floor to join in with the punters. Everyone talks to everyone else, and three thousand people is a small enough group that you're soon bumping into people you've met earlier. There's no posing or trying to look cool and, certainly, despite all the hours of boozing, no aggro. It's all about being silly, friendly and happy.

Maybe I'm getting a bit tired and over-emotional, but then, it has been a very long night.

1 *Suggs from Madness plays the coldest gig of his career*
2-3 *Dancing on ice in the Arctic Disco*
4 *Comedy breakdance crew the Cuban Brothers*
5 *Snowbombers are never out of fancy dress*
6 *Live music is never far away, however odd*

The Knowledge
Mayrhofen, Austria

STATS **Town altitude:** 630m **Highest lift:** 2,500m; **Lifts:** 48 **Pistes:** 157km
Lift pass: €36 per day **Closest airport:** Innsbruck – 65km

➔ WHY? Mayrhofen is party-mad all winter long, but nothing in the mountains can rival the revelry that takes place in the final week of the season, when Snowbombing hits town **➔ GETTING THERE** Innsbruck is closest, an easy hour's drive, but some flights there stop at the end of March, before the Snowbombing week. Instead, fly to Munich (190km away, but the drive is almost all on motorway so it takes a little over 2 hours), or Salzburg (170km and 3 hours) **➔ TRANSFERS** A taxi is reasonable value from Innsbruck, but it will probably work out cheaper to hire a car from Munich. A taxi pick-up from Innsbruck will cost around €100 for up to 3, €140 for up to 7 (+43 (0)528 562260; www.taxikroell.com) and €260/€320 from Munich. From Innsbruck airport you can reach Mayrhofen by train in under 2 hours – take a taxi or shuttle bus from the airport to the main station (15 minutes), then take a train to Jenbach (33 minutes) and connect with the train that runs along the Ziller valley to Mayrhofen (56 minutes). See www.oebb.at for timetables **➔ WHERE TO STAY** Sporthotel Manni (+43 (0)528 5633010; www.mannis.at; doubles from €150, including breakfast) is a friendly four-star with good food and a dramatic roof-top pool. The Sporthotel Strass (+43 (0)528 56705; www.hotelstrass.com; doubles from €164, including breakfast) is the epicentre of Snowbombing – lively and noisy round the clock. The Gasthof Brücke (+43 (0)528 562232; www.gasthof-bruecke.com; doubles from €110, including breakfast) also gets good reviews **➔ WHERE TO SKI** The Ahorn sector to the south-east of the village is a great spot for learners. Others should head up to the far larger Penken area on the opposite side of town. Boarders and freestylers will love the Penken Park, a huge area of jumps and half-pipes beside the Sunjet lift. Off-pisters should take the nearby 150er-Tux cable car to access some excellent faces (but take care, some are very avalanche prone). Intermediates will enjoy long blue run 7a from the Horberg peak and blue piste 6 from the top of the Horbergjoch chair, the highest lift. Good piste skiers should have a go at the Harakiri, supposedly 'Austria's steepest piste' with a gradient of 78 per cent – although it sounds less impressive when you convert that to 38 degrees

WHERE TO EAT On the mountain, relax on the terrace of the Grillhofalm (+43 (0)664 5403066), just at the bottom of the Penken Park – so you can watch the stunts as you chill out (it also has rooms if you want a night away from the action in town). Back in the high street, Coup (+43 (0)528 563665) is a relaxed, upmarket bar/restaurant. If you're in need of belly timber to soak up the booze, head to the Kebab Shop, opposite the Penken cable car and slightly up the hill, which also does huge pizza slices, or Hans, the butcher directly opposite the cable car, which does great roast-pork rolls. For something different, try Wirtshaus Zum Griena (+43 (0)528 562778; www.griena.at) a 440-year-old former farmhouse serving traditional dishes like venison and dumplings **WHERE TO PARTY** During Snowbombing there are at least seven main music venues and nightly one-off parties in lots of different locations. The biggest venue is the Europahaus, a converted conference hall which does a good impression of a cavernous nightclub. Then there is the Schlüssel, a Tirolean, wooden-beamed après-ski joint close to the Ahorn cable car. The Garage, underneath the Hotel Strass, goes on till 7 a.m. **HELP!** Snowbombing (0161 610 2000; www.snowbombing.com) acts as a tour operator for the event, selling packages including accommodation and a festival wristband that gives access to all the clubs and bars. It can also arrange transfers, lift passes and ski hire. The packages are for a minimum of six nights but are cheap enough to still be the best option for most weekenders – a 6-night package in the Strass or Manni hotels costs around £379, including the festival wristband (which in 2008 cost £149 if sold separately) but not flights. Packages staying in self-catering apartments cost from £239 **TOURIST OFFICE** +43 (0)5285 6760; www.mayrhofen.at

DJ Krafty Kuts (and friend) in the icy booth of the Arctic Disco

Three More... For Partying

ISCHGL, AUSTRIA

➔ STATS: **Town altitude:** 1,400m; **Highest lift:** 2,872m; **Lifts:** 40; **Pistes:** 235km; **Closest airport:** Innsbruck – 86km

➔ **WHY?** Ischgl may be little known in Britain (although it's becoming more so), but its nightlife is famous across Europe. Several times a season there are big-name concerts up at Idalp, a confluence of pistes at 2,320m – recent headliners include Elton John, Diana Ross and Rihanna. Down in the village, the streets are jammed full of drinking skiers by 4 p.m. and, in the evening, there is a huge range of clubs and even Vegas-style music and dance spectaculars. There's great skiing too. Intermediates will love the long run that takes you away from the pistes and lifts, down a long ravine and through a forest to Samnaun, an isolated Swiss village. Experts will be pleasantly surprised – a guide can reveal some serious couloirs and powder fields that stay untracked for days after snowfall because most people in town are too busy partying to care

➔ **GETTING THERE** Hire a car for the hour-and-a-half drive, or take a taxi, which will cost €150 each way (+43 (0)544 45757; www.taxi-ischgl.at). Alternatively, take the shuttle bus from the airport to Innsbruck station, train to Landeck (direct, 45 minutes), then Postbus 4240 to Ischgl (leaving hourly, and taking 55 minutes)

➔ **WHERE TO STAY** The Hotel Madlein (+43 (0)544 45226; www.madlein.com; doubles from €320, half board) was the first Design Hotel in the Alps and is by far the coolest place to stay in town. Or try the Jägerhof (+43 (0)544 45206; www.jaegerhof-ischgl.at; doubles from €150), which is central and friendly

➔ **WHERE TO PARTY** Après-ski hotspots are the Schatzi Bar in the Hotel Elizabeth, close to the bottom of the Pardatschgrat lift (complete with saucy dancers in traditional Austrian dirndl dresses) and the Trofana Alm, an old wooden barn near the bottom of the Silvrettabahn. Later on, head to Pacha, the club in the Hotel Madlein, one of the best in the Alps. The Madlein also has Coyote Ugly, a table-dancing bar, one of three in town

➔ **TOURIST OFFICE** +43 (0)509 90100; www.ischgl.com

LAAX, SWITZERLAND

➔ STATS: **Town altitude:** 1,100m; **Highest lift:** 3,018m; **Lifts:** 27; **Pistes:** 220km; **Closest airport:** Friedrichshafen – 100km

➔ **WHY?** The hip Riders Palace crossed design hotel and backpacker hostel to create a mecca for young snowboarders and put the beautiful village of Laax on the party map. Really, though, if you're looking to party, you need to come during the Brits (usually late March or early April), a major snowboarding and freestyle-skiing competition which is the excuse for a week of full-on parties, gigs and special events

➔ **GETTING THERE** The tourist office arranges a transfer bus from Zurich (150km away) on Thursdays, Saturdays and Sundays, and daily to meet Ryanair flights into Friedrichshafen. It costs CHF135/£66 return and takes 90 minutes; details from the tourist office, as below. Or hire a car, or take the train from Zurich airport station to Chur, from where regular local buses take 50 minutes to Laax (see www.sbb.ch)

➔ **WHERE TO STAY** The Riders Palace (+41(0)81 927 97 00; www.riderspalace.com) has 3-night packages, including 3-day lift pass, from CHF224/£110 per person in a 5-bedded 'back to basics' room, or CHF379/£186 per person in a 'multimedia double', with surround sound and Xbox gaming system

➔ **WHERE TO PARTY** The Crap bar, at the bottom of the lifts, is the place for après ski and gets wild during the Brits. The Riders Palace has its own Lobby bar and Palace Club, which are good fun. There's also the Chesa Veglia disco

➔ **TOURIST OFFICE** +41 (0)81 927 77 77; www.laax.com

SAUZE D'OULX, ITALY

➔ STATS: **Town altitude:** 1,510m; **Highest lift:** 2,825m; **Lifts:** 78; **Pistes:** 400km; **Closest airport:** Turin – 84km

➔ **WHY?** Back in the 1980s, when skiing was enjoying its first boom, Sauze d'Oulx and, in particular, Andy Cap's bar, got such a reputation for the antics of its binge-drinking Brits that it started making tabloid headlines at home. Today, it's slightly more sophisticated, with some cool bars in the attractive core of the medieval village, but Sauze remains a hard-drinking party hotspot, with a decidedly British flavour. It's also part of the Milky Way ski circuit, with good links to Sestriere and Sansicario, so there's plenty of piste

➔ **GETTING THERE** The resort is just off the motorway, so driving should take under an hour. Hiring a car also means you can drive up to the neighbouring resorts like Montgenèvre and Sestriere (to where the skiing link sometimes doesn't open in times of poor snow). A taxi

will cost around €150 each way; book through the hotel, as it's hard to find a taxi driver who speaks English. Public buses run from the airport twice a day on Saturdays and Sundays (see www.cavourese.it). Finally, you can taxi from the airport to Turin Porta Susa station, take the train to Oulx (about an hour), then a taxi for 10 minutes up the hill to the resort

WHERE TO STAY The slope-side Stella Alpina (+39 0122 858731; www.stellalpinahotel.it; doubles from €90, including breakfast) welcomes short-break bookings, and the British owner Caroline Eydallin will arrange taxis, ski hire, lessons and lift passes

WHERE TO PARTY The New Scotch Bar, under the Stella Alpina, does excellent mulled wine and is good for après ski. Later on, head for Moncrons (a cocktail bar) the Cotton Club, Max's, Scatto Matto, Gran Trun and Ghost. The Schuss disco is open till 4 a.m.

TOURIST OFFICE +39 0122 858009; www.vialattea.it, and www.montagnedoc.net

MORE FESTIVALS

Inspired by the success of Snowbombing and the Brits, festivals are opening up all over the Alps. These are some of the key ones, although they have a habit of changing names and times, swapping resorts and going out of business, so double check this season's dates before booking flights

TIGNESFEST: Tignes, France, mid-April. Started in 2008 and boasted one key advantage – it was totally free. See www.tignesfest.com

X-BOX: Val d'Isère, France, first weekend of March. One of Europe's top snowboard and freestyle-ski competitions, it's also the wildest weekend of the year in the resort. See www.valdisere.com

ALTITUDE: Méribel, France, mid-April. A comedy festival organized by stand-up Marcus Brigstocke. In 2008 it featured performances by Lee Mack, Rich Hall and Ed Byrne, as well as freestyle skiing events and music from bands like the Dub Pistols. See www.altitudefestival.com

18

Late Snow

RIKSGRÄNSEN, SWEDEN

WHEN EUROPE'S RESORTS are winding down, Riksgränsen is only just beginning to swing.

IT'S THE FIRST WEEKEND in June. London has been sweltering for weeks, the grass in Hyde Park is turning yellow, Wimbledon is only three weeks away, and we are pushing through Paddington station with skis on our shoulders.

Sometimes, the ski season simply isn't long enough. You come down the final run of the winter and the despondency swells as you contemplate the nine long months stretching ahead before you get to take the next chairlift back up. But there is a solution: a tiny, remote outpost where snow addicts can quietly slip off for a weekend fix to get them through the summer.

It's almost unknown among British skiers but, as the last snows melt in St Anton, Verbier and Engelberg, the name Riksgränsen begins to be passed in excited whispers between ski bums who don't want to go home. When summer comes to the Alps, the serious skiers head to the Arctic.

As Robin and I sit, sweating, on the packed Heathrow Express, Riksgränsen seems like the stuff of fantasy. It is 360km north of the Arctic Circle, in Swedish Lapland, the most northerly ski resort in the world. When Europe's resorts are winding down, its season is only just beginning to swing; its lifts start in mid-February and run almost until the end of June. Because it is so far north, they can't open the lifts any earlier because it would be dark for most of the day but, by May, the opposite becomes true – the sun never properly sets, so the lifts can stay open until after midnight. But perhaps what's most amazing of all is that travelling from summer back to winter can be done in just a few hours.

We fly from London to Kiruna, a coal-mining town in northern Sweden, changing planes in Stockholm. Snow is lying on the ground as we emerge from the tiny terminal, blinking in the harsh light, and it feels like we've come to the very edge of civilization. Snowfields stretch away all around, and the dreary bulk of Kiruna's ice-encrusted slagheap looms in the distance. And yet, waiting alongside us for the bus are at least twenty American ski dudes in caps, sunglasses, studded belts and low-slung jeans – professional skiers and boarders heading to a freeride competition at Riksgränsen. Their West-coast accents couldn't be more at odds with the surroundings, and they round off what has already been quite a surreal morning.

The bus appears and we set off on the 130km ride north to the resort, dodging the reindeer which wander into the middle of the road, oblivious. The road skirts huge sparkling fjords, and pure-white pyramidal peaks tower above us. To the left runs a single-track railway, built at the end of the nineteenth century to transport the iron ore north from Kiruna to the port of Narvik, on Norway's coast. Ironically, it was this arduous industrial feat which helped create the skiers' playground we're heading for.

In 1902 the rails being built from the Swedish and Norwegian sides were finally linked at the border, Riksgränsen (which literally means state border). To celebrate, an elaborate wooden station was built, second in size only to that in Stockholm, with covered platforms to keep travellers warm, numerous waiting rooms and an adjoining hotel. Of course, there was nothing else there at all, and no reason to get off the train, so the vast white elephant was demolished after just twelve years. In 1930 the railway company tried again to promote Riksgränsen as a destination, this time building a modest hotel for visiting skiers, later run as a sort of youth hostel. It never looked back: the country's first ski school was established there in 1934, and more lifts and holiday houses were gradually added.

Today, the railway line still cuts through the centre of the resort, and with snow falling hard as our bus pulls up, it's easy to imagine that not a vast amount has changed since the 1930s. There's just one central hotel building, surrounded by a variety of smaller

Après ski on the terrace of the Riksgränsen Hotel

ICY PEAKS, glaciers and snowfields stretch away in every direction, all turned a hundred exquisite shades of pink and red by the weak midnight sun.

houses, huts and outbuildings. All are clad in wooden clapboard and painted in the same dark red. Against the treeless, snow-covered mountains and rocks, the place looks a little like a polar research station. Inside, the main hotel still feels a bit youth-hostelly too. There's waterproof rubber flooring in the lobby, a noticeboard announcing the day's activities and a small shop and café.

Actually, for one establishment, the hotel does a remarkable job of catering for all tastes and budgets. For the cash-strapped ski bum, there are 'skiers' rooms' – tiny cabins off a long corridor sleeping two or three on various combinations of sofa-beds and fold-down bunks. There's a TV, a phone, a Lilliputian bathroom with shower and a laughably flimsy curtain, given the twenty-four-hour sunlight (do not forget an eye mask). Moving up the scale, there are some standard-size double hotel rooms, kitted out in contemporary Scandinavian style, and self-catering apartments sleeping between two and eight. A few metres from the main lobby is a separate building that once housed a meteorological research station and in 2006 was converted into Meteorologen, a four-star, boutique hotel within a hotel, with fourteen stylish rooms and a funky bar and restaurant.

We shower, have a burger and a few rounds of Spendrups, the local lager, then, at about 9 p.m., head back to our rooms to get into our ski stuff. On Fridays, from mid-May onwards, the lifts close at 4 p.m. but reopen at 10 p.m. for skiing under the midnight sun.

The drinks are expensive, the heliskiing is a bargain

So, on the same day we left baking London, we are riding up a chair lift in the Arctic, shivering slightly and anxious to get moving. The resort sits huddled close in to the bottom of a steep, snowy slope but, as the chairlift takes us up over the brow of the hill, a huge view of the high Arctic plateau opens. Icy peaks, glaciers and snowfields stretch away in every direction, all turned a hundred exquisite shades of pink and red by the weak midnight sun. In the far distance, beyond miles of barren wilderness, we can just make out the frozen waters of Norwegian fjords.

It has to be said, though, that while the light and the views are enough to bring a lump to your throat, especially with emotions sharpened by Spendrups, the skiing itself is a bit sketchy. Those watery red sunbeams carry no heat, and it's bitterly cold. The pistes, which had become slushy in the afternoon sun, have now frozen into rock-solid ruts and bumps, making our skis clatter about manically. Falling is not comfortable, either. So, shortly after midnight, we retire back to the bar for the second bout of après ski in a single day.

Next morning, we're up early to explore the area properly. While Riksgränsen's latitude is unrivalled, its altitude and other vital statistics look downright weedy. There are just six lifts, rising to a high point of 909m. Ski from very top to very bottom and you drop just 400m. The sixteen pistes, almost all blues and reds, are enough to keep an early intermediate busy for a couple of days, but little more. At first, it seems

1|2
3
4
5
6
1329
HELINORD

as if it doesn't add up – how can such a place have earned the right to be talked of in tones of reverence by gnarly freeriders across Europe?

But, as the morning wears on, it starts to become clear. While the odd family is pootling down the pistes, pretty much everyone else is ignoring them completely, heading off wherever they fancy to get fresh tracks in the soft spring snow. 'Riksgränsen is all about freedom, exploring and finding your own way down,' Robert Lindstedt, the resort manager, tells me later. 'Some resorts take your lift pass away if you go off piste – not here.'

Occasionally, we see small groups gathered to watch each other take off from the wind-lips and rocky outcrops which provide natural launching points across the area. These lumps and bumps are the terrain that has made the place famous, and draw freeriders and boarders from around the world.

But even if, like me, you have no desire to throw yourself off cliffs or find yourself in thin air, the off-piste skiing here has one great advantage. The entire Riksgränsen hotel complex can host a maximum of six hundred people. It's a tiny number of people on the mountain (some Alpine resorts get ten thousand skiers a day). The result is that you can be close to the marked runs, a ten-minute ski from a beer back at base, and find yourself utterly alone, with a field of untouched powder stretching before you.

For keen skiers, there's another major draw too – probably the cheapest heliskiing in the world. Sign up for a heliski trip in Canada and you're looking at thousands of dollars. Here, you can get to taste the sport's most exclusive delights for around £60 a go. We sign up for a package of three helicopter lifts, each taking us to the top of a different nearby peak. Including guide and equipment hire, it came to just 2,195 kronor – £180. It's all done with the minimum of fuss too. You just put your name on the list in the morning and the guide calls you on your mobile when it's time for you to go.

We're led down to the helipad, actually a little gravel area at the side of the hotel car park, and given a safety briefing. I'm not sure if this is a reason why it's so cheap, but the little red helicopter doesn't look hugely hi-tech or state of the art. Instead of light-weight fibreglass and carbon, this has big metal door handles that look as if they're from a 1960s Ford Transit. It's an Alouette 3 of a type first built in 1970, but the guide assures us that the exhaustive maintenance regime means age makes no difference.

Soon, we're soaring up over the slopes and touching down on the 1,463m-high summit of Vassitjåkka. We crouch in the snow as the pilot lifts off and veers sharply away. It's an amazing moment, the absolute silence all the more startling after the clatter of rotors and buffeting downdraft.

The descent is simply fabulous. We carve huge, high-speed arcs in the buttery spring snow, leaving enormous S-shaped signatures on what had been an untouched mountainside. The initial steep slopes level and open out into a wide hidden valley where

1 *The ski resort grew out of a border-post railway station*

2 *Skiing under the midnight sun*

3 *The helipad, right beside the hotel*

4 *Traditional turf-roofed huts*

5-6 *Though in the middle of nowhere, in May and June Riksgränsen draws ski fanatics from around Europe*

Anna and Tom labour up Nordalsfjäll

we ski past a family of reindeer before pulling up to wait for the chopper. Saturday afternoons really don't come better than this.

That evening we treat ourselves to a meal in Lapplandia, the hotel's gourmet restaurant. It serves traditional Lapland food but with a decidedly chi-chi twist – the reindeer comes lightly smoked with chanterelle sformato and parsley root, the elk has a chilli and liquorice marinade. It's delicious, but not cheap: the set menu costs £39 per person, à la carte mains as much as £18, and a bottle of house red £16.

But the high drink prices don't appear to put people off. Next door, the bar/nightclub is heaving. It's still half light outside, but the dance floor is rocking. 'Swedish men are so nervous,' one girl tells us mournfully at the bar. 'They can't actually talk to girls so they just get really drunk, then lurch over and ask if we'll sleep with them . . .'

On Sunday morning one of the guides, Anna Thoursie, leads us up Nordalsfjäll, a peak just behind the main ski area. We traverse over from the lift, put skis on our rucksacks then start slogging up the slope, hearts pounding and heads throbbing. Thankfully, frozen footsteps remain from the previous day to ease the way and in forty-five minutes we reach the top. From here, there are numerous routes, ranging from white open powder-fields to seriously steep 50- degree rock-strewn chutes. This really is the beauty of the skiing here – that a short hike from the lifts, there is so much off-piste terrain. But it's not just that . . .

On Monday morning we have to take the 11 a.m. bus to get back to Kiruna for our 2 p.m. flight. Robin sleeps in, but I take the first lift up then quickly retrace our steps to the top of Nordalsfjäll. Standing at the top, alone, all I can see for miles and miles is white, frozen wilderness, rolling peaks, distant fjords and the blue ice of glaciers. At 9 p.m. that night, I'll be back having a pint in my local in London, worrying about the week ahead at work but, for now, I'm a tiny dot in the Arctic wastes, with nothing between me and the North Pole and not a care in the world.

THE INSIDE TRACK

Krister Jonsson Heliski Guide

'Don't miss a drink in Låktatjåkko Lodge, the highest bar in Sweden. It's an old wooden mountain hut, 1,228m up, with a small bar, ten beds and a sauna. There are no roads, but you can get there on skis, snowshoes, snowmobiles or in a helicopter. I usually do a ski tour, starting at Kopparasen, which is fifteen minutes by car from Riksgränsen, then climb up the Låktatjåkka peak at 1,404m, before dropping down to the hut. There, we have waffles, for which it's famous, with cloudberry sauce and some schnapps, then watch the sunset through the big windows before skiing back down.'

Låktatjåkko Lodge: +46 (0)980 64100; www.bjorkliden.com

In the nightclub the blinds are drawn to keep out the midnight sun

THE HIGH DRINK prices don't appear to be putting people off.

The Knowledge
Riksgränsen, Sweden

STATS **Town altitude:** 504m **Highest lift:** 909m; **Lifts:** 6
Pistes: 45km **Lift pass:** £22 per day **Closest airport:** Harstad-Narvik – 85km

WHY? Unless you go to Chile or Argentina, there's no better place to extend your ski season. The lifts run until 24 June **GETTING THERE** It's literally in the middle of nowhere – 360km north of the Arctic circle on the Swedish/Norwegian border – but travel is surprisingly easy. Harstad-Narvik in Norway is the closest airport, but more people fly to Kiruna in Sweden, 130km away. SAS (for contact details, see Airline Directory, page 286) fly from Heathrow to Kiruna, via Stockholm. It costs from £180 and journey time is about 5 hours and 30 minutes. Beware Ryanair: their flights to Stockholm go to Skavsta and Västerås airports, 112km and 72km from Arlanda, from where all connecting flights to Kiruna depart. If the flight times don't suit, look into the Norwegian option. Flights from Olso International to Harstad-Narvik with Norwegian Air Shuttle cost as little as £75, and you can get to Oslo International from Stansted, Gatwick and Edinburgh with Norwegian Air Shuttle, or Nottingham and Gatwick with Sterling, or from various other departure points with BMI and SAS. The disadvantage is that the timetables mean you may have to overnight in Oslo on the way out. Finally, tour operator Discover the World (01737 218800; www.discovertheworld.co.uk) runs direct charter flights from Heathrow to Kiruna, available if you book a package including accommodation and transfers **TRANSFERS** From Kiruna, regular buses run direct to the resort, taking 90 minutes (details: +46 (0)771 100110; www.ltnbd.se). From Harstad-Narvik, there are buses (www.nordtrafikk.no), but you need to change in Narvik town centre. Better to hire a car for the incredibly scenic drive (Avis, Europcar, Hertz and Budget have desks at the airport) **WHERE TO STAY** All the accommodation options are booked through Hotel Riksgränsen (+46 (0)980 40080; www.riksgransen.nu). Hardcore ski bums on a budget can share a tiny 2- or 3-person 'skiers' room' for £32pppn, including a great breakfast buffet. For something more romantic, get a room in the funky, boutiquey Meteorologen Lodge, from £135 for a double room

Anna braves the wind at the summit of Nordalsfjäll

➔ WHERE TO SKI The long, red, Gränsleden piste has amazing views and a unique selling point – it starts and ends in Sweden but switches for most of its length into Norway. Really, though, it's all about the off piste: hiking up Nordalsfjäll for a huge choice of lines or making the most of the bargain heliskiing (book on arrival through the hotel) **➔ WHERE TO EAT** The restaurant of the Meteorologen Lodge, open to non-residents, wins on ambience and its fine wine list. A 3-course meal with wine will cost about £45. Bookings are essential (+46 (0)735 032417 or via the hotel reception) **➔ WHERE TO PARTY** There's only one option: the Grönan bar and nightclub in the basement of the main hotel. There are live bands (look out for Kelly Bacon and the Rocker), DJs and lots of serious drinking. It's not cheap – a Spendrups beer will set you back around £5 – but this doesn't seem to deter anyone

➔ HELP! If you'd like someone to arrange your trip for you, Original Travel (0207 978 7333; www.originaltravel.co.uk) offers a 4-night package from £850 **➔ TOURIST OFFICE** +46 980 18880; www.lappland.se. See also www.swedishlapland.com. Or contact Visit Sweden in London on 0207 108 6168; www.visitsweden.com

Five More... For Late Snow

KAPRUN, AUSTRIA

➜ STATS: **Town altitude:** 785m; **Highest lift:** 3,029m; **Lifts:** 28; **Pistes:** 59km; **Closest airport:** Salzburg – 80km

➜ WHY? During the main ski season, Kaprun is overshadowed by larger, livelier, Zell am See (which has 77km of its own pistes and is included on the same lift pass). But when Zell's lifts shut around 14 April, attention turns to Kaprun, where the lifts on the Kitzsteinhorn glacier remain open year round, apart from a short summer break, usually 2–20 June
➜ GETTING THERE Until the end of March, there are shuttle buses 4 times a day from Wednesday to Sunday, taking 90 minutes and costing €51 return (booking and timetables: +43 (0)654 25499; www.vorderegger.at). Later than that, hire a car or book a taxi, which will take just over an hour and cost €120 each way for up to 8 (+43 (0)650 8502501; www.taxi-oberkofler.at)
➜ WHERE TO STAY The four-star Hotel Rudolfshof (+43 (0)6547 7183; www.rudolfshof.com; doubles from €140, half board) is good value, with excellent 4-course dinners, plus a spa with indoor pool and 4 saunas
➜ WHERE TO PARTY Kaprun's Baum Bar is the busiest nightclub in the region, open until early morning. Also try Kitsch & Bitter, which does good cocktails and has live bands on Fridays
➜ TOURIST OFFICE +43 (0)654 2770; www.zellamsee-kaprun.com. For skiing info, see www.kitzsteinhorn.at

VAL THORENS, FRANCE

➜ STATS: **Town altitude:** 2,300m; **Highest lift:** 3,230m; **Lifts:** 183; **Pistes:** 600km; **Closest airport:** Chambéry – 112km

➜ WHY? The superlatives are hard to ignore – this is Europe's highest ski resort, and sits at the top of Les Trois Vallées, the world's largest interlinked ski area. The season usually runs from 24 November all the way to 4 May. Some people complain that it's an ugly, purpose-built resort, and that it's so high there are no trees but, in April, nowhere else offers such a good guarantee of snow, over so many miles of piste
➜ GETTING THERE TransSavoie (+33 (0)4 79 68 32 90; www.transavoie.com) runs buses direct from Chambéry to Val Thorens, which take 2 hours 45 minutes and cost around €70 return. A hire car is a far better option from Chambéry or Geneva airport unless you're alone
➜ WHERE TO STAY You can ski right to the door of the three-star Le Val Chavière (+33 (0)4 79 00 00 33; www.hotel-valthorens.com; doubles from €140, half board)
➜ WHERE TO PARTY Val T is shaking off its once dour reputation and becoming known for nightlife as well as skiing, helped by the TransalpineXS dance-music festival in late March. Head for the Frog and Rosbif and take the Frog Yard Challenge – down the selection of shooters in under 30 seconds and you drink for free all night
➜ TOURIST OFFICE +33 (0)4 79 00 08 08; www.valthorens.com

HINTERTUX, AUSTRIA

➜ STATS: **Town altitude:** 1,500m; **Highest lift:** 3,250m; **Lifts:** 62; **Pistes:** 227km; **Closest airport:** Innsbruck – 90km

➜ WHY? Because it's one of the very few places you can ski 365 days of the year. In the main ski season, Hintertux's 21 lifts and 86km of piste are linked by shuttle bus, taking 20 minutes, to Mayrhofen and Finkenberg, together forming the 'Ski and Glacierworld Zillertal 3000' ski area, with 227km of pistes. Mayrhofen and Finkenberg shut down around 18 April, but Hintertux keeps going, with around 60–70km of skiing up until 24 May, and usually at least 9 lifts and 18km of piste operating right through the summer
➜ GETTING THERE Hire a car for the 90-minute drive. A taxi will cost €150 each way for up to 3, or €40pp for larger groups (+43 (0)528 71718; www.taxi-tux.at). You can take the train from Innsbruck station to Mayrhofen (change at Jenbach) then a bus/taxi, but this will take about 2 hours and 30 minutes
➜ WHERE TO STAY The four-star Vierjahreszeiten (+43 (0)528 78525; www.vierjahreszeiten.at; doubles from €162, half board) is close to the lifts and has a sauna and gym. Or try the Neuhintertux (+43 (0)5287 8580; www.neu-hintertux.com; doubles from €194, half board)
➜ WHERE TO PARTY The place to go for après ski is the Hohenhaus Tenne, a wooden chalet at the bottom of the cable car, which has a good sun terrace. Later on, the action heads inside to the Tux 1 disco, also part of the Hotel Hohenhaus. Also try the Batzenkeller. For a big night out, take a taxi down the valley to Mayrhofen, or there's a nightbus that runs till 2 a.m.
➜ TOURIST OFFICE +43 (0)528 78506; www.tux.at. See also www.hintertuxergletscher.at and www.zillertal.at

HEMSEDAL, NORWAY

➲ **STATS: Town altitude:** 640m; **Highest lift:** 1,450m; **Lifts:** 22; **Pistes:** 43km; **Closest airport:** Fagernes – 80km

➲ **WHY?** With a vertical drop from top to bottom of 810m, Hemsedal is by far the most serious ski resort in Norway, and the season runs from the middle of November until the first week of May. It's a much more rounded resort than Riksgränsen, and what it lacks in terms of cosy Alpine chalets, traditional village centre and dramatic soaring peaks, it makes up for with a thrilling sense of being in the remote wilderness

➲ **GETTING THERE** The closest airport is Fagernes, just over an hour's drive away, but you have to fly there with Air Norway (www.airnorway.no) via Oslo or Aalborg. So better to use Olso (157km), or Torp (served by Ryanair, 209km away). The best thing is to hire a car for the 3-and-a-half-hour drive – through beautiful, empty countryside. Hemsedal guests can get special rates with Hertz (see www.skistar.com). Transfer buses run on Fridays and Sundays from Oslo Gardermoen, NOK490/£49 return, taking between 3 and a half and 5 hours (details and booking via tourist office), but only until 19 April

➲ **WHERE TO STAY** The Skogstad Hotel (+47 (0) 32 05 50 00; www.skogstadhotell.no; doubles from NOK2240/£224, including breakfast) is a focal point of Hemsedal village, which is a 3km shuttle bus ride from the modern 'Skisenter' at the base of the lifts. To really get a taste of the wilderness, stay at the Skarsnuten (+47 (0)3206 1700; www.skarsnutenhotell.no; doubles from NOK2900/£290 half board), which is in a beautiful setting up the mountain at 1,000m

➲ **WHERE TO PARTY** Bar(t) and Garasjen are the places for après ski, and there's often live music in the Elgen bar of the Skogstad hotel. The Fjellbekk, also in the Skogstad hotel, is the main disco, and has a special room for tasting 'high end' whiskies (before you get stuck in, remember you are in Norway, and you may need to remortgage when the bill arrives)

➲ **TOURIST OFFICE** +47 (0) 32 05 50 30; www.hemsedal.com, and see www.skistar.com

ARGENTIÈRE, FRANCE

➲ **STATS: Town altitude:** 1,240m; **Highest lift:** 3,842m; **Lifts:** 62; **Pistes:** 210km; **Closest airport:** Geneva – 80km

➲ **WHY?** About 10km down the valley from Chamonix (see Chapter 1), the village of Argentière sits beneath the area's most snow-sure pistes – the Grands Montets. Up here, the lifts usually run till at least 8 May, giving access to north-facing slopes, super-long descents and some classic off-piste. During the main ski season, it makes sense to base yourself in Chamonix itself and take the free ski bus, which takes 20 minutes to reach the Grands Montets lifts. Towards the end of the season, though, the serious ski bums start basing themselves in Argentière to ensure they get the first lift and first tracks

➲ **GETTING THERE** There is a conventional coach service from Geneva (run by SAT Montblanc; +33 (0)4 50 53 01 15; www.sat-montblanc.com), but this takes just over 2 hours. Instead, use one of the numerous private minibus operators who will do the journey in an hour and a quarter and charge as little as €25 per person each way, depending on group size. Try Mountain Drop-offs (0871 5754810; www.mountaindropoffs.com), Chamvan (0208 144 6347; www.cham-van.com) or AlpyBus (01509 213696; www.alpybus.com)

➲ **WHERE TO STAY** The hotels are generally cheaper than in Chamonix. The three-star, family-run Montana (+33 (0)4 50 54 14 99; www.hotel-montana.fr; doubles from €190, including breakfast) is just 200m from the Grands Montets cable car, with good food. Or try Le Dahu (+33 (0)4 50 54 01 55; www.hotel-argentiere.com; doubles from €50)

➲ **WHERE TO PARTY** For full-on clubs, you'll have to take a taxi into Chamonix (head for Le Garage or La Cantina). In Argentière, the social hub is the Office – a wood-panelled pub with live music and an army of loyal devotees. It also serves morning-after fry-ups

➲ **TOURIST OFFICE** +33 (0)4 50 54 02 14; www.chamonix.com

Snowfinder
Airport
White Weekends featured resorts
Other resorts
GERMANY
FRANCE
SWITZERLAND
ITALY
LIECHTENSTEIN
Friedrichshafen
Basel
Zurich
Bern
St Anton
Arosa
Davos
Andermatt
Grindelwald
St Moritz
Borm
Whitepod
Sion
Geneva
Avoriaz
Verbier
Zermatt
Lyon
La Clusaz
Chamonix
Champoluc
Chambéry
Tignes
Val d'Isère
Milan
Les Trois Vallées
Grenoble
Alpe d'Huez
La Grave
Turin
Sauze d'Oulx
Serre Chevalier
0 50 100 km
0 50 100 miles

Munich
Salzburg
AUSTRIA
Kitzbühel
Schladming
sbruck
Saalbach
Graz
17 Mayrhofen
7 Neustift
rgurgl
Almdorf
15
Klagenfurt
Nassfeld
9
Badia 10
Cortina
Ljubljana
SLOVENIA
Trieste
Venice
Riksgränsen, Sweden 18
Cairngorm, Scotland 12
Krasnaya Polyana, Russia 14
Granada, Spain 3

Directory

AIRLINES

Adria Airlines: 020 7734 4630; www.adria.si
Aeroflot: 020 7355 2233; www.aeroflot.co.uk
Air Berlin: 0870 7388880; www.airberlin.com
Air France: 0870 1424343; www.airfrance.com/uk
Alitalia: 0870 5448259; www.alitalia.co.uk
Astraeus: 01293 819850; www.flystar.com
Austrian Airlines: 0870 1242625; www.austrianairlines.co.uk
BMI: 0870 6070555; www.flybmi.com
BMI Baby: 0871 2240224; www.bmibaby.com
British Airways: 0870 8509850; www.ba.com
Darwin: +41 (0) 84 817 71 77; www.darwinairline.com
Eastern Airways: 0870 3669100; www.easternairways.com
Easyjet: 0905 8210905 (65p/min); www.easyjet.com
Flybe: 0871 7002000; www.flybe.com
FlyGlobespan: 0870 5561522; www.flyglobespan.com
Helvetic: 020 7026 3464; www.helvetic.com
Jet2: 0871 2261737; www.jet2.com
Lufthansa: 0870 8377747; www.lufthansa.co.uk
Norwegian Air Shuttle: +47 (0) 21 49 00 15; www.norwegian.no
Ryanair: 0871 2460000; www.ryanair.com
SAS: 0870 6072772; www.flysas.com
Scotairways: 0870 6060707; www.scotairways.com
Sterling: 0870 7878038; www.sterlingticket.com
Swiss: 0845 6010956; www.swiss.com
Thomsonfly: 0871 2314691; www.thomsonfly.com

For private jets, contact Jeffersons: 020 8746 2496; www.jeffersons.com

CAR HIRE

Alamo: 0870 4004562; www.alamo.co.uk
Avis: 0870 0100287; www.avis.co.uk
Budget: 0870 1565656; www.budget.co.uk
Europcar: 0870 6075000; www.europcar.co.uk
Hertz: 0870 8484848; www.hertz.co.uk

There are also large numbers of car-hire brokerages. The two that we found most reliable during the research trips for this book were:
Auto Europe: 0800 3581229; www.autoeurope.co.uk
Holiday Autos: 0870 4000000; www.holidayautos.co.uk

NATIONAL TOURIST BOARDS

Austria: 0845 1011818; www.austria.info
France: 0906 8244123 (60p/min); www.franceguide.com/uk
Italy: 020 7399 3562; www.enit.it
Spain: 020 7486 8077; www.tourspain.co.uk
Sweden: 020 7108 6168; www.visitsweden.com
Switzerland: 0800 10020030; www.myswitzerland.com

TRAINS

EUROSTAR SKI TRAIN

During the winter Eurostar runs direct services from London to Moûtiers (for Les Trois Vallées), Aime (for La Plagne) and Bourg-St-Maurice (for Val d'Isère and Tignes), taking as little as 6 and a half hours. Unfortunately, these aren't of much use for weekenders – there is one service which leaves London on Friday night and one on Saturday morning, but both return on Saturday night, meaning you'd get at most a single day on the slopes.

The overnight Eurostar isn't the most comfortable experience either – it's not a sleeper train with beds, just ordinary seats. You arrive in the Alps at 6 a.m. in the morning, having spent all night trying to rest your head on the little table that folds down from the seat in front, and the last thing you want to do is go skiing. See www.eurostar.com/ski

RAIL EUROPE SNOW TRAIN

Another alternative is the famous Snow Train, organized by the British company Rail Europe. You take the normal Eurostar to Paris, then change to the overnight Snow Train (which departs from the same station, the Gare du Nord). It has the advantage of proper bunks, not to mention the legendary, sound-proofed disco carriage. It stops at Chambéry, Albertville, Moûtiers, Aime, Landry, and Bourg-St-Maurice. Again, though, it's of little use to weekenders, as it only runs out on Friday nights, and back on Saturday nights. See www.snowtrain.co.uk

BERGLAND EXPRESS

A Snow Train equivalent for Austria. You take the Eurostar to Brussels, then change on to the Bergland Express, which has bunks, and arrive the following morning at stations including Innsbruck, Kitzbühel, St Johann in Tirol and Zell am See. Again, it's for full-week skiers, though, running out on Friday night, back Saturday night. See www.berglandexpress.com

REGULAR TRAINS

The good news is that new high-speed rail links are making it far easier to get to resorts across the Alps on ordinary scheduled trains which run every day and so are perfect for long weekends. For example, from St Pancras, getting to Grenoble, gateway to the southern Alps, takes just 6 hours and 12 minutes. Geneva is about 6 and a half hours, Annecy just over 7 hours. All three require just one change, in Paris. For bookings and advice contact:

Rail Europe: 0870 5848848; www.raileurope.co.uk. A specialist rail-travel agent that can arrange tickets for any European journey
Seat 61: www.seat61.com. An independent site giving advice on rail journeys
Eurostar: 0870 5186186; www.eurostar.co.uk
Eurotunnel: 0870 5353535; www.eurotunnel.com
Railteam: www.railteam.eu. An alliance of 7 European high-speed-rail operators, designed to make it easier to get information and tickets for international journeys

NATIONAL RAILWAY WEBSITES FOR TIMETABLE INFORMATION

Austria: www.oebb.at
France: www.sncf.com
Italy: www.trenitalia.com
Switzerland: www.sbb.ch

SWISS TRANSFER TICKETS

The Swiss tourist board and national railway operator together run the Swiss Travel System (0207 420 49 00; www.swisstravelsystem.co.uk), which sells tickets and rail passes to tourists before they leave their home country. Most relevant for skiers is the Swiss Transfer Ticket, which allows you to travel from the border or any airport to any resort and back at the end of the holiday. At the time of going to press, it costs £67.

FLIGHTFINDER

	Heathrow	Gatwick	Stansted	London City	Luton	Birmingham	Manchester	Bournemouth	Bristol	East Midlands	Edinburgh	Glasgow	Leeds/Bradford	Liverpool	Newcastle	Belfast	Southampton	Exeter	Aberdeen	Cardiff
Geneva	BA	E; BA	E	AF;BA;S	E	E; BB	BB;J;FB	E	E	E; BB	E;FG;FB	E;FG;FB	J	E	E	E	FB	FB	FG	BB
Grenoble		E; BA; T	R		E	E		E	E	R		R		R						
Chambéry		AS					J				FG		J		J		FB	FG		
Zurich	BA; S	BA		BA; S; AF	E	S	S				BM									
Innsbruck		E					E		E					E						
Lyon	BA		E			AF	BM													
Bern						FB											FB			
Basel	BA		E	S	E		S							E						
Turin		BA	R		E				R											
Milan	AL; BA	E	R		R	FB; BB	R; FB; J	R	E	R	E; J	R	J	R	R	J				
Friedrichshafen			R																	
Venice	BM	E; BA	R				J; T		E	E			J	R		E				
Munich	BA; L		AB; E	L		L	L				E									
Salzburg		T; BA	R							R			J	R			FB	FB		
Klagenfurt			R																	
Ljubljana		AA	E				AA													
Trieste			R			R														
Verona		BA	R																	

AA: ADRIA AIRLINES **AB:** AIR BERLIN **AF:** AIR FRANCE **AL:** ALITALIA **AA:** ADRIA AIRLINES **AS:** ASTREUS **BA:** BRITISH AIRWAYS **BB:** BMI BABY
BM: BMI **E:** EASYJET **FB:** FLYBE **FG:** FLYGLOBESPAN **J:** JET2 **L:** LUFTHANSA **R:** RYANAIR **S:** SWISS **T:** THOMSONFLY

Index of Resorts